CHURCHILL

The Battle of Britain

JOHN WILLIS

MENSCH PUBLISHING

Mensch Publishing
51 Northchurch Road, London N1 4EE, United Kingdom

First published in Great Britain 1985
This edition published in Great Britain 2023

ISBN: PB: 978-1-912914-64-7; e-Book: 978-1-912914-06-7

To Janet, Tom and Beth

CONTENTS

FOREWORD

Many years ago, I made a film about a group of First World War veterans from Leeds on their annual return visit to the muddy battlefields of Passchendaele and Ypres. They were old men, but their common characteristics were immediately striking. If your concern is for peace, it is hard to accept that war brings out the best in people – but all these veterans possessed a rare tolerance towards the frailties of their fellow men. Their months in the trenches of Flanders had been the most significant event in their entire lives. At seventeen or eighteen they had reached a peak of experience they could never hope to match again. Those who had survived had grown up almost overnight in the mud and chaos, and returned from the war changed men.

I feel exactly the same about the six lives explored in this book. Alongside Hastings, Trafalgar and Waterloo, the Battle of Britain ranks as one of the most famous military events in British history (though its significance is scarcely recognised by German historians and it lasted only a few months). There were many key turning points in the Second World War but, as it was so early in that war, the Battle of Britain carries extra significance as the pivotal moment. At that point, Hitler had ripped quickly through France and driven British forces back across the Channel from Dunkirk. If the German invasion of Britain had been successful then the history of that war would have been completely different.

In that 'queer, golden time', as one pilot's wife called it, the lives of the six men portrayed here changed forever. The pilots are largely unknown – a world apart from the Douglas Baders and Bob Stanford Tucks – but, for them, the consequences of the Battle of Britain were even more profound than they were for their more famous counterparts. So, in this book I have tried not only to capture the day-to-day drama of the air battle, and to look afresh at the rather romantic portrait of the Battle of Britain that has developed, but to reach beyond the strict ending of the battle and explore its long-term effects on these men.

It had been my original intention to concentrate only on RAF pilots, but, having met former Oberleutnant Ulrich Steinhilper of the Luftwaffe, I thought his experiences so dramatic and revealing and his character so far from the popular image of the wartime German, that I decided to write his story too. I hope that the inclusion of an enemy of Churchill's Few throws additional light on the other five characters and adds an extra dimension to the whole book.

To all the pilots whose stories are told here and all the others who gave their time, I offer thanks. On a handful of occasions, I have changed a pilot's name in order to avoid distress after all these years. The six central characters put up with the difficulties with grace and good humour, and I grew to like and respect all of them enormously. In the intervening years since this introduction was first written, my admiration and liking for the men portrayed here has only deepened. Time has only served to show their courage as even more remarkable.

John Willis
August 2019

PROLOGUE

Spitend Point, near Dutchman's Island on the Isle of Sheppey, lies at the tip of a dank waste of Kentish marshland. Inhospitable and flat, it is a remote, friendless place that no man visits without good reason.

On Sunday 29 September 1979 the strange, almost sinister, atmosphere of the mudflats at Spitend Point was heightened by whiskers of early morning mist. A few hundred yards from the sea half a dozen men in their twenties and thirties were gathered in a circle. A farmer, an accountant, a local government officer, a coalman and two builders, they were all dressed in boiler suits and armed with spades and metal detectors.

These men were members of the Wealden Aviation Archaeological Group. They had come to this isolated corner of Britain to dig for what, in their narrow world, was buried treasure. They were searching for the remains of a Hurricane fighter which had been shot down during the Battle of Britain by Messerschmitt 109s before crashing into the boggy land at the edge of the sea.

For nearly forty years the plane had been entombed in the dark soil of the Isle of Sheppey. Now this small group of enthusiasts were hoping to recover the Hurricane from its marshy grave, preserve as much of the plane as possible, and so put the full stop on another line of Battle of Britain history.

Preliminary research had indicated approximately where the Hurricane had crashed, but the recovery party was not sure whether the pilot's body would still be in the wreckage if they found it. In several years of Sundays spent digging for Battle of Britain planes, they had discovered a body only four or five times.

What they did know was that the pilot of the Hurricane reported missing had been Flight Lieutenant Hugh Beresford, flight commander of 'A' flight 257 Squadron, based at Martlesham Heath, near Ipswich. Born at Ampthill in Bedfordshire in 1915, Beresford had joined the RAF straight from school and by the age of twenty-four, at the time of the crash, was almost a veteran. Handsome and sporty, he reflected perfectly the classic image of the fighter pilot. Young and charming, with the well-bred good looks of the English public schoolboy, he was a popular figure in the tiny Leicestershire village of Hoby, where his father was rector. 'Hugh did not feel he had any vocation,' said his sister, Pamela. 'He liked to play cricket, kick a ball around. He had a rifle and a gun. The air force seems to have fascinated him.' Soon after war broke out in 1939, Hugh Beresford married Pat Kemp, the nineteen-year-old daughter of a fellow RAF officer.

When, in the late afternoon of 7 September 1940, 257 Squadron had 'scrambled' from Martlesham Heath, it had been Hugh Beresford's fourth sortie of the day. The squadron had flown along the Thames estuary before Beresford alerted others that four Messerschmitts were attacking from above and that he was unable to fire at the enemy because another Hurricane was in his way. A few minutes later Hugh Beresford was dead. The official record coldly noted the event:

> The Squadron intercepted a formation of about fifty
> enemy bombers flying up the Thames Estuary. The
> bombers were escorted by a great number of fighters
> flying above them. In the ensuing combat F/Lt
> Beresford, 'A' flight commander, and F/O Mitchell, 'B'
> flight commander, were lost and posted missing.

From earlier researches, the Wealden recovery group had narrowed the crash site down to an area a few hundred yards from the sea. As the autumn sun tried to force its way through the mist, the six aviation archaeologists got to work with their metal detectors. A pungent smell hung over the dark soil. Except for a handful of sheep grazing in the distance, they had seen no sign of life since arriving. The nearest farm was over a mile away. Probably, the only humans who had passed this way since 1940 were a few birdwatchers and the occasional escaped inmate from HM Prison at nearby Eastchurch. The search was expected to be long and difficult. The mudflats were so boggy that the team even began to build an elaborate ramp to extricate the wreckage – in the end, it was not needed. Surprisingly quickly, the metal detectors indicated that there was an object below. The men started to dig. Twenty-five feet down, they found the first piece of wreckage and soon located the aircraft identity plate. With the mud wiped off, it read: *Gloster Aircraft, Date 5/40,* followed by a number which looked like P 3048 or P 3049. Careful inspection revealed that the final digit was in fact a 9 which had been double-stamped. P 3049 was the number of Hugh Beresford's Hurricane.

The Hurricane had crashed from about twenty thousand feet while travelling at 750 mph so its wings had broken off on impact. The rest of the plane, including the tail and the engine, had been compressed into a space of no more than ten feet. Bit by bit, pieces of wreckage were pulled from the hole – a wheel, the joystick, sections of fabric. The parachute was found neatly packaged and as good as new, with the tail wheel on top of it. Underneath lay what remained of Flight Lieutenant Hugh Beresford.

By now the diggers were thirty feet down. As they carefully tried to free the pilot's remains from the mud, the stench became almost unbearable. The handful of bodies the aviation archaeologists had discovered in the past had been mere skeletons. This was much more difficult to take. Entombed in the clay, petrol and oil, cut off from the air which would have caused rapid decomposition, Hugh Beresford was surprisingly well preserved. His head had disintegrated when the Hurricane hit the ground, but the torso had stayed relatively intact, held in place by the straps and harness. The legs had been smashed off at the knees. His flying boots were still neatly in place. Some of the men turned their heads away.

Official records show that almost since the day Hugh Beresford had crashed the Ministry of Defence had known where he was but had been either unwilling or unable to recover the pilot and his plane. On 4 October 1940, No. 49 RAF Maintenance Unit had reported that a Hurricane:

> ... has crashed in marshy land a mile and a half from
> the nearest hard road ... it will be necessary for the
> vehicle removing the aircraft to travel over the marsh.
> It would appear that a tractor is most suitable for this
> clearance. I suggest as an alternative that the RAF
> stationed at Eastchurch might drag this wreckage
> across the marsh by means of their Bren Gun Carrier.

Thirty-nine years later this had still not happened. As one of the recovery party said, 'The ministry knew about it. They knew Hugh Beresford might still be in his plane but they left him there for nearly forty years.'

On this dismal September day, the aviation archaeologists had no time to ponder such matters. It was very unpleasant in the dark, marshy hole. They wanted to finish their unhappy task as quickly as possible. The six men meticulously placed the shattered remains of the Battle of Britain pilot into black plastic rubbish sacks and sat down to take stock of their discovery.

By law, the authorities had to be informed immediately. One of the diggers trudged through the treacly mud to the nearest village. From the public telephone box he made what must have been one of the oddest calls ever received by the Isle of Sheppey police. 'I'd like to report,' he said, 'the finding of some human remains from thirty-nine years ago.' The switchboard operator was extremely matter-of-fact. She could have been taking details of a minor traffic accident or a lost dog. 'Oh, a body,' she said. 'Hold on a minute.'

PART ONE

BEFORE THE BATTLE

1

The Build up

On 10 July 1940 – according to official RAF view, the date when the air Battle of Britain began – Lord Beaverbrook, Minister of Aircraft Production, urged the British public to support the aircraft industry by providing it with aluminium. 'We will turn your pots and pans into Spitfires and Hurricanes, Blenheims and Wellingtons,' he said. Accordingly, thousands of saucepans were loyally sacrificed.

Beaverbrook's plaintive appeal was indicative of the parlous state into which the RAF had fallen during the interwar years. The minister was trying to compensate for lost time by speeding up the rate of modern aircraft production and strengthening the essential repair services that would be crucial to the defence of Britain in an air war. Beaverbrook's task needed all the dynamism that had characterised his career as a newspaper tycoon.

The seeds of the RAF's swift decline were sown in the aftermath of the 1914–18 war. When the armistice was signed in November 1918, the British people needed time to recover from the bruising conflict which had supposedly been 'the war to end all wars'; few could contemplate another one. At this time the RAF, which had become an independent service on 1 April 1918, was a formidable force. It had 181 squadrons, comprising nearly 300,000 officers and other ranks flying 22,000 aircraft, some of high technological sophistication. By 1920, those squadrons had shrunk to just twelve, and the number of aircraft from 22,000 to 371. The RAF salvage store near Croydon was crammed with unwanted machinery, including 30,000 engines and a third of a million spark plugs. As Denis Winter in *The First of the Few* noted, 'This spirit of the bargain basement seemed to apply to the whole air service after the war as if it were an unwanted illegitimate child.'* Indeed, Lloyd George decided in December 1918 that the Air Ministry was not to remain as a separate department, but was to be subsumed into the War Office or the Admiralty.

It was against this background of political indifference that, in 1919, Sir Hugh Trenchard became the first Chief of the Air Staff. His brief was to develop the core of an air force that could be swiftly expanded in times of crisis. He was also keen that the air force remain independent of both army and navy, and that it should act on the lessons learned by the Royal Flying Corps in 1914–18. Trenchard – influenced by the successful and largely undefended attacks from June 1917 on London and the south-east of England by twin-engined Gotha bombers – was convinced that the key to maintaining independence for the RAF was to place emphasis on bomber forces. Consequently, the limited resources available were poured largely into bomber production, leaving the fighter relegated to an interception role. Even after his retirement in 1929, Trenchard's policy was to shape the battle order for 1940. As late as 1936, fewer than a third of the RAF's home-based squadrons were equipped with fighters, many of which were obsolete anyway.

*Allen Lane, 1982.

Meanwhile, the Germans were formally prevented from building up their air force by the Treaty of Versailles, signed in June 1919. The treaty, with its territorial penalties in Saarland Alsace-Lorraine and the Polish Corridor, was a national humiliation for Germany. In meticulous detail it laid out the restrictions to be placed on the German forces. The number of fighting men was to be drastically reduced; submarines, tanks and armoured cars were banned: and severe limitations were imposed on small weaponry and ammunition. The air force was equally hard hit. No air arms of any kind were allowed, and all aeronautical material had to be handed over to the Allies. Over 15,000 aircraft and 27,000 engines were surrendered.

Yet, for all its harshness, the Treaty of Versailles failed to prevent the rise of the Luftwaffe. The significant loophole in the treaty was its relative lack of control over civil aviation, which was burgeoning the world over. Moreover, the treaty had rubbed the Germans' noses into the ground, and national pride dictated that the German government must avoid complete military emasculation at all costs. As Lloyd George had said, even if Germany were made to 'reduce her armaments to a mere police force … in the end if she feels that she has been unjustly treated in the peace of 1919 she will find means of exacting retribution on her conquerors'.

A small band of regular officers (among them Hugo Sperrle and Albert Kesselring, both later to become air fleet commanders in the Battle of Britain), working from a tiny base in the defence ministry that Versailles had left intact, set about making Lloyd George's prediction come true and, soon after Versailles, most of the famous German aircraft factories were operating on a small scale but well-organised basis. Although unable to manufacture the bombers and fighters they would later want, the Germans nonetheless produced a wide range of aircraft, some of which were later converted for military use.

In 1926, the Paris Air Agreement removed any remaining constraints on civil aviation, and the formation of Lufthansa proved a perfect wooden horse. As it grew into a technically sophisticated airline, Lufthansa offered enormous opportunities for pilot training and advances in communication, airfield construction and aircraft design. The Germans also made a secret agreement with the Russians by which a small but influential group of German pilots were provided with military training at Lipetsk in Russia. So, when Hitler took hold of the political reins in 1933, a skeleton Luftwaffe was already in existence.

To advance Germany's international position, Hitler poured resources into his air force. The man entrusted with masterminding the air expansion was of course Hermann Goering, a First World War pilot who had risen to the highest levels within the National Socialist Party. A large, fat, popular man who delighted in power and ostentatious wealth, Goering had the personal flying experience to equip him for the job but had shown little or no skill in the strategy of aerial warfare. His deputy at the air ministry, Erhard Milch, who had skilfully built up Lufthansa as a civil airline, undertook most of the detailed work in reorganizing the structure of the Luftwaffe and stepping up aircraft production and personnel training. However, it was clear that the growing reservoir of pilots emerging from Lufthansa or from the rapidly developing air sports clubs needed the kind of military training precluded by the

Treaty of Versailles, so an agreement was made with Mussolini to secretly train Luftwaffe pilots in Italy.

By March 1935 the Germans felt confident enough for Goering to admit officially what the other Versailles signatories already knew: that they had flagrantly breached the Treaty of Versailles. The Germans revealed that they now had a force of nearly 2000 aircraft with 20,000 men to fly and service them. German intervention in the Spanish Civil War in 1936 presented Hitler and Goering with a perfect opportunity to experiment with the modern aircraft and growing professionalism of the new Luftwaffe in war conditions. The Dornier 17, whose elegant slim fuselage earned it the nickname 'Flying Pencil'; the Heinkel III bomber, whose speed made it almost untouchable by the Republicans; and, above all, the Messerschmitt 109 fighter, with its sharp acceleration and excellent diving speed: all were successfully tested by the Condor Legion in the Spanish Civil War. Even the horror of the bombing of Guernica was lost on most German people in the heady excitement of Luftwaffe success and the crude outpourings of German propaganda.

It was only in 1936, after Hitler had unveiled the might of the new Luftwaffe, that the RAF at last began to tackle its weaknesses. The service was split into separate commands – Bomber, Fighter, Coastal and Training – and it was decided to more than double the number of squadrons. The number of flying training schools also doubled and opportunities for short-service commissions and promotion of NCOs to pilots were greatly expanded. The austere, rather remote Sir Hugh Dowding became commander-in-chief of Fighter Command in July 1936. Although the command was still badly understrength, with insufficient squadrons adequately to cover large tracts of Britain outside the home counties, Dowding vigorously set about co-ordinating defences and skilfully integrated the early-warning potential of radar and the Observer Corps with Fighter Command.

While Germany re-armed, Hitler trod relatively cautiously on the international stage. Although as the Luftwaffe increased in both power and sophistication, he grew more ambitious. The occupation of Austria in March 1938 provided him with more pilots, airfields and greater aircraft production capacity. The events that followed are well known.

As Europe prepared for war, young men in both Britain and Germany looked forward to the thrills that the rapid development of more powerful and sophisticated aircraft would bring. As Hitler cut through Europe, thousands of eighteen- and nineteen-year-olds were eager to become one of what would later be known as 'Churchill's Few'. Most of them cherished a romantic view of warfare, in which Spitfires and Messerschmitts were like racing cars, the instruments for a sporting duel. The young men hailed from a wide variety of social backgrounds, but they all had a great deal to learn about the realities of war.

2

THE FLYING ACE

Bob Doe was born in 1920 at Reigate in Surrey, where his father was a gardener on an estate. His strong and domineering mother was thirty-three before she gave birth to her only child. It is hard to imagine a future Battle of Britain pilot in the sickly boy who was breastfed until the age of two and a half – which may have caused the rickets that afflicted him as a child. Once a week, Bob and his mother would take the train to London for treatment for the disease. When Bob was five it was discovered that he also suffered from tubercular glands.

Bob Doe did not attend school for the first time until the age of seven and a half. His ill-health, lack of siblings and late start in the education system made him withdrawn. His isolation was not helped by the behaviour of his father, who – apart from telling occasional stories of his experiences in the First World War – never talked to his son, preferring the company of flowers and plants to that of humans.

Bob's first day at school coincided with the Doe family's moving to Walton-on-the-Hill, between Epsom and Reigate, where Mr Doe had been appointed head gardener to Emsley Carr, owner of the *News of the World*. They lived in one of a pair of cottages owned by Carr. Mr Doe's wages were three pounds ten shillings a week and as head gardener he was firmly established in the upper-working-class bracket.

Bob went to the local church school and, although the rickets and tubercular glands were behind him, he remained a lonely child throughout his primary education. At school, the boys formed naturally into groups or gangs of friends. Bob was always excluded. When he came home in the afternoons he would go straight onto the common, where he ran and played for hours with his sole companion—his dog.

It was only at the age of ten, when he moved to what was then called a central school in Leatherhead, that Bob's life started to expand. Leatherhead was five or six miles from home and Bob was expected to cycle there and back. Although it often seemed arduous, especially in bad weather, the long ride strengthened his legs, which had been weakened by the rickets and he developed into a tall, sturdy young boy. At school his obsession was maths, the only subject he was good at. He also began to enjoy cricket, in which he was an admirably fast bowler, and athletics, in which he hurdled for his county in the All-England Schoolboys' Championships. At home his mother encouraged Bob to learn the violin and he became good enough to play in a local orchestra.

When he was thirteen, Bob saw his first aeroplane. Cycling home one afternoon, he spotted overhead an RAF fighter biplane which seemed to be in difficulty. To Bob's surprise, the pilot force-landed the plane in the field about twenty yards away from the road. Bob pushed his bicycle into the hedgerow, ran into the field and walked round the plane, staring in wonderment. The pilot was unhurt and smiled at him. That the plane should have landed so close was an almost mystical experience for the young boy. Bob cycled home excitedly to tell his mother, who merely scolded him for being late for tea.

The dramatic exploits of men such as Lindbergh or Alcock and Brown, the pioneers of aviation, thrilled schoolboys of Bob Doe's generation. Bob himself read avidly the romantic stories of the Royal Flying Corps in the 1914–18 war, in which the pilots were portrayed as twentieth-century equivalents of Galahad and Lancelot. On one side were aerial knights such as Albert Ball, VC; on the other, the 'Red Baron' of Germany, Manfred von Richtofen. However, for the moment, the nation had grown tired of war and to the young gardener's boy from Surrey, becoming a fighter pilot seemed an unattainable dream.

At fourteen it was time for Bob to leave school. The horizons that had expanded so much since he had begun secondary education were soon to grow further. He had no idea what job he wanted but, as his father worked for Emsley Carr, Bob found work in Fleet Street as an office boy at the *News of the World*.

Every day he would walk the two miles to Tadworth station and catch the 7.15 a.m. train to London. During the day he worked in the share transfer department, delivering shares to various offices around London. Two or three times a week, he would attend night school before making the long journey home.

Bob enjoyed the job and took pleasure in exploring London. His cricketing skill was noticed and he began to play for the *News of the World* and the Newspaper Publishers' Association. All these activities left no time for his other gathering enthusiasm: aeroplanes. He was too busy with cricket to spend weekends at air shows, but he began to cut out every photograph or article he could find about planes and all the money he saved went on aviation magazines.

In 1936, Bob's dream began to come true. Hitler's development of a secret air force had finally persuaded Britain that the RAF needed to expand. As part of the process of increasing the number of pilots, the Volunteer Reserve was formed for the training of pilots in their spare time. Here was a chance even for young men like Bob Doe, from relatively humble backgrounds, to stop fantasising about flying and become pilots – being paid in the process.

Bob Doe was just eighteen when he became one of the first six hundred young men to join the RAF Volunteer Reserve. 'When I reported to RAF Hanworth, my chest stuck out a mile. I was delighted.'

At Hanworth, Doe learnt to fly B2 biplanes, which looked a bit like Tiger Moths. The B2 was 'a wonderful aeroplane to fly', he said, 'but I believe it flew better upside down than the right way up.'

Doe enjoyed flying so much that he gave up his weekend cricket and in summer would cycle the sixty-mile round trip to Hanworth to continue his training. He was given the rank of sergeant and the payment for hours attended was a useful supplement to his office boy's salary. Yet Doe was still a lonely figure. His lack of confidence and absence of social graces meant that he kept himself apart from others whom he instinctively felt were superior both as pilots and people. Indeed, some of the other young men in the Volunteer Reserve came from quite wealthy families and owned cars; while Doe began his weary cycle home, they would go for a drink at the hotel in the middle of the airfield. He never once went with them.

By his own admission, Doe was slow at learning to fly, but on 4 June 1938 he flew solo for the first time. Although he was frightened, he landed the B2 safely and was delighted with himself. In the coming months, he logged seventy-five hours training on B2s and Hawker Harts. On his own in the air he felt more confident, but he was inclined to fly the way he thought best, rather than conforming to what was expected – and, as a result, was criticised for not always adhering to discipline in the air. He passed his course with an 'average' rating, but the instructor added that RFT Doe was 'rather over-confident'. The pilot himself felt that the opposite was much nearer the truth.

By early 1939 it was growing obvious to Doe that war was imminent. The *News of the World* had become a rather tedious five-day interlude between weekends in the air, so he decided to apply for a short-service commission. 'Being young, brash and naive, I walked into the Air Ministry in Holborn and announced that I wanted to be a pilot.' To his surprise, he was ushered into an office occupied by a man in a uniform covered in gold braid. After some initial questions, a medical and an exam were arranged. 'My exam was very basic and I had no problems with it. To my surprise, they offered me a short-service commission; they must have been scraping the barrel.'

By March 1939 Hitler had annexed the whole of Czechoslovakia. That same month, a few days after his nineteenth birthday, Bob Doe, now an acting pilot officer on probation, began his four-year commission at Redhill, Surrey. A contemporary photograph shows a ruggedly handsome young man with black hair wearing an ill-fitting uniform comprising of a shapeless jacket and rather baggy trousers. Most young pilots used their uniform grant to go to smart tailors, but Doe found a tailor to make his uniform as cheaply as possible. The result was awful, but he saved himself five pounds on the grant.

At Redhill the new acting pilot officer learned to fly Magisters, early biplanes which had a reputation for being impossible to get out of a spin – so everyone was a little scared of them. Despite his long experience at Hanworth, Doe was slow to go solo on the Magisters, but he eventually passed the course, again as 'average'.

After a spell of drilling and square-bashing at Uxbridge, he moved on to No. 6 Flying Training School at Little Rissington in Gloucestershire; the plan was for him to become a bomber pilot, learning on the twin-engined Avro Ansons. Like many young flyers, Doe still harboured a desire to be a fighter pilot, the most glamorous role in the RAF, but as long as he was flying he was happy to join any command. At Little Rissington he still largely kept himself to himself. By the time the mess bill of twelve pounds a month was paid out of his eighteen to nineteen pounds a month salary, there was little spare money available for socialising – especially as, unlike many others, he had no financial support from his parents.

Doe was again slow to adapt to flying the new aircraft. When the young pilots were not learning how to fly, they spent hours being drilled on the square, being taught how to march and carry a rifle and bayonet properly. Doe found it hard to see how this would help him become a better pilot, but stuck at it nonetheless. He found two weeks gunnery training in North Wales of more practical benefit. His self-confidence increased a little when he met his first girlfriend, whose father managed the local aerodrome. 'I began to realise,' he said, 'that I was quite a pretty boy.' The situation, even in late August 1939, was still rather unreal. According to Mass Observation, only one person in six would admit at that time that they were expecting war. Two days after Hitler had invaded Poland, on the morning of 3 September 1939, Bob Doe and several other pilots went down to the airfield as usual. At 11.15 a.m., the young men stood outside the hangar and listened to Chamberlain's momentous speech on the radio.

Afterwards, everyone was quiet. 'It was a funny feeling. All of us knew what we were there for, but we didn't know what to expect. In many ways we were keen for it to happen.'

However, before Bob Doe could fly against the Germans, he had to complete his course. He knew his own limitations all too well and worked desperately hard for his Wings exam, scraping through by 2 per cent. He passed out of his advanced bombing at Little Rissington as, again, 'average'; this time, it was noted that he was 'rather under-confident and below average at navigation'.

Whatever his defects as a pilot, the RAF needed men and on 6 November 1939, Doe was dispatched to RAF Leconfield on Humberside to join a newly formed squadron – 234. Thirteen other graduates from the bomber course at Little Rissington also started the new squadron, among them Cecil Hight from New Zealand, Pat Horton from Australia and Richard Hardy. Other pilots came from Poland and Canada.

When Doe arrived at Leconfield he anxiously asked what kind of station it was, hoping that he might have found himself transferred into Fighter Command, but was disappointed to discover that it was a bomber station.

Formed on 1 November, the squadron had been ill- starred from the start. On 2 November, their squadron leader, W. A. J. Satchell, was injured in a car accident which forced him out of immediate active service. The squadron also did not seem to have the up-to-date aircraft needed to allow the newly arrived pilots to gain enough experience to take on the Luftwaffe. At the beginning, the total flying complement for training was just three Magisters and three Gloucester Gauntlets. By early December this had been supplemented by two Tutors, one Battle and two Blenheim bombers.

For a month the members of the new squadron took it in turns to fly the handful of old-fashioned planes at its disposal. On 12 December, Doe flew a Blenheim for the first time. He landed safely, but on the same day two other pilot officers crashed a Magister; they wrote off the aircraft and both of them broke their spines.

Five days later, Pilot Officer Geoffrey Gout failed to raise his undercarriage before becoming properly airborne and struck rising ground, damaging his plane. It gradually became clear that the new commanding officer was not going to give the squadron the firm leadership it needed to bolster confidence, after these crashes.

Squadron Leader Satchell, then in Hull Royal Infirmary, had been replaced by Squadron Leader Dickie Barnett, MBE. Barnett was in his mid-thirties, dark-haired, with a military moustache. A rather distant, retiring character who rarely flew, he had been trained in what might be called the 'old school'. Leader of 'A' flight, Flight Lieutenant Thielman, suffered badly from asthma. 'B' flight was led by Pat Hughes, a tough but intelligent Australian. Even at this stage of the squadron's development, it was Hughes who emerged as the real force. The young pilots looked to him for guidance and inspiration.

Pat Hughes hailed from Haberfield, New South Wales and liked to wear his Royal Australian Air Force uniform. Like most of the twenty-two Australians who flew in the Battle of Britain, Hughes had paid his own fare to England. To the other pilots, he seemed older and more mature than they were, but he was only in his early twenties. He was famous for having a small dog, 'Flying Officer' Butch, whom he took everywhere with him, including the air. 'Hughes was the one who taught me everything in the air,' said Bob Doe. 'We respected him, listened to him. But he was not a remote figure like the other two; he was one of the lads as well. He was the real power behind the squadron.'

The difficulties created by Barnett's lack of leadership were compounded by further bewildering shifts in the squadron's planes. In December the Blenheim bombers were converted into fighters and sent to Finland to fight the Russians, leaving 234 with only Fairey Battles, planes which were both under-powered and seriously underarmed, with only one forward machine gun. This was a matter of grave concern to Bob Doe: 'They were appalling aeroplanes to go to war in, dangerous; we were very worried.' Although, to their two-man crews, the Battles were flying death-traps, more than three thousand of these machines, which were destined to prove so slow and vulnerable against the modern aircraft of the Luftwaffe, had been built.

Although, the squadron's first fatality was unconnected with the inadequacy of the aircraft availability.

In February 1940, Pilot Officer David Coysh, a quiet young pilot, was taxiing in a little Magister round the corner of the hangar, unable to see a Spitfire of 616 Squadron on the runway on the other side of the hangar. Seemingly, the control tower had failed to warn either pilot of the other's presence. The Spitfire ripped right through the Magister, killing David Coysh. Unit 234 had not even seen action yet.

At this time, as the nation geared up for war, training accidents were an inescapable reality of RAF squadron life, but they never reached the extraordinary level of 1914–18 training casualties: 14,166 pilots died in that war; more than half of them, 8000, killed in training accidents in Britain.

In March 1940, to the squadron's relief and delight, Mark I Spitfires began to arrive for them at Leconfield; by the end of the month they had twelve. After training for so long on bombers, 234 was to be a fighter squadron after all. When the first Spitfire appeared, all the pilots came out to inspect it. 'This beautiful thing arrived. We walked round it, stroked it. We took turns sitting in it,' said Bob Doe. 234 was becoming a realistic fighting unit at last.

The Spitfire was a joy. To Bob Doe it was the only plane: 'After you'd flown it once, you realised you weren't flying an aeroplane anymore; you just strapped wings on your back and you flew. Flying a Spitfire was like playing a fiddle. If you played it right, you got the music you asked for.'

Training intensified, with Pat Hughes increasingly taking responsibility for the seemingly uninterested squadron leader. The pilots learned to fly the Spitfires in strict formation, according to RAF instructions. Doe instinctively felt that these rigid formations were wrong, but was still too shy to speak out against them.

On 6 May Doe had his first and only gunnery practice in a fighter, firing his guns into the sea. Fortunately, his training on the Anson bomber at Little Rissington, when he had spent two weeks in the turret as a rear gunner, had given him some idea of deflection techniques and the other arts of gunnery. Two days later, 234 Squadron became operational. During May the squadron had several practice night flights. Then, on 18 June 1940, they moved from Yorkshire to St Eval, near Newquay in Cornwall, on the same day Winston Churchill made his famous speech:

> 'What General Weygand called the Battle of France is over. I expect that the Battle of Britain is about to begin … The whole fury and might of the enemy must very soon be turned on us. Hitler knows that he will have to break us in this island or lose the war. If we can stand up to him all Europe may be free and the life of the world may move forward into bright sunlight uplands. But if we fail, the whole world, including the United States, including all that we have known and cared for, will sink into the abyss of a new Dark Age made more sinister and perhaps more protracted by the lights of perverted silence … If the British Empire and its Commonwealth last for a thousand years, men will still say, "This was their finest hour."'

3

THE POLE

Joseph Szlagowski was born in 1914 in the Polish market town of Koscierzyna, tucked inland from the Baltic in flat farming country. It was an attractive little town, with a pleasant market square and neat, well-laid-out parks. Joseph's father was the town's stationmaster, a cheery, happy-go-lucky man who was completely bald by the time he was thirty. With the stationmaster's job came a house about five minutes' walk from the railway station set on a triangle of green where the road to the Baltic port of Gdansk began. In front of the house was a small children's park, where Joseph and his two brothers and sisters could play.

Joseph had a happy childhood. His mother was a warm and gentle woman, with long, dark, curly hair all the way down her back, which she assiduously combed every night. His father worked long hours at the station but, when he came home, he often brought sweets or some other gifts for his children.

In the summertime, Joseph and his brothers and sisters would swim in the lake on the edge of town or pick wild mushrooms in the nearby forest. In winter, the children of Koscierzyna would ice skate or sledge in the deep snow.

The only intrusion into Joseph's idyll was the outbreak of the First World War. The Germans requisitioned all the furniture in the Szlagowskis' house and food was in short supply. For days at a time the family would be without bread. Like most other families in Koscierzyna, they now lived on credit. Compared to many, however, a stationmaster was financially quite well off, and privileged to be in a reserved occupation; but one day the Germans arrived to search the house because Joseph's father was suspected of being a conduit for illicit arms. Although Joseph was only a small child at the time, he can still remember being terrified by the stiff-looking Germans with their tall pickle-helmets and fierce Alsatian dogs. The children hid under the bed, screaming as the Alsatians barked at them. Eventually the Germans went away, having found nothing.

At fourteen, Joseph left school and went to work in the local power station as an apprentice electrician. Like his father, he was easy-going and popular with his workmates. He immediately settled into the job, proving himself to be an adept electrician from the start. He was always keen to have a go at anything, willing to take a risk – a quality that was to become evident in the Battle of Britain. On one occasion, for example, when the lightning conductor on top of one of the huge chimneys at the power station needed replacement, no one apart from Joseph was prepared to undertake the task. He climbed up inside the chimney and, although in places the steps which fitted into the bricks were loose, he made it to the top. As he looked down at the tiny figures below, he realised that the chimney was swaying from side to side. When Joseph climbed down, the manager of the colliery congratulated him and gave him a handsome bonus.

In the early 1930s, when he was given the job of installing motors at a new bacon factory and slaughterhouse in Koscierzyna owned by an English company, Joseph had his first contact with the British. He was fascinated by the sound of the English language, but at that time the prospect of ever visiting what seemed a strange, faraway land, seemed remote. From the beginning the new factory (from where meat was sent by sea to England) did a brisk trade – and its presence had a profound effect on the whole Szlagowski family. Joseph's father, already fond of a drink or two, found that, as station-master, he was in a powerful position. Bottles of drink and other gifts were slipped to him to ensure that the products from the factory were freighted from the station as fast as possible, with the result that his social drinking turned into regular drunkenness.

In the summer of 1933, when he was nineteen, Joseph went by train to stay with his cousin at the seaside town of Gdynia on the gulf of Danzig. The port was in the 'Polish Corridor', which had been established in the Treaty of Versailles and divided East Prussia from the rest of Germany. On his first day in Gdynia, as he lay on the beach soaking up the sun, Szlagowski spotted a rotary-engined biplane overhead. It was performing aerobatics, looping, rolling and spinning. The young man stood up, entranced, and in that instant, he decided he was going to be a pilot: 'The instinct that had spurred me to volunteer to climb that chimney came to the fore. I thought it must be a lovely life up there in the sky and that was it.'

Returning home at the end of the holiday, Szlagowski told no one of his plans – least of all his mother, who, he feared, might not be best pleased. The next day he went into the recruiting office in Koscierzyna and joined up. Six months later, in March 1934, his papers came through, and he was called up in the Polish air force. He plucked up courage to tell his mother: 'She looked at me and said, "If that's what you want, then go, but take care." I was thrilled. My father just gave me a pat on the shoulder and said he wished he was young enough to fly.'

Szlagowski was posted to the Polish air force training school at Torun, about halfway between Koscierzyna and Warsaw, where he adapted easily to his new life as a pilot. He particularly enjoyed a six-week glider course in southern Poland, where he was allowed to fly solo. Like most young men in their twenties, he enjoyed the freedom of being away from home. Though a more self-contained and private person than most of his friends realised, he was handsome and sociable and took pleasure in the comradeship of young men of his own age with similar ideas. When he went back to Koscierzyna on leave, he was the centre of attention in his uniform, being one of the first boys in town to join the air force.

After completing his training, Szlagowski's wish to join a fighter squadron was granted. He was sent to a fighter training school near Torun. Here he had a close brush with death when the fuel tank on his Polish-built PZL dropped through the undercarriage while he was performing acrobatics. It was held on by pipes and wires and, on landing, cleared the ground by only a couple of inches.

In 1937, the young man was posted as an instructor to the Polish air force officer cadet school at Deblin on the Vistula river, eighty miles south of Warsaw. He enjoyed teaching and although he was not an officer and only aged twenty-four, his flying skills earned him the respect of the eighteen- and nineteen-year-olds in his charge, several of whom were also to become Battle of Britain pilots.

By the spring of 1939, Hitler had annexed Austria and Czechoslovakia. The threat to Poland, with its fifty-mile-wide corridor to the Baltic dividing Germany from East Prussia, was growing, and Joseph Szlagowski was anxious to be transferred back to a fighter squadron, but there seemed no hope of that at the time. In July, a heavy presence of German troops built up along the borders with Poland and in East Prussia. Hitler had a million and a half troops available on the frontiers, backed up by two thousand Luftwaffe planes. Two months later, on the flimsy pretext of the need to retaliate against Polish border violations, Hitler attacked. The Germans stabbed deep and fast into the rump of Poland, whose army had no answer to the enemy tanks. The plan was to nip Poland in a sharp pincer movement between two huge, heavily armed groups of soldiers, one cutting south, the other north. The Luftwaffe, who were to act as a spearhead, bombing airfields, roads and bridges, had more than five times the number of front-line aircraft the Polish could muster, including 648 modern Heinkel III and Dornier 17 bombers. Apart from a few dozen medium bombers, most of the approximately four hundred Polish aircraft were disastrously old fashioned. Their fighter pilots were equipped with Polish-made PZL P11 fighters, monoplanes whose basic design dated back to 1931. Lightly armed, lacking in climbing power, with a top speed of nearly 100 miles an hour slower than the Messerschmitt 109s, they had a hopeless task against a German air force already battle-hardened in Spain.

In September 1939, Wladek Gnys, who was later to fight in the Battle of Britain, was stationed near Cracow: 'My bed was directly under the window. I raised the blind and looked out. To my horror I saw all Cracow was burning. The sky was scarlet from the flames.'*

The Luftwaffe moved on at will, smashing key railway junctions and obliterating strategic roads, railways and bridges. With no efficient communications or early-warning system, the Polish air force was never able to organise an adequate defensive campaign. Only around Warsaw, which had installed an early warning system a few months before, was resistance possible.

On 8 September, Deblin was badly hit by German bombers. At the officers' cadet school on the edge of town, Joseph Szlagowski had grown increasingly frustrated. As he was not attached to a fighter squadron, he still appeared to have no prospect of flying in action.

The whole world was stunned by the German *Blitzkrieg* in Poland. The combination of armoured forces and modern, high-powered aircraft was awesome. Even Warsaw was doomed to swift defeat: after more than seventeen hundred bombing attacks in two days, Poland's capital city succumbed. As the German air fleet commander Albert Kesselring wrote, 'The Polish Campaign was the touchstone of the potentialities of the German air force and an apprenticeship of special significance.'

On 17 September, as part of a secret agreement between Germany and Russia signed before the war, Stalin annexed the eastern part of Poland. The defeated Polish air force could do

*Wladek Gnys, *First Kill*, William Kimber, 1981.

nothing but fly as many planes and pilots as possible out of the country, in the hope of carrying on the struggle elsewhere in Europe. On the day that Stalin's troops moved in, the Polish air force commander, General Pilot Kalkus, ordered Poland's three thousand pilots, including Joseph Szlagowski, to escape from Poland, taking an aircraft if possible. Rumours abounded that, if only the Polish pilots could reach Rumania, RAF Spitfires and Hurricanes were waiting for them. To Szlagowski, who had seen photographs of the Spitfire and understood that here at last was a machine that could take on the Messerschmitt 109 on equal terms, this sounded a thrilling opportunity. He grabbed a small reconnaissance aircraft, pushed his mechanic, Johnnie Cieslik, on board, and took off from Deblin over the Vistula river. For about three hours they flew south-east, between Czechoslovakia and Hungary on one side and Russia on the other, heading for Rumania.

That first night, the two men gobbled all their meagre rations and slept fitfully in their plane somewhere in southern Poland. At dawn the next day, fog lay thick on the field. Szlagowski could hear the rumbling sound of tanks in the distance: he could not afford to wait for better weather. As the plane lifted off into the fog, the Russian tanks fired; one bullet pierced the left wing, leaving a neat hole.

To Szlagowski's relief, as they gained height, the sun broke through the fog and the sky cleared. The two men flew on, below them mountains which they assumed to be the Rumanian border. Suddenly the engine began to cough: the plane had run out of petrol. Szlagowski's glider training came to his aid as he glided down searching for a place to force-land. Beneath him on the ground he could see people in what looked like white overalls: 'Oh, my God, I thought. I am in Russia! But I had to land. As I finished taxiing, the right wheel dropped into a hole. The plane dropped on its nose, but luckily the propeller was not damaged.' As the men in white ran up to the plane, Szlagowski realised that he had landed on an athletics field; the athletes were speaking not Russian but Rumanian. They were just inside the border.

One of the Rumanians drove off in his car for some fuel. Others hurried to find food for the hungry Poles. Fortified by a meal of beef goulash and with fifteen gallons of fuel in the plane, they took off again as soon as possible.

After a second brief refuelling stop at a nearby aerodrome, the Poles proceeded to the southern Rumanian city of Constanza, east of Bucharest on the Black Sea. Szlagowski had no map in his plane, and little knowledge of Rumania, but he knew that a certain valley led into Constanza and eventually found it. With great relief, the two men landed, to be met by several other newly arrived Polish pilots. Their aeroplanes were confiscated, and Szlagowski and Cieslik were taken to a small hotel.

The situation in Rumania was complex. The Polish pilots were well trained and experienced, and the Germans were determined that they would not be able to continue to fight. Although the Germans did not control Rumania, the Rumanian leaders recognized that, after Austria and Czechoslovakia, they were clearly in Germany's sphere of influence. Moreover, Rumanian oil was crucial to the German war effort. The Rumanians could scarcely jeopardise their position by insisting on independence in dealing with escaping Polish pilots. Therefore, many of the escaping Poles, including several who had been Szlagowski's pupils, were interned. Szlagowski and Cieslik heard from the Rumanian underground that the authorities planned to intern all Polish military personnel. With about fifty other Poles, they were taken in secret to a farm outside the town. After a few days in hiding they moved on to the port.

Escaping from Rumania was not easy. There were huge crowds trying to get away, and thousands milled around at the port. The Poles were advised that the best chance was to look like wounded refugees. 'I was trembling as I came to the gate,' said Szlagowski. 'I feigned a very bad limp. As Johnnie and I reached the head of the queue I gave the guard a wad of Polish and Rumanian money. He just let us go. Others were not so lucky, and were sent back to internment camps.'

On the boat, which was heading for Beirut, they were advised by Polish officers to destroy any evidence that they were either Polish or pilots. 'With great sadness I bundled up photographs and papers with my revolver,' said Szlagowski. 'I threw them into the Black Sea.'

The voyage gave Szlagowski his first chance to catch his breath and think about what was happening to his country. He began to worry if his family were still alive. Hundreds of people were waiting to greet them in Beirut. On the quayside a band played a welcome. The Polish pilots were given priority treatment and were soon put aboard a second boat, to Marseilles, from where they were taken up to Lyons to the Polish refugee camp.

In France, Szlagowski received the first news of his family. A letter arrived from his mother via the Red Cross. Since the German invasion, his parents had kept moving eastwards from

Koscierzyna, and were safe. The only family casualty was his grandmother, who was aged ninety-two. A strong and healthy woman despite her great age, she had been moved by the Germans across Poland in an open cattle truck. It was so cold that she had frozen to death.

On 16 February 1940, Szlagowski joined the French air force, but he never fought in France because he was a flying instructor and still needed combat training. By 9 March he was in Cherbourg, about to embark for further training in England – one of the first eighteen Polish pilots to do so. In Cherbourg, the Poles were told by Winston Churchill himself that they had not lost their battle with the Germans yet.

On landing in England, the Polish pilots were taken by bus to Sheerness on the Isle of Sheppey. Here was flat, agricultural land similar to parts of Poland. As the men marched to the camp, Joseph Szlagowski spotted something by the roadside. It was an English pound note: 'I jumped out of line and picked it up. It was very green, in good condition. I'd never seen an English pound note before. In those days a pound really was a pound. My mates all gathered round and looked at it. We began to wonder if the streets of England were paved with gold. Anyway, it paid for our first English booze-up.'

4

THE INTELLIGENCE OFFICER

Geoffrey Myers was born in 1902 to a north London Jewish family. His father was a stockbroker and at the end of Geoff's schooldays at University College School in Hampstead, Mr Myers decided to send his son to Germany and France to learn languages. The young man managed to land a job as an office boy with the *Morning Post* in Berlin, where the bureau chief soon recognised that the newcomer was blessed with intelligence and steely determination.

In 1925, when he was just nineteen, Geoff Myers became a journalist and embarked on a hectic life, making his way in his career while taking full advantage of Berlin's rich cultural life. The city was a thrilling place to be at the time – art, music, literature and café society all flourished. Hitler's accession to power in January 1933 was still several years away. Yet, beneath the superficial glitter of café life, Myers was aware of the looming postwar economic crisis and the lack of social and political cohesion. He watched the rise of National Socialism and saw it make headway even in liberal Berlin. As a journalist it was his job to coolly report the rapid and significant changes in German political life. However, as a Jew, he understood only too well that in Germany he was becoming an enemy.

So, when his father fell seriously ill in 1931, Myers was in some ways pleased to return home. He transferred to the *Daily Telegraph* in London as a temporary sub-editor. In at a time of worldwide economic depression, permanent employment in Fleet Street was hard to come by and when his temporary job was over Myers was out of work for several months. In 1932, he was offered a summer relief job at the *Telegraph's* Paris office.

Soon after his arrival in Paris, Myers fell in love with a friend of his sister, an attractive young music student named Margot. It seemed an odd match. Margot was nineteen, rather young and naive. Geoff was twenty-seven and by now an experienced journalist. Even though her daughter had fallen for an English Jew eight years her senior, Margot's rather strict mother was content. 'He's a very, very decent fellow,' she told her daughter. In 1933 the couple married and Geoff got a job with the Jewish Telegraphic Agency in London. Margot was still a music student and so at first the two of them could meet only for irregular weekends. The following summer, Myers returned to Paris, this time as a temporary replacement for a *Telegraph* journalist who was ill. Six months later, at the end of 1934, his appointment was made permanent.

In the five years before the outbreak of war, Geoff and Margot Myers were settled and happy in France. Margot taught music and played in concerts. Geoff translated a novel by the Provençal writer Jean Giono for publication in America. The couple bought a flat of their own; a son was born in 1936 and a daughter two years later. The only threat to this cosy world was the dramatic change taking place in Germany.

In Paris the fear of impending war began to grow pervasive. Two of the newspapers there were openly anti-English and antisemitic, and the arrival of German refugees in Paris stoked up anti-Semitism further. Even Margot's previously liberal brother began to suggest that Hitler would bring order to the chaos of Europe. Italian fascists strutted about near the Myers's flat, loosing off the occasional volley of bullets. As a Jew, Myers was acutely aware of the danger. Determined to defend freedom against the Nazis, he went to the British embassy in Paris to volunteer. At his interview the air attaché asked him languidly whether he wanted to be an officer. 'I don't give a damn,' Myers replied.

To his surprise and disappointment, the only prewar training Myers received was a few days of drill with three other volunteers in the embassy cellars. A tailor was even sent over from Savile Row in London to measure the four Parisian volunteers for their uniforms. Myers was desperate to get into the front line.

When his papers arrived, he was indeed an officer – Pilot Officer Myers. A fellow volunteer, an intelligent, talented accountant who had not been blessed with a public school education, was made a sergeant.

In July 1939, the Myers family took a gentle holiday on the Isle of Wight. The tense events taking place on the continent of Europe seemed a long way from the tranquillity of the very British little island. One day Myers slipped over while wheeling his son's pushchair and hurt his back. The boat back to Le Havre was virtually empty. In the Channel, the ferries going the other way were full of families escaping from France. In Paris, Myers hobbled ignominiously on his crutches back to the embassy, ready for action.

He had to wait until the day before war broke out. Two RAF squadrons – 142 and 12 – were sent to Rheims, and Geoff Myers, now mercifully free of his crutches, was dispatched to join them. He had no knowledge of flying, but he was keen to learn; so he was bitterly disappointed when he realised that, as a French-speaker, his role was confined to liaison officer and interpreter.

The squadrons were stationed on twin airfields at Berry-au-Bac near Guignicourt, north of Reims. The group captain seemed to know how things should be done in the RAF and told his new liaison officer to use his French-speaking skills to requisition the local chateau. Although rebuilt after sustaining damage in the First World War, it was still spacious and beautiful. It was owned by the Marquise de Nazelle, who agreed to move into a small but elegant servant's house to make way for the RAF. The group captain took the stylish state room for himself, but never slept on the four-poster bed, preferring his camp bed which was placed alongside. About one hundred and twenty men lived at the chateau. Forty of them were batmen, waiters and cooks; the rest were officers. These men had all come to fight, but through the phony war of the winter of 1939–40 they lived in the lap of luxury. Geoff Myers did not learn to fly or fire a gun during that time, but with his knowledge of French language and cuisine he was soon put in charge of running what was, in effect, a Grand Hotel.

The good weather of September 1939 gave way to a wet autumn, which made the rather featureless countryside around Guignicourt look even more grey. The nearby grass airfield became muddy and difficult to negotiate. When he was not busy at the chateau, Myers used a caravan at the airfield as his office, where he could analyse intelligence reports and deal with language difficulties. He seemed middle-aged to the younger pilots, but convivial and tolerant nonetheless.

There was, of course, the occasional disaster at the chateau – the worst being when the boiler burst in the severe winter weather and the group captain was prevented from having his daily bath. A further crisis was averted when, in an effort to improve the food, the wife of the local innkeeper was seconded to the chateau as a chef. The male RAF cooks were appalled by the idea of working for a woman, but the food was so good under her direction that their revolt was soon quashed. The chateau was in Veuve Cliquot country and so champagne was the staple drink. As winter passed, tins of RAF-issued bully beef piled up in the bar, beer tankards overflowed with Veuve Cliquot and dustbins were stuffed full of champagne bottles.

However, this wasn't to last. One day his Savile Row tailored uniform arrived at Guignicourt out of the blue. To Myers, it seemed to fit perfectly. As time went on, the squadrons at Guignicourt began to listen ever more intently to the radio. One or two still thought the war might pass them by, but Geoff Myers knew that it was just a matter of time.

His wife Margot had little idea of what was to come. Her father had been a naval officer in the 1914–18 war and had returned home safely. She assumed it would be the same for Geoff and so when her husband was dispatched to Guignicourt she had taken the children to Beaurepaire, the family house at Lucenay-les-Aix between Vichy and Nevers in central France. Large and square, built in French pisé and neatly whitewashed, it still seemed as solid and secure a refuge as it had been in 1914–18. Geoff's exact station was supposed to be a military secret, but Margot managed to meet him once in Paris just before Christmas. When she got off the train, Geoff was waiting. It was the first time she had seen him in his uniform. She roared with laughter. The uniform was big and baggy, the hat was ill-fitting and the coat could be wrapped around him twice. It had been months since Geoff had been measured for the uniform and now he had obviously been given someone else's. Margot immediately made him take it to a tailor at the back of the Madeleine and have it altered.

Guignicourt was in a *Zone Interdit:* outsiders were forbidden to enter. To Geoff's embarrassment, a close American friend of his, Steve Jocelyn, found a way of smuggling Margot in. Geoff maintained that it was not allowed, but Jocelyn got permission for his 'niece', with her son Robert, to stay in the local hotel for three weeks. Geoff was still very uneasy but was able to spend time with her. The family took their meals discreetly in a back dining room and Geoff's friends were brought into the hotel to meet his wife.

Margot sensed her husband's anxiety at the quickening pace of events in Europe. He was worried about the capabilities of the aircraft at the RAF's disposal. Yet the young pilots she met in the hotel seemed blissfully unaware of any cause for concern, despite Hitler's attacks on Norway and Denmark, launched on 9 April.

In early April, 1 Squadron, stationed near Nancy and equipped with Hurricanes, was temporarily quartered at the chateau at Guignicourt. One of the resident squadrons – 12 – was equipped only with the inadequate Battles. Paul Richey, one of 1 Squadron's best pilots, wrote:

We had already done a certain amount of liaison and co-operation with the Battles – practice attacks on them and so on – and we sympathised with 12 in their slow, under-armed machines. But they were pathetically confident … Although we gave them as much practice and encouragement as we could, we privately didn't give much for their chances.[*]

In spring Geoff Myers was sent back to England. He reported to Hendon, where he joined a course to become an intelligence officer. His duties were to learn how to investigate and collate all aerial incidents involving a particular squadron. The aim was to accurately record how many planes had been shot down, under what circumstances and by whom, and to draw an intelligence picture of the enemy's strengths and weaknesses. Although he was pleased to return to England, it meant leaving his family in central France, so contact with them was restricted even further. Beaurepaire seemed reasonably safe but, as his children were half Jewish, it was difficult for Myers to be completely confident. When his training was completed, Myers returned to France, where he was attached to a section dealing with photographic intelligence in Arras. His job was to classify aerial photographs, mainly of Holland and Belgium, which identified potential targets.

As 10 May 1940 dawned at Guignicourt, Bill Simpson of 12 Squadron heard the distinctive low hum of Heinkels over the chateau. Suddenly the sky was full of aircraft. There were bombs falling everywhere, but the automatic reactions of RAF training left the pilots little time to be frightened as

[*]Paul Richey, *Fighter Pilot,* Jane's, 1980.

they hurried to the airfield. The German invasion of France had begun.

The Germans moved fast, sending wave upon wave of bombers to hit the airfields. After that first dawn raid the runway at Berry-au-Bac was pitted, making take-off difficult. 12 Squadron now flew into combat for the first time. Bill Simpson, in his Battle, was hit on a low-level bombing run against German troops entering Luxembourg. He was engulfed in flames and burned so badly that he subsequently spent eighteen months in hospital. Two days later, five 12 Squadron pilots attacked the bridges at Maastricht. All five were shot down.

The RAF forces in France had no chance. The might of the Luftwaffe paved the way for the army and then provided cover as they moved forward. Escorted by fighters, the German bombers efficiently attacked Allied troops and strategic targets such as railway marshalling yards. British and French air force buses suffered continuous bombing. Whenever the advance was held up, Stuka dive-bombers maintained particularly devastating offensives.

The Battles and Blenheims proved, as some had predicted, no match for the Luftwaffe's Me 109s and 110s. On the first day of the German advance, out of thirty-two Battles airborne, thirteen were shot down and destroyed and many others were damaged. On 14 May, forty Battles were shot down in one attack. In the first five days the British lost over two hundred planes. Those aircraft not destroyed in action were hit on the ground. Against an air force that boasted a total strength of three and a half thousand front-line aircraft, the British force with its limited numbers of Hurricanes was hopelessly outnumbered.

At the aerodrome at Arras the news came through that German tanks were pouring through Luxembourg on their way to France. As bombs began to fall on the airfield, Geoff Myers and his colleagues in the intelligence unit spent more time sheltering in the cellars than analysing intelligence reports.

After several days of frightening chaos the British started to move out of Guignicourt. It was a horrendous job: vehicles, equipment, mobile office, petrol tankers and mobile landing lights, all had to be shifted. Pilots and groundcrew watched in agonised silence as the last remaining petrol and bomb stores were spectacularly blown up.

The German *Blitzkrieg* ripped through northern France at an astonishing pace, reaching Arras by 21 May. As the bombs fell and lines of terrified refugees began to rapidly flee the town, Geoff Myers volunteered to go to the house where the intelligence unit had worked. He went to remove the most secret documents and burn the rest before they were seized by the enemy. He wrote later:

> I said to Major Chase, 'If I get caught in the house, should I shoot myself? I'm wondering what to do, because I'm a Jew, and I don't know how things are.' Major Chase said, 'Oh, that makes things different,' and he gave me a look of such kindness that I thanked him inwardly. I also handed him my wife's name and address on a slip of paper, in case he got out and something happened to me.

But the mission was accomplished successfully and, with boxes of documents stuffed in a car, Myers headed for Wimeureux, where orders were received to destroy all but two of the most secret.

In a field beside the Picardy hotel, Myers and two colleagues started a giant bonfire. They then proceeded to Bergues, five miles inland from Dunkirk, where headquarters had been established. Everyone was so relaxed that the enemy could have been hundreds of miles away rather than just fifteen. Myers wrote:

> I felt as if we were caught like rats in a trap. So did the others. Unarmed men in uniform feel silly facing tanks. They were fifteen miles away and we had two hundred clerks, batmen and waiters with a few dozen rifles to defend us.

Myers never had to use a rifle. He was sent to Belgium with an urgent message, and then ordered to head for Dunkirk. By 24 May the Germans had taken Calais and reached Boulogne. Dunkirk was the only escape route available for the British and French troops, who were surrounded on all sides.

On the evening of 26 May – just sixteen days after the end of the phony war – the Dunkirk rescue operation was launched. More than 330,000 troops were evacuated. Among them was Geoff Myers:

> We dumped the car and ran up the ship's gangway just before it was lifted. Four minutes later we left for England … At Dover, people were enjoying the warm spell. Near the jetty people were playing tennis. We had come from another world.

5

THE GUINEA PIG

For Geoffrey Page, as for so many young men who fought in the Battle of Britain, flying was an obsession, the ruling passion of his life. However, Page's ambition was more specific than simply to become a pilot. He wished to emulate his hero, Captain Albert Ball, VC, the legendary First World War fighter ace, credited with shooting down more than forty German aircraft. Ball was the first pilot to be revered as a national hero. Although the twenty-year-old Ball had been killed in 1917 – the year of Geoffrey Page's birth – to a young flyer his achievements still seemed romantic:

> I also thought I knew about war in the air. I imagined
> it to be Arthurian – about chivalry. Paradoxically, death
> and injury played no part in it. I had not yet seen the
> other side of the coin, with its images of hideous vio-
> lence, fear, pain and death. I did not know then about
> vengeance. Neither did I know about the ecstasy of
> victory. Nor did I remotely suspect the presence within
> my being of a dormant lust for killing.*

*All the quotations in this chapter are taken from Geoffrey Page, *Tale of a Guinea Pig*, Pelham, 1981.

As a boy, Geoffrey Page spent endless happy hours tinkering with model aeroplanes. His uncle was an aircraft manufacturer but, despite the family connections his parents, who were separated, were implacably opposed to their son's joining the air force. So in 1937, aged seventeen, Page enrolled as a student at Imperial College London, where he soon discovered a way around his parents' opposition. He joined the University Air Squadron, eventually spending more time flying from Northolt than he did on his studies. When war came, the University Air Squadrons were to provide a fruitful supply of recruits for the RAF; although not quite ready-made, the young flyers from London, Oxford and Cambridge were nonetheless 80 per cent trained.

Geoffrey Page, like other young aviation enthusiasts, actively welcomed the war. It meant he could abandon his studies and fly all the time, and in the finest planes. Two weeks after war began, he received his call-up papers and joined several hundred other hopeful young pilots from the University Squadrons at the Aircrew Receiving Centre in Hastings. Apart from the rigours forced upon them by the NCOs, the centre must have been like a continuation of university life for these high-spirited, innocent young men who faced the future as if it was to be no more than an exciting adventure. Within a few weeks, Page was lucky enough to be one of the twenty-five pilots at Hastings to be selected for entry to RAF Cranwell in Lincolnshire, thus embarking on one of the several routes to Fighter Command.

The establishment of Cranwell in 1920 was part of Chief of the Air Staff Sir Hugh Trenchard's plan to ensure that the nation's newest force was not regarded as second-rate by the other services. It was designed to perform the same function for Britain's most recent service as Sandhurst and Dartmouth were doing for the army and navy. The approximately fifty graduates Cranwell produced a year were expected to be not just pilots, but leaders too: they were the élite.

Pilots of more humble origin such as Bob Doe found entry to the RAF via the Royal Air Force Volunteer Reserve, and numbers were augmented by apprentices who came up through the ranks, from the tough Apprentices' School at Halton, where boys from secondary school were trained as skilled groundcrew. All in all, by 1939, Britain was producing about two hundred pilots a month.

The well-organised German training machine, meanwhile, was turning out twelve thousand pilots a year from one hundred schools. On the outbreak of war, the Germans had sixty thousand aircrew available, with more in training.

When compared to the extent and quality of the German training, the programme at RAF Cranwell had its limitations, being remote from the realities of war in the air. As Geoffrey Page soon realised, the training aircraft were like dinosaurs when set beside Spitfires or Messerschmitt 109s. Even when Page's pilot intake moved into the advanced flying training school in January 1940, by which time the war was already nearly four months old, the planes remained unchanged. Most training at Cranwell was carried out in Hawker Hind biplanes, which had no flaps or retractable undercarriage. Page enjoyed his time there nonetheless, feeling at home among the small band of young men who could talk of nothing else but their passion for flying.

At the end of his course Page qualified as a pilot with an exceptional rating, and as a result was initially allocated to

Training Command at Meir airfield outside Stoke-on-Trent. This tribute to his skill meant he was considered good enough to teach others, but to a young pilot whose idol was Captain Ball, VC, of the Royal Flying Corps, Training Command was nothing short of disaster – depriving him of the opportunity of seeing action. Fortunately for Page, almost as soon as he arrived his posting was cancelled, and he was transferred to a Spitfire squadron, **66**, stationed in Norwich. For this improvement in his fortunes Page had the enemy to thank. In an attempt to halt the deep swathe that Hitler was cutting through Europe, relatively inexperienced young men were being summoned to the front line.

The squadron commander at Norwich was appalled to discover that his new recruit had never flown a Spitfire. 'Damned disgrace,' he said, 'sending along a young boy who's never flown anything more advanced than a Hind. If you get killed, it will be Group's fault. I've done my best to warn them.' Within half an hour of arriving, the nervous, slightly confused young pilot was sitting in a Spitfire for the first time. Trickling with sweat, he tentatively launched the sleek machine along the runway and eased it into the air. A mistake with the control column made the plane lose height and nearly hit a tree, but the nineteen-year-old from Cranwell soon relaxed and managed to land the machine successfully. He thought that he would never feel more exhilarated in his life.

Geoffrey Page was happy at 66 Squadron. He delete made good friends and worked hard learning how to fly Spitfires. Naturally he was thrilled when he was made operational. Although, within minutes of receiving the good news he came out of the hangar to meet the squadron commander, whom he heard telling another senior officer, 'They've made a mistake with Mounsden's and Page's postings; they should have been sent to 56 Squadron instead.'

Geoffrey Page was shattered by the Air Ministry's bureaucratic error. In just a few days he had come to adore Spitfires. Now he was off once again, this time to North Weald at Epping in Essex. Even worse, his new squadron flew Hurricanes, a rugged and effective plane but nowhere near as romantic as the Spitfire. Page's only consolation was that Captain Albert Ball had once been flight commander in 56 Squadron. Indeed, 56 had been the only squadron to produce two VCs in the 1914–18 war, Ball and Major James McCudden, the latter of whom was killed when his plane crashed after take-off on 9 July 1918, soon after he had shot down his fifty-eighth enemy aircraft.

North Weald had been opened in 1916 as a landing field on the eastern approaches to London. In the interwar years Epping had fallen victim to the unrelenting spread of suburban housing, but in May 1940, when Pilot Officer Page arrived from Norwich, it still seemed a tranquil place to be. By the standard of the more hastily converted airfields, it was well appointed, with a large flat grass strip and a solid officers' mess on the other side of the Epping to Ongar road. Page was delighted to discover that, despite his earlier misgivings, the Hurricane was a pleasure to fly. Admittedly, it was less sleek than the Spitfire, but it had clear advantages over the other plane, among them a roomier cockpit with a less restricted view: 'I was given a lovely fast aeroplane to fly for nothing and was paid the glorious sum of five pounds a week to do it.'

When Page joined the squadron at the end of May, 56 had already been badly hit over France and had since withdrawn to recuperate. Sent there as reinforcements on 16 May, they had lost their flight commander, Ian Soden, and Sergeant 'Tommy' Rose, who had previously survived being shot down by an RAF Spitfire in the week war broke out. Nerves were frayed and, according to Pilot Officer Barry Sutton, men like Page were a good influence on morale. Barry Sutton, was a tall, thin, distinguished-looking man who had been wounded in France and was now reunited with his depleted squadron said of Page, was new blood, he was keen, was a good flyer, and I think people liked him; two or three came at the same time and put heart into people like me. Geoffrey was obviously mad keen to get on with it. He was the sort of chap one needed.'

A few days later, 'Minny' Ereminski, the acting flight commander of 'B' flight in 56 Squadron – an extraordinary character who resembled a Nordic god, although he was in fact a white Russian – told Page over breakfast one morning to prepare for renewed action over France. Immediately, Page began to feel sick. As he waited at dispersal he was paralysed with fear, unable to read a newspaper or write a letter. He and his colleagues were to sweep across part of northern France with the aim of keeping the German fighters away from those British ground troops who were not surrounded at Dunkirk and who were retiring southwards to St Valery. Looking back, Page now regards this as the day on which he began to grow up:

> For us young airmen winging our way over the
> Channel, life had taken on a new meaning ... all that
> remained of youth in those swiftly moving Hurricanes
> were the physical attributes of our bodies; the minds

were no longer carefree and careless. The sordid reality that our task implied banished lighter thoughts for the time being.

Page was halfway across the Channel before he realised the impossibility of wearing a collar and tie when flying on operational sorties. In desperation, he ripped the collar away, tearing the shirt. Moments later he saw ahead the astonishing sight of a gigantic black cloud caused by oil burning from storage tanks below. Then through his earphones a voice said, 'Look out! 109s above.' By the time another message had reassured the young pilot that the aircraft above were, after all, British Hurricanes, Geoffrey Page was in a panic. His mind went blank as he looked anxiously round the sky for German planes. Suddenly, there was a gigantic shudder as he inadvertently flew through the slipstream of a colleague's aircraft. The shock jolted Page back to life and he began to pull himself together. By now the inexperienced pilot had lost contact with his squadron but he had enough nerve to creep back home, flying low over the Channel. His first sortie was over.

It was becoming obvious that other squadrons such as 56 stationed in Essex could not give adequate support for their army in France. The range was too great. The flight from North Weald, for example, gave the Hurricanes about fifteen minutes' worth of fuel left for combat before they were forced to return. Yet Page and his colleagues were lucky in some ways; other pilots were not even equipped with adequate planes. Patrols were flown by obsolete planes, which were sitting targets for the Luftwaffe. On one patrol, thirty-seven Fleet Air

Arm Skua and Roc dive-bombers and two-seater fighters set off from southern England and only nine returned.

Six days after the opening raid on the airfield at Berry-au-Bac, with RAF losses mounting, Commander-in-Chief Sir Hugh Dowding told the government that no more fighters would be sent to France. Any further weakening of the RAF's defensive capabilities would leave her extremely vulnerable in the coming defensive air battle over Britain. At first, Churchill insisted on sending the equivalent of ten more squadrons; it was not until 19 May, when four squadrons had already been sent, did the Prime Minister yield to pressure and agree to support Dowding. Instead, in a crucial decision, units were posted to airfields on the south coast of England.

Two days after Geoffrey Page's first hair-raising flight over France, his romantic view of war was shattered. Standing outside dispersal, he saw Hurricanes from 151, the other squadron based at North Weald, flying low over the airfield. As they began to pull away, the right-hand plane hit the ground. There was a loud explosion. As the plume of black smoke curled silently upwards, men ran through the grass towards the wreckage from all corners of the airfield, followed by a clanging ambulance. Page knew that there was no hope but kept on running. He stood in a helpless group as the firemen searched for a body:

> I was aware of two definite reactions to the scene
> before me. The first was one of nausea from the
> combined smell of the wreckage and burnt flesh. The
> other sensation was more powerful than that of a
> queasy stomach. I realised with surprise that the death
> of this recent companion did not disturb me very

much. It was as if a wave of shock radiated out from
the mangled debris, but just as it approached, the wave
passed on the other side leaving the senses high and
dry on a little island, erected by nature to protect the
occupant from the drowning effect of the horror of
the event.

'How about a drink?' Geoffrey asked a friend, almost casually,
and they led each other away from the wreckage so that they
might, in the time-honoured way, anaesthetise themselves
against all memories of what they had just seen.

6

THE SERGEANT PILOT

The pilots based at Hooton Park airfield in rural Cheshire in the early thirties were too busy flying to notice the regular presence on the boundary fence of a stocky boy with red hair and a cheery smile. The boy would stand there watching the planes for hours on end, his nose up against the wire, his bike leaning against the fence.

From that time forward, Cyril Stanley Bamberger, better known as Bam, longed to fly: 'If a boy is brought up by the sea, he's almost certain to be fascinated by ships. We lived so close to the airfield that I became addicted to planes.'

However, for Cyril Bamberger, the rigidity of the class system within the RAF made his hopes of becoming a pilot seem slim. Bam had been born at Port Sunlight, a pleasant Merseyside village created by Lever Brothers in the shadow of their own factory a few miles from the airfield at Hooton Park. His father was a clerk in the Lever bought-ledger department.

Bam and his two sisters lived with their parents in a neat house with a postage-stamp front garden and a back yard. Although the family was not well off, they never went hungry. A clerk was slightly better paid than a shop-floor worker, and Bam's father had been lucky enough to hold down a job during the difficult years of the thirties. At fourteen Bam left school and took a job selling fish from a bike, but was clever enough to, a year later, secure an electrical engineering apprenticeship at Lever Brothers.

610 (County of Chester) Squadron was part of the Auxiliary Air Force that had been conceived in 1924 as a reserve to help compensate for the enormous postwar decline in RAF numbers. Recruits tended to be drawn from the wealthy young men of the county or town. The squadron's motto was CERES RISING IN A WINGED CAR; and in 610's case the car would almost certainly have been a Rolls-Royce. Like all the Auxiliary Air Force squadrons, 610 was a reservoir of snobbery and class prejudice.

On the day of his seventeenth birthday, the boy whose nose had been enthusiastically pressed against the Hooton Park fence joined his idols as an auxiliary. As part of 610 Squadron, he trained every Saturday, Sunday and Thursday evening, eventually rising to the dizzy heights of leading aircraftsman and aerial photographer, and gradually losing interest in his apprenticeship.

In 1937 the RAF announced that each auxiliary squadron could appoint four trainee sergeant pilots. This was a golden opportunity for Bam and all the other aircraft fanatics who had the desire to fly but neither the money nor the position to be accepted for training.

Such was Bam's determination to become a fighter pilot that, when he was eighteen, he volunteered for the Chinese (Nationalist) air force. Answering a newspaper advertisement for pilots, he went along with a friend to the Chinese consulate in Liverpool. The two young men were disappointed to discover that the Chinese air force did not seem to want aerial photographers.

So, the trainee sergeant pilot scheme seemed to be Bam's only chance of fulfilling his growing ambition. Unfortunately, over two hundred auxiliaries at Hooton Park, many of whom had a university education, had the same idea. The interview went surprisingly well though and, thanks to his night-school training at Lever Brothers, Bam passed the mathematical test easily. The third requirement was a medical. The auxiliary medical officer was so drunk – he had been working onboard a ship in Liverpool and the seamen had plied him with cheap drink – that he just waved his stethoscope at Bam and pronounced him fit.

That evening, Cyril Stanley Bamberger was told he was to be trained as a pilot. His mathematical skills had been crucial. 'It was unbelievable. I wanted to scream and dance and shout. But the others were so disappointed I couldn't. Some were furious. One other applicant who later became a famous test pilot went mad when he heard that I'd got it.' As he cycled home to Port Sunlight, Bam was at last able to scream at the top of his voice with excitement. 'There were ten thousand men in Port Sunlight and I was the only one training to be a pilot. To some of them, Amy Johnson and Cyril Bamberger were the only pilots they knew.'

Flying then became Bam's whole existence: 'I must have been so naive; it was a wonder I clung on and qualified. I was so coarse, so unpolished compared to everyone else – especially the officers, who were all so well off and well bred.'

Some months later Bam flew solo for the first time. At about 8.00 p.m. on a calm Thursday evening he took off in an Avro Tutor, a large, clumsy plane for learners. With so much to think about, there was no time for him to feel nervous.

Only momentarily did the nineteen-year-old have a chance to appreciate the peace and tranquillity of flying on a still evening in an open-cockpit plane. Bam managed the difficult three-point landing, and his first solo flight was over. His logbook records that he was airborne for exactly five minutes.

Afterwards, he cycled furiously home to Port Sunlight, thrilled with his success, but in the village the novelty of having a trainee pilot had worn off and, although they listened, friends and neighbours were more concerned with their own problems. Here we are, thought the trainee pilot, waiting to fight a war, and Port Sunlight seems so insular, so blind to what is happening in the rest of the world.

By the time war broke out, the conflict between his desire to fly and his job at Lever Brothers had become almost impossible for Bam to cope with: 'War happening was, for me, the finest thing possible. It put me where I really wanted to be – flying.' As he had completed only thirty-six hours of solo flying time, he was still a leading aircraftsman (LAC).

Bam's family had a tradition of common soldiering. His grandfather had been a private and then a sergeant in the regular army. His father, who had followed suit and been invalided out of the First World War, now, at the age of forty-nine, also joined the RAF as an aircraftsman. Yet, for all his military background, Cyril Bamberger had no patriotic thoughts about war. He accepted it, and he welcomed it, but he didn't feel he was fighting for freedom, or to defend the British way of life. He simply wanted to fly. But the trainee sergeant pilot still had a long way to go to reach his mandatory hundred hours' solo. Thus, in September 1939, when 610 Squadron moved to a base at RAF Digby in Lincolnshire, Bam stayed behind in Port Sunlight.

A few weeks later, on 23 October 1939, he flew down to the No. 8 Flying Training School at Woodley, near Reading, the airfield where Douglas Bader had lost his legs in a prewar crash. Training was not really on a war footing yet; the instructors were civilians who had been given honorary rank in the RAF. Although they worked hard, an old-fashioned unhurried peacetime system operated for the trainees. Much to his frustration, Bam was taken back to basics, flying Magisters: 'It was as if I'd never flown before.' But he was so pleased to be flying that he never questioned the way things were done. He was a leading aircraftsman, he had a place in the order of things, and that was that.

For both officers and other ranks, the peace of the quiet ordered world of Woodley was very soon to be shattered. Today, Cyril Bamberger has a group photograph of the men on his training course at that time. It shows twenty-two shining young faces. He has marked with a red cross those who were killed in the war. There are eleven crosses. In October 1939, Bam's statistical chance of survival was one in two.

7

THE GERMAN

Ulrich Steinhilper grew up in Ochsenwang; a small, neat village of about a hundred and twenty inhabitants tucked away on a hillside fifty kilometres outside Stuttgart. It was a delightful place for children; traffic was virtually non-existent, and in summertime they could freely explore the surrounding woods and rocky countryside. In winter the village was cut off from neighbouring communities by snow. For adults, winter was a desolate time, but for Ulrich and his friends it brought the delights of sledging and ice skating.

Ulrich's father, Wilhelm, was the only teacher in the tiny village school, responsible for children from seven different age groups. He was a tolerant, understanding, popular man. However, it was Ulrich's mother, Paula, who was the dominant character in the partnership. She played the organ in the local church and taught children the piano. Her crisp manner and strictness made her a formidable figure in the eyes of her pupils. A village schoolmaster was poorly paid and, although their education placed Ulrich's parents firmly in the middle class, their meagre income meant that they could not always fulfil the aspirations of their class. The family could not even afford a bicycle – until 1924, when they acquired a lady's second-hand model. Until then, Ulrich helped with the weekly purchase of provisions, which involved a walk of nine miles in each direction.

This secure but isolated upbringing came to an end for Ulrich when, at the age of seven, he moved with his family to the larger community of Creglingen on the other side of Stuttgart. Ulrich's father now headed a staff of four at the local elementary school and the family's living standards improved, but the strong local dialect in Creglingen and an inherent resistance to newcomers made Ulrich feel like an outsider. In fact, resentment towards the Steinhilpers smouldered on for years, particularly among the professional classes. Ulrich himself had a reputation for always getting into trouble. When he fell off his bicycle one day, a local forestry worker, instead of helping him, beat him up with a bottle. Ulrich's parents took the man to court, but this merely increased local ill-will.

Ulrich's main passion as a young boy was machinery. In his spare time, he worked in a local garage, washing down the cars in the hope of earning himself a ride. Once, he was amazed to see a glider in the village. It was very exciting, yet the chance of a village boy ever flying one seemed so remote that the thought of becoming a pilot never even occurred to him.

In 1933, Ulrich was sent to school in Stuttgart itself. As a boy from the country he hated the crowds in the city and was always happy to go home at the weekends. Initially, when in Stuttgart, he lived in the YMCA. He had already been a member for a couple of years, and enjoyed the outdoor activities and sense of fellowship; but he was soon forced to swap the green shirt of the YMCA for the uniform of the Hitler Youth.

To Ulrich the Hitler Youth did not at first seem markedly different from the YMCA. All the usual activities, the camping and marching, continued, but in another shirt. The one change was that in the Hitler Youth young Germans were systematically indoctrinated with Nazi propaganda.

Until 1932, Ulrich's father had been fundamentally non-political, but the power of Hitler's speeches and the economic stability that he offered to bring to a system in difficulty began to make their mark on the headmaster. In 1934, Wilhelm Steinhilper joined the National Socialist Party, three years before it became compulsory for all teachers to join the National Socialist Teachers' League. This new political allegiance immediately caused trouble for the Steinhilper family. Among Ulrich's mother's pupils for piano lessons were eight Jewish children. Indeed, Creglingen had quite a strong Jewish community, particularly among the traders and shopkeepers. The local Nazis put pressure on Ulrich's father to stop his wife teaching Jews. But Mrs Steinhilper was not having her precious piano lessons disrupted, and continued to teach the Jewish children. Despite her husband's membership of the National Socialists, the family maintained normal relationships with the local Jewish community, until they moved to the town of Ludwigsburg, fifteen miles north of Stuttgart. Ulrich transferred to the senior school in the town.

Like many young German men, Ulrich Steinhilper was carried along on the tide of newfound national self-respect that Hitler helped stimulate. His interest in machinery and this growing nationalism made him keen to join up when Hitler's accession to power led to increased development of the armed forces. In late 1935 he applied to join a local infantry regiment at Ludwigsburg. At the same time, he had begun to resent the pressure the town's National Socialists were putting on his family. If he joined the army, he reasoned, he would be beyond their reach. The ammunition for this pressure came from a widely-known affair that his mother was having with another teacher. One faction in the National Socialists, dominated by pre-1933 members, wanted to use this knowledge to remove Ulrich's father from his influential job. Meanwhile, they informed the army about the affair and Ulrich's application was turned down.

Ulrich was bitterly disappointed, but in early 1936 a second chance presented itself when a Luftwaffe officer visited his school looking for recruits. Nervously, Ulrich applied, hoping that the Luftwaffe would not find out about his mother. He was delighted when his application was accepted, and he was dispatched to Berlin for further suitability tests. He arrived in Berlin, where he stayed with distant relatives, on the opening day of the 1936 Olympics – an occasion which Hitler exploited to convince the rest of the world that Germany was settled and content. The air force tests – physical, technical and intelligence, were intensive. To Ulrich's relief, there was little or no compulsion to toe the party line. Only about ten of the fifty teenagers were accepted, and Ulrich was one of the lucky ones.

Ulrich could have stayed in Berlin a further week to watch the Olympics, but for a country boy the city seemed crowded and noisy, so he hurried back to Swabia. Perhaps if he had stayed and witnessed the gap between the way the Jews were treated for those few weeks when the city was in the world spotlight and the day-to-day persecution they usually suffered, the young trainee pilot might have better understood what was happening in his beloved country. In many towns it was already extraordinarily difficult for Jews to purchase food or medicines at all. Yet, in Berlin before the Olympics, signs over shops saying JEWS NOT ADMITTED were taken down. During the Berlin Olympics, the Nazi terror campaign against the Jews was virtually halted.

Back home, Ulrich's parents asked eagerly what Berlin had been like during the Olympics. Although they were both teachers, they came from small isolated communities, had never travelled and had little conception of the monster that Germany was becoming. One of Ulrich's uncles, a Liberal Democrat, warned that Germany was proceeding along a slippery and unpleasant path. Similar warnings came from his girlfriend's father and from an academic family in Stuttgart whom he knew well. But a young man not yet eighteen, with a National Socialist for a father, who had already been accepted as a trainee officer in the Luftwaffe and had chanted the slogans and digested the philosophies of Hitler Youth, was unlikely to heed such warnings. He was too excited at the prospect of joining an air force that was beginning to make an indelible mark on the world.

In the autumn of 1936, Ulrich Steinhilper completed his two months of labour service, the pre-military training where uniformed young boys and girls dug ditches or shovelled snow. Such service was designed to introduce all young people to hard physical labour and provide a stepping stone between Hitler Youth and military service. The climax was a visit to the annual rally of the Nazi Party at Nuremburg in early September. Steinhilper was one of the lucky teenagers chosen to go. Among all the marching and crowds it was the aerial displays, particularly those of dive-bombers, that most excited him.

Steinhilper was next posted to the tough officers' training school at Werder, twenty miles outside Berlin, where the old-fashioned NCOs behaved very roughly if a uniform was not clean or a bed not properly made. In May 1937, after six months of basic training, he began his pilot's course, which included night-flying, blind-flying and gunnery. Again, the going was tough. On his first night-flight, one of the instructors, who had a reputation as a playboy, turned up completely drunk. Steinhilper could smell the stench of whisky on his breath and was terrified as they took off. When the drunken instructor began to mistake the local street lights for landing lights, the younger man was forced to take over and made the night landing on his own. Ironically, Steinhilper was described by his instructors generally as 'undisciplined and raw'.

At the end of his two year training, Steinhilper was sent to join a fighter squadron at Bad Aibling, south of Munich, which was still equipped with Heinkel 51 biplanes – much to the annoyance of those senior pilots who had been better equipped while flying with the Condor Legion in Spain.

As part of Hitler's operation to annex Czechoslovakia, in 1938 the squadron was sent to Eger near Carlsbad. On the journey, the squadron completely lost its way. Unlike the latest Luftwaffe aircraft, the Heinkel 51 had no radio communication, and maps were in such short supply that only the squadron leader had one. Several aircraft ran out of fuel and two were force-landed and written off. At Eger the squadron saw no action. Steinhilper met a pretty girl from a prominent National Socialist family and spent most of his time with her.

After six weeks in Czechoslovakia the squadron moved back to Germany.

Soon afterwards, Steinhilper was moved to what was to be his Battle of Britain fighter wing, the new Jadges Schwader (JG) 52 at Strubling, close to the Czech border, where he was promoted to lieutenant. JG 52 was equipped with brand new Me 109s. When the planes arrived the pilots walked round them in amazement and sat delightedly in the rather cramped cockpits.

Like each fighter wing, JG 52 was divided into groups, each comprising about thirty-six aircraft. The groups were then split into 'squadrons' of about twelve aircraft each. After a three-minute interview, Lieutenant Steinhilper was assigned to a 'squadron' in 1 Gruppe, under Squadron Leader Adolf Galland, who was already on his way to becoming a legend.

At 1/JG 52, Steinhilper was immediately diverted from conventional fighter-pilot duties, being appointed group communications officer. His group commander had not been in Spain and had little wartime service, but followed his directives and told the young man to set up a communications system from scratch. After his initial disappointment, Steinhilper warmed to his new role. Within a few months he had telephone equipment, switchboards and radios installed and working. For a twenty-year-old, this was all good experience in leadership and organisation.

The attacks on Jews in Germany were growing ever more excessive. Legislative restrictions on employment and education were followed by violence and persecution, which reached a new height on Crystal Night, 9 November 1938, and in the early hours of the following morning. The Nazis organised demonstrations against the Jews and all over Germany Jewish shops were smashed and looted and synagogues burned to the ground. Scores of Jews were murdered, and those responsible went virtually unpunished. The ordinary German people seemed to have lost their voice. To Steinhilper and his friends the crude brutalities of Crystal Night could be laid at the door of a few wild people; one way to come to terms with the cancer that was spreading through German society was to close your mind to it and concentrate on flying.

In the summer of 1939, JG 52 moved to Boblingen, the former Lufthansa airport in Steinhilper's home town of Stuttgart. Although he now had time to see his parents and friends more regularly, much of the young man's time was taken up with a huge Luftwaffe manoeuvre – a simulated bombing attack on Stuttgart. More than two hundred Do 17s, He IIIs and Ju 87s were involved. As communications officer, it was Steinhilper's job to decide when the air-raid sirens should be sounded. The simulated attack was a success. Steinhilper was delighted with the efficiency of the communications system he had set up, but the manoeuvre contributed towards a deterioration in his relationship with Galland. At the huge debrief afterwards, Galland, who from the start had belittled the importance of communications, criticised the ground-station procedure in front of more than two hundred other pilots.

Worse was to follow. Me 109s with new Daimler engines had arrived at the *Gruppe*. Steinhilper could not wait to try his new plane and, although flights in them had not yet been officially sanctioned, he skipped lunch the day they arrived and took his plane up for a quick spin. On his fourth landing he came in too fast. The plane jumped up and turned to the side. The undercarriage was broken off and the propeller bent. The brand new Me 109 had been with JG 52 for less than three hours. Justifiably, Galland was furious. After a dressing-down, Steinhilper was made to land endlessly in an old-fashioned Heinkel 70 which had a pumped undercarriage. Soon afterwards he was transferred to Gruppe 3. 'Galland and I,' said Steinhilper, 'were not entirely of the same wood. He was very autocratic. I didn't always agree with him.'

His new squadron leader was Helmut Kuhle, an amiable, humorous twenty-four-year-old who was respected and liked by his junior pilots. It was Kuhle's job to instil in his pilots the techniques they would need in war. It was essential, for example, for fighter pilots to develop expertise in aerial gunnery. Comparable training in the RAF was random and often brief, but Ulrich Steinhilper and his colleagues in 3/JG 52 were well equipped from the start. During 1939 they regularly practised gunnery techniques, usually shooting a hundred or more shots each session into marked squares on the ground. In the same year, Steinhilper also attended a two-week gunnery course in the North Sea. Pilots practised shooting at the shadows of other aircraft, then discussed and practised air-to-air gunnery tactics. The six hundred or so shots fired by the young German on that course were a far cry from the brief bursts of fire that was all too often the RAF trainee pilot's only gunnery experience.

Late into 1939, it was not certain that aerial combat against Britain would be necessary. Not that the men of JG 52 were afraid to go *to* war. 'On the contrary,' said Steinhilper, 'we were trained for it. When the *Blitzkrieg* in Poland happened, I didn't say to myself, I'm glad I can't get killed in Poland. I felt left behind.'

If the French could be dealt with efficiently, the thinking went, perhaps the British would see the sense in not fighting. So, in April, JG 52 moved to Neustadt, east of Kaiserslautern, to prepare for the war against France. Soon afterwards, during training, Steinhilper was rammed from below by his flying partner by mistake. The accident scarcely made any noise, but the plane's pedals felt loose and he noticed a hole in the bottom of his Me 109. Immediately he threw himself out of the plane. By the time his parachute had opened, the plane had hit the ground. Steinhilper knew that he was fortunate not to have been killed before he had even flown in combat.

3/JG 52 were to take part in the second wave in the attack on France, but after the initial wave resistance was limited and once again Steinhilper's fighting ambitions were frustrated. Even when the *Gruppe* moved to Laon inside France the squadron did not have a single victory or loss. Steinhilper's direct war experience was limited to flying over Dunkirk, after the evacuation, where all he could see was smoke rising upwards. Once again, he felt that the war had passed him by, though by now the German pilots were supremely confident that their machines and men were superior. Germany had taken Poland, Norway, Denmark, Holland, Belgium, Luxembourg and now France – but Flying Officer Ulrich Steinhilper had yet to fire a single shot in combat.

8

BATTLE ORDER

On 1 July 1940, Ulrich Steinhilper was waiting for his squadron to be moved to the French coast in preparation for the air battle with England. Geoff Myers was on a course at RAF Manston, near Folkestone in Kent, preparing to join a squadron as an intelligence officer. Bob Doe was flying his Spitfire miles away from the action, at RAF Leconfield in Yorkshire. Cyril Bamberger and Joseph Szlagowski were both desperate to move into the front line but were still undergoing training in the west country. Only Geoffrey Page, at nineteen the youngest of these six men, had tasted war. The chance for the others would come soon enough.

With France defeated, the Germans began to turn their attention to the invasion of Britain. After Dunkirk, the German military machine had temporarily come to a full stop. Hitler had never given adequate thought to how a war against Britain would be fought; he lacked an overall strategy. Virtually all the German experience and expertise was in waging war on land. The Strait of Dover was a formidable obstacle, especially as the Germans in 1940 were short of both landing craft and aircraft carriers. At the time, Britain was not to know the extent of the

German indecision. Until now, Hitler had acted with extreme confidence and calculated efficiency. The British knew that, if an invasion ever succeeded, Hitler's powerful army would smash Britain's limited defences relatively easily. After all, the Germans had just driven the British back across the Channel in a desperate escape. Since entering Poland, Germany had lost 27,000 lives; her enemies had lost 135,000.

Fighter Command was in disarray. The RAF had lost over 900 planes and 435 pilots, many of them experienced, in just three weeks. Morale was at rock-bottom. If Dowding had not shown his intuitive skill at pacing an air war, by husbanding his precious resources against pressure from Churchill and others who wanted to commit more squadrons to France, Fighter Command would have been even more seriously damaged.

The British were undoubtedly vulnerable and it might have been a good moment to attack, but Hitler felt that an Aryan nation like Britain, with its impressive achievements of empire and its racial strength, was a natural ally rather than an enemy. Moreover, expansion eastwards was more central to his thinking, and in June Stalin moved into Lithuania, Estonia, Latvia and eastern Rumania.

As Hitler and his advisors weighed up the pros and cons of invading Britain, Dowding took the opportunity to rebuild and regroup his forces. If the Luftwaffe were going to be prevented from winning supremacy in the skies, then a Fighter Command still recovering from the hammering it had suffered over France was going to have to fight a bitter, defensive air battle over southern England.

The government at last decided to substantially increase the amount of money committed to the war effort; it rose from a weekly average of £33 million in April to £55 million in June. Priority was given to building front-line fighters and bombers – beginning with an increase in Hurricane output.

Furthermore, the appointment, in May 1940, of the energetic newspaper tycoon Lord Beaverbrook as Minister of Aircraft Production speeded up the rate of manufacture. The number of Rolls-Royce Merlin engines, for example, produced in June was 839 – an increase of 500 over the April figure. The Civilian Repair Organisation (CRO) similarly beefed up its activity, raising its repair level from 20 a week in February to 160 per week in mid-July. Much of the increased repair work was done by motor mechanics and other inexperienced men, under the guidance of RAF technicians.

Modest food rationing began. A second wave of children were evacuated. Rumours of spies and enemy parachutists arriving were rife. German and Austrian nationals living in Britain were classified, and eventually the majority of them were interned. Early June saw the widespread removal or obliteration of road and rail signs. Holiday beaches were covered with barbed wire.

On the other side of the Channel a supremely confident Luftwaffe moved into positions to prepare for the defeat of Fighter Command. Bases were established in Holland, Belgium and, in particular, northern France.

Skirmishes between the RAF and the Luftwaffe started at the beginning of July, but it was not until 16 July, six days after what was later seen as the official start to the battle, that Adolf Hitler finally issued his Directive No.16:

> As England, despite her hopeless military situation,
> still shows no sign of willingness to come to terms,

I have decided to prepare, and if necessary carry out,
a landing operation against her. The aim of this operation is to eliminate the English motherland as a base
from which war against Germany can be continued
and if necessary to occupy the country completely.

Directive No. 16 was intercepted and its code name, 'Operation
Sealion', became known. Even this directive states that occupation of Britain would only happen 'if necessary' – indicating
that Hitler's plans for invasion were still not clear-cut. Famous
Luftwaffe ace Adolf Galland called the invasion 'a necessary
evil' for Hitler, 'with which he had to cope somehow – just
how, he was not quite sure'.[*]

In a speech on 19 July, Hitler made what sounded like a
final peace offer. After accusing Churchill of warmongering,
he said, 'I feel it to be my duty before my own conscience
to appeal once more to reason and common sense in Great
Britain … I can see no reason why this war must go on.' When
he received no response to this rather vague overture, Hitler
was able to turn to the German people and blame Britain.

Preparations for Sealion now began in earnest. Plans were
laid for six infantry divisions to land on the beaches between
Ramsgate and Bexhill. Three more divisions would land
between Weymouth and Lyme Regis. By the time a third
wave of forces had landed it was intended that 260,000 men
should be ashore in Britain. German navy commanders were
unhappy, doubtful that they could protect such a wide front
of soldiers. So far, the *Blitzkrieg,* combining the army and air
force, had been strikingly effective. Now the Germans were

---

[*]Adolf Galland, *The First and the Last,* Methuen, 1955.

expected to land a huge force of men with very little experience of amphibious craft on such a large scale, and little time for adequate preparation. The British navy was strong and supported by an air force which, although seriously damaged in France, still had enough planes and pilots left to offer her navy some protection.

During July 1940, the German aircraft took their places along the Channel coast. Luftflotten (Air Fleet) II and III were moved into key positions with a force of 2600 planes, nearly a thousand of which were fighters; the remainder were bombers, plus a few reconnaissance aircraft. A further 190 planes of Luftflotten V were based in Norway. With impressive speed the bases in France, including a communications network and repair facilities, were set up.

Commanded by Albert Kesselring, who had led his air fleet with such distinction in the *Blitzkrieg* in Poland and France, the pilots of Luftflotte II included Oberleutnant Ulrich Steinhilper, who had moved with the rest of 3/JG 52 up to Calais. Their headquarters was a tiny monastery at Coquelles a few kilometres inland from Cap Gris-Nez, the nearest point of mainland France to the southern coast of England. Some of the pilots stayed in the barnyards of nearby farms, but most of the accommodation was in tents. The airfield incorporated a meadow, a cornfield and a potato field. For quick take-offs, 3/JG 52 had to taxi across the soft part of the potato field, but the Me 109 was well equipped to deal with such conditions. Steinhilper and his colleagues knew quite clearly that an invasion was in preparation. Barges with specially fitted ramps were arriving in Boulogne and Calais. Though, at the same time, there were persistent rumours of a deal between Hitler and Britain.

On the other side of the Channel, Fighter Command was divided into four groups. All the famous fighter stations – Tangmere, Biggin Hill, Northolt, Manston – were in II Group, commanded from Uxbridge by Air Vice Marshal Keith Park, a quiet New Zealander possessed of great tactical intuition. 10 Group, established as late as 17 July, covered the south-west with the vital job of protecting Southampton and other local ports, but was otherwise outside the central battle area. Its commander was the solid South African Air Vice Marshal Quintin Brand. 12 Group, under the ambitious Air Vice Marshal Trafford Leigh-Mallory, was based at Watnall in Nottinghamshire, but its key bases like Duxford were in East Anglia just to the north of the II Group ring of fighter stations. Headquartered at Newcastle, 13 Group under Air Vice Marshal Richard Saul controlled airfields in Scotland, Northumberland and North Yorkshire.

Against the 2600 aircraft (1900 serviceable) deployed in Luftflotten II and III, Fighter Command had 900 aircraft, but only 591 of these were serviceable. With bomber and reconnaissance aircraft removed from the total figure, the Luftwaffe had 1055 fighters against the RAF's 900: a much more even balance than is commonly supposed.

The bulk of the German fighter planes were Messerschmitt 109s, which had proved themselves the greatest fighter planes in the world. They were light, but steady and stable, with good acceleration, turning circle and diving speed. However, difficulties with visibility and a tendency to swing at take-off and landing made the Me 109 prone to accidents.

Over half of the 900 British fighters were Hawker Hurricanes, sturdy aircraft outclassed by the Me 109s in terms of speed and diving power but extremely resilient, particularly against cannon shell, and easy to repair. There were also the Supermarine Spitfires. Light and sleek, with better visibility than the Me 109s, the Spitfires matched the German planes in every respect, except when the two aircraft flew over 20,000 feet. However, by 1 July only 286 of them had been built, greater resources having been poured into the Hurricanes and less worthwhile aircraft.

The rest of the German fighter strength was taken up by 246 Me 110 twin-engined fighters. Designed as escort planes for bombers, they were well armed and faster than the Hurricane, but their acceleration was poor and their turning circle wide, so they presented easy targets for the Spitfires.

The Hurricanes and Spitfires of Fighter Command were supported by Blenheims and Defiants, which were not as effective even as the 110. Slow and old-fashioned, both planes were to suffer heavy losses at the hands of the Me 109s.

The Germans appeared to have a distinct advantage at the beginning of the Battle of Britain, with battle-hardened pilots flying a superior number of first-rate, proven fighters, against a demoralised and under-equipped enemy. Yet, in terms of strategy and tactics, the RAF had the upper hand. Much of German success to date had depended on the use of bombers, particularly the rapid-striking Stuka dive-bomber, rather than on the attacking qualities of its fighter force. The German bomb-making and aircraft industry were not geared to anything more than a short decisive campaign and, despite the undoubted quality of the Me 109 fighters, the German High Command continued to place more emphasis on the production of bombers. In Britain, on the other hand, Beaverbrook was dramatically increasing the output of Hurricanes and Spitfires. In the third quarter of 1940, fighter production hit a monthly average peak of 563 compared with the Luftwaffe's monthly average of 156. Germany was capable of producing more. Indeed, she ultimately raised her aircraft production output to 2500 a month – but that wasn't until 1944, when it was too late.

A second crucial advantage for Fighter Command was the successful application of its radar network, but the greatest advantage of all was the fact that the battle was fought over home territory. The Me 109s were not equipped with a second petrol tank, so were reduced to fifteen minutes or so of combat before being forced to head home. If a Luftwaffe pilot had to bail out, he risked drowning or being taken prisoner. His plane was lost. On the other hand, an RAF pilot who bailed out could easily rejoin his squadron. Even those who were burned or injured could be patched up and sent back to the front line. If damage was not too extensive, their planes could be repaired and used again. Furthermore, fighting over Britain gave the RAF pilot a psychological boost. At night he could drink or socialise in familiar places; contact with his family was easy, and below him as he flew was the land he was defending. The Sussex downs and the Weald of Kent were permanent reminders of the battle's purpose.

Yet, for all these advantages, the RAF had inherited many of the prewar qualities of a gentlemen's club. It was elitist, amateurish and unrealistic in its preparations for war. Against this, the professional efficiency of the men and machines at the disposal of a so-far invincible Luftwaffe meant that British victory was far from a foregone conclusion.

As Dowding set out to replace the pilots who had been killed or captured in France, a restless Cyril Bamberger could see that his chance of action was coming at last. For nine months a war had been going on while he marked time on Darts and Magisters, without getting anywhere near a Spitfire or Hurricane. However hard-pressed the RAF might be, Bamberger was still expected to finish his course at No. 9 Service Flying School at Hullavington. 610 had already had seven pilots killed over France. As Bam spent a final frustrating fortnight waiting to rejoin his squadron at Biggin Hill, they suffered further losses.

Within a few days of the start of the Battle of Britain, one of Bam's fellow sergeant pilots, twenty-two-year-old Sydney Ireland, had been killed while practising dogfighting. The next day on 13 July, Sergeant Patrick Watson-Parker was killed during a routine patrol, followed by Pilot Officer P. Litchfield, killed after an engagement with the enemy north of Calais. A close knit Auxiliary squadron such as 610, whose pilots all came from the same one or two towns, was particularly badly hit by such losses, which damaged morale and changed the fundamental nature of the squadron for ever.

But to Cyril Bamberger, training at Hullavington still seemed gentle and unhurried, with the realities of war as remote as ever. He had to occupy himself with petty rules and regulations when all he wanted to do was to fly in action. One day Bam broke bounds with a fellow sergeant and walked to the local village. As a result, he was given the Black Book: this had to be signed at certain times of the day to ensure that the offender was still on the airfield. Once a day the duty officer had to sign. 'For this I had to go to the officers' mess – to us, the ultimate holy of holies. He would sign the book and while I stood there helpless, like a lemon, he would shout and bawl at me in front of the officers. I suppose it was part of the system, but it made me feel so small, so humiliated. It was so needless. I imagine it was like a public school.'

Despite its unnerving losses in France, the RAF was in no hurry to push its experienced Polish recruits into action. Indeed, for the Polish pilots newly arrived in Britain the opening few months were deeply frustrating. Many had already fought the Germans in Poland, albeit briefly and painfully, and some had gone on to fly with the French. As one put it, 'It was always in our minds to avenge Poland. Nobody could stop us. We had more hate than anybody. On a couple of occasions Poles still attacked Jerries even though they had run out of ammo. They just flew straight in.' Yet the very speed with which the superior German aircraft had ripped through the Polish opposition made some senior RAF figures uncertain about the pilots' ability. The need to retrain them on Hurricanes and Spitfires and their lack of facility with the English language also militated against the Poles' chances of exacting swift revenge. Their subsequent success was so spectacular, however, that the RAF came to feel guilty about being overcautious in the early phases of the battle.

In July 1940, 303, an entirely Polish squadron, was set up at RAF Northolt. All the senior British officers were shadowed by Poles of the same rank. 'A' Flight was led by the distinguished Canadian flyer Johnnie Kent, with the Polish Flight Lieutenants Henneberg and, later, Urbanowicz by his side. As RAF pilots began to die in considerable numbers elsewhere, the Poles were still learning the basics of English and radio transmitter

(RT) technique. In the mornings, 303 Squadron would go to Uxbridge, nine miles away from Northolt, to learn the rudiments of RT procedure. They were taught the classic RAF language such as 'bandits' for enemies, 'pancake' for landing. Some days, the Polish pilots were reduced to riding round RAF Uxbridge on bicycles while instructions in English were barked at them over headphones.

Joseph Szlagowski was one of the lucky ones. As one of the first eighteen Polish pilots to arrive in Britain, he was due to be posted to an English squadron. By July, Szlagowski had already flown six different types of aircraft. Early that month he flew a Spitfire for the first time at the training school at Aston Down, Gloucestershire. He was initially wary of the retractable under-carriage, but he soon grew to love the plane: 'You sat there in the cockpit and the rhythm of the engine made you happy singing to it; you could fly that aircraft without touching the controls.'

On 18 June, Bob Doe's Squadron 234 had finally moved south from Yorkshire to RAF St Eval, near Newquay in Cornwall. At Leconfield no one had believed that the war was real, but at St Eval the mood changed dramatically. 234's role was to protect British shipping convoys and to patrol Plymouth. Gregory Kirkorian, Armenian-born but every inch the English gentleman, was the squadron's intelligence officer and, like Geoffrey Myers at 257, a father confessor to the young men: 'All those early patrol convoys made everyone nervous and angry,' he said.

The tension between the commanding officer, Squadron Leader Barnett, and the rest of the squadron grew even more marked in Cornwall, as Kirkorian remembers: 'It was clear at St Eval that Barnett couldn't and wouldn't lead the squadron into battle.' Indeed, the squadron record book mentions no flights by Barnett in May and June, four solo patrols in mid-July, and not a single flight in the second half of July and August when the Battle of Britain was heating up. He appears never to have flown in action.

At the same time, Bob Doe and other 234 pilots were being scrambled three or more times a day. Yet, compared to many pilots who were to fly later in the war after only five or six hours on Spitfires or Hurricanes, the 234 pilots had already been in training for several months. Doe said, 'I think I'd done about four hundred hours in Spitfires when the Battle of Britain started, so I was a pretty experienced pilot, except as far as gunnery was concerned. I'd just fired my guns once, into the sea.'

St Eval, a grass airfield with runways under construction, was a coastal command station, flying Ansons, with a fighter sector attached. The operations room was tiny. Intelligence Officer Kirkorian recalled, 'We messed in wooden huts and messing arrangements were odd. I seem to remember that for five or six weeks we had an uninterrupted diet of Spam, tinned grapefruit and champagne.'

Between the start of the battle and early August the squadron was concerned mainly with routine patrols, although some of these were tricky ones undertaken at night. Squadron Leader Barnett, who led from the hangar, was conspicuous by his absence in the air, and some of the young pilots felt lost. Despite the hours of flying practice, 'We were all amateurs,' said Kirkorian. 'Yet, the young pilots lived their lives to the full because they knew that any day they'd be dead.'

In early July, Geoff Myers returned to Hendon to join 257 Squadron, which had been earmarked to go back to France and needed a French-speaking intelligence officer.

257 was a former training squadron that had been adopted by the people of Burma. The Burmese motto on its badge was translated as DEATH OR GLORY. Disbanded in 1919, the squadron had been reformed as recently as 17 May 1940 as a fighter squadron. In those few weeks they had already changed aircraft once: having started with Spitfires, 257's pilots had to be retrained when these planes were replaced by Hurricanes in June.

On his first day with 257 at Hendon, the newly arrived intelligence officer was struck by one thing about his colleagues – their youth. As he looked round the room, many of 257 Squadron appeared to him to be no more than boys. At thirty-four, Myers was almost twice as old as the youngest, who was eighteen; few of the others were older than twenty. They seemed so fresh and innocent.

One of the most senior pilots, a handsome flight lieutenant of twenty-four, introduced himself as Hugh Beresford. Apart from his age and rank, Beresford was set apart from the younger pilots by the additional responsibility of marriage. To the sergeant pilots such as Glaswegian Ronnie Forward, he seemed remote, even aloof: 'He was a bit above my station in civilian life. We christened him "blue blood Beresford".'*

On 4 July, 257 Squadron moved from Hendon to Northolt on the western edge of London. During the months that followed, Geoff Myers kept a unique record of his experiences. His wife and family were hidden away deep in occupied

*BBC TV *Forty Minutes*, 1980.

France. Communication with them was almost impossible, so Myers wrote letters to them in a notebook – letters which were never posted but kept safe so that, if he survived, his wife and children might understand what their father had experienced:

> Three months of it now and I have kept silent. I have been hoping to write letters to you, letters that would reach you. I have been wanting to do something that would help you to escape from occupied France and get us all out of this living grave.

I haven't had the courage up to now to write letters to you like this, in a notebook, with the knowledge that you may never see them.Most of the young pilots had no family responsibilities, and in those first few weeks in July, Myers felt out of tune with their needs and preoccupied with the safety of his own family:

> I was like a living ghost. I knew it, but try as I might, I couldn't shake off the pall. I couldn't help getting those day nightmares about you in German-occupied France. At first they were such that I longed for the night, because although I had nightmares, they were as nothing compared with those of the day. But I've almost stamped them out. I'm calmer now and I'm more useful again to the boys.

In the first three weeks of July, 257 worked to become a cohesive operational unit. This was obviously more difficult for a new squadron, whose pilots were drawn from several different sources, than it would have been for a well-established squadron with prewar experience. But the whole squadron felt confident in the skills of Squadron Leader David Bayne. Myers wrote:

Just the sort of man we needed. Determined, conscientious and brave. Two years ago he had a flying accident which left him with a wooden leg. You couldn't scarcely have guessed this, because he walked around with a stick and scarcely limped. That was the sort of man he was.

As 257 waited for their first operational orders, a new officer, a rather aloof man called Hill Harkness, was posted to the squadron as an 'observer'. Both Myers and the adjutant, who was also some years older than most of the other pilots, were concerned:

We felt sorry for him, because he seemed like a lost sheep, so we gave him as much encouragement as we could.

One day, Myers and the adjutant were called into the squadron leader's office to be told that Bayne had been promoted to wing commander and that Hill Harkness was taking over. Harkness was from Belfast and his combat experience was much less than that of his predecessor. However capable a leader Bayne was, the RAF obviously did not want an operational commander with a wooden leg. Myers wrote:

Nothing in his face betrayed his anger and dismay at being deprived of the leadership of the squadron just as it was becoming operational. He knew that he was being posted to a fighter control room on or below the ground. He tried to talk casually to us about the squadron, but his voice almost dried up.

PART TWO

THE BATTLE

9

THE CLOSING DAYS OF JULY

The first phase of the air battle began with a succession of skirmishes, as the Germans launched attacks on Channel convoys with their heavily escorted bombers. Despite the speed with which Fighter Command had patched up the gaping holes left by the battle for France, Dowding knew that British cover remained thin and that his fighters had to be used economically and warily. If his pilots did not fly a protection role, then Channel convoys would be sunk, but each sortie represented a great risk; he could not afford to commit too many squadrons in one go.

The Luftwaffe, on the other hand, confident of early victory, were simply waiting for Hitler to announce the total commitment to attack that would pave the way for Operation Sealion. In the meantime, they planned to draw the fighters based in southern England into the air and destroy them by superiority of numbers and technique. Alternatively, Air Fleet II's fighter force might engage the enemy planes and, when the enemy had to withdraw for refuelling, the German bombers would move in and attack the Channel convoys.

Until now, Ulrich Steinhilper's view of the war had been limited to circling over the smoking debris of Dunkirk. But at Coquelles, twenty-odd miles from Dover, JG 52 were at the centre of the action. One evening, on a routine search for convoys near Dover, Steinhilper saw a group of about ten Spitfires flying below him. One of the most effective features of the 109 was its diving power; the German now put this to the test. Although the sea beneath the enemy looked black and unfriendly, the group of Spitfires were bathed in a beautiful red light. Steinhilper fired a brief burst and hit the leading aircraft, which spiralled downwards. 'It was my first victory but I felt no special satisfaction,' he said. 'I was just doing my job. The cruel thing about war in the air is that you rarely acknowledge the fact that you have killed a human. It blunts the senses.' The next day, Steinhilper was told that his victim had been a squadron leader. The news unnerved him: 'I didn't like the feeling of the victim having an identity, a name.'

When they were not in action, life for JG 52 was very similar to that of their RAF counterparts across the Channel. Sleep was fitful, and they hated the sound of the telephone. They would sit around in deckchairs playing cards or reading papers. Steinhilper had a mongrel dog which followed him everywhere, and he would sometimes take it with him shooting in the woods. Among his friends was Albert Waller, a tall, blond farmer's son from outside Hamburg whom he had trained with three years before. Waller was a hard-working and reliable colleague. Another linchpin of the squadron was Lothar Schieverhofer from Hanover. Although Schieverhofer had not fought in Spain, he was an experienced pilot with five years of experience. He was rather formal and disciplined, and not interested in fooling around either in the air or on the ground. In contrast, Steinhilper himself was sporty and sociable, always happy to have a drink or a laugh. His fresh face and dark good looks made him attractive to women. Wine and champagne were freely available at Coquelles and helpful for steadying the nerves. One day, Steinhilper and a friend noticed half a dozen barrels floating in the harbour at Dunkirk. They opened one and found it contained red wine. Next day, they returned with a truck and helped themselves.

The Battle of Britain was only three days old when, on patrol off the Kent coast, 56 Squadron found itself facing an enemy force of about seventy Me 109s and 110s. A tense battle developed, with Geoffrey Page working hard to stay alive as the 109s attacked out of the sun. His attempts at firing back always seemed a moment too late. One minute, the sky was streaked with tracer as scores of warplanes turned and attacked; the next, everything was still and all Page could hear was the distant sounds of the air battle carried on the wind. Then, in front of his Hurricane, he spotted a solitary 109. The two pilots headed towards each other at a great pace. Neither would give way. Both fired. The planes were so close that Page was certain that they would collide and finish up as one ball of flame.

The 109 passed by with inches to spare and the two planes broke away. As he made his way back to base, Page felt only a sense of disappointment at his failure to hit an enemy aircraft. But twenty-seven years later, when the German pilot, Flight Sergeant Dau, recalled the incident in *The Luftwaffe Diaries,* Page realised that he had in fact hit Dau's 109. The German wrote:

The whole cockpit stank of burnt insulation. But
I managed to stretch my glide to the coast, then made
a belly landing close to Boulogne. As I jumped out the
machine was on fire and within seconds ammunition
and fuel went up with a bang.[*]

Like Ulrich Steinhilper across the Channel, when Geoffrey Page
was not in action he spent his days at dispersal in North Weald
waiting for the telephone to ring. He too sat in deckchairs,
read the papers, played cards and caught up on missed sleep.
Initially, the pilots slept in the solid officers' mess on the other
side of the main road to the airfield, but soon beds were put
in the wooden huts at dispersal so the young men could sleep
near their planes. They lived next to their machines from half
an hour before first light in the morning until after last light
in the evening.

At night, 56 Squadron grabbed at pleasure with the desperation of young men who knew they were running out of time.
If Geoffrey Page and his friends were not to be found in the
King's Head near the airfield, they would be propping up the
bar of the RAF pub in Shepherd's Market in the West End. On
one occasion they spent the night at a club off Regent's Street.
It was nearly first light by the time Taffy Higginson's car,
Esmerelda, chugged back into North Weald full of drunken
and sleepy pilots.

Inevitably, that same morning, 20 July, brought a particularly early start, despite an overcast sky. At 5.00 a.m.,
Page had only just slipped into bed and fallen asleep when
the phone rang. Hardly awake, he rushed from his bed at

[*]Cajus Bekker, *The Luftwaffe Diaries,* Macdonald, 1967.

dispersal and clambered into his Hurricane. He had been air-borne a few minutes before he noticed that, although he had on his life-saving jacket and his flying boots, in place of his flying suit was a pair of summer pyjamas. It was too late to turn back. At 18,000 feet Page, feeling bitterly cold, noticed a Ju 88 on a photo-reconnaissance trip emerge from a cloud. Flight Lieutenant Jumbo Gracie, Flying Officer Weaver and Geoffrey Page all went for the Junkers. They saw the plane hit. Page fired again and saw a further strike on the German before it disappeared into a cloud. It was still only 5.45 a.m. The three pilots were disappointed, but when they returned to North Weald they heard that the Ju 88 had crashed in flames off St Osyth near Clacton. Four Germans had been taken prisoner. Despite the pyjamas, Page had scored his first recognised victory.

The squadron combat report records a further success for Geoffrey Page a few days later. On 25 July, 56 Squadron arrived in the Channel to take over protection duty for a convoy. The Germans had already successfully caught the ships between Fighter Command patrols. They had sunk five and hit four more before 56 Squadron arrived to see Stukas still diving on the convoy. The sea seemed to be ablaze and the sound of bombs and machine guns filled the sky. With great bravery 56 attacked the German bombers, in defiance of the Messerschmitts escorting them. Then Page managed to shoot down a Stuka. All he could make out after the German hit the sea was one solitary wheel bobbing on the water and a patch of burning oil.

At Coquelles that day, Ulrich Steinhilper and his colleagues mourned the loss of their first pilot, Lieutenant Schmidt, who was shot down at 6.40 p.m. off the Kent coast. JG 52 had run into Cyril Bamberger's Squadron 610 for the second day running. The wing had lost six planes in two days.

That same evening, fifteen minutes before midnight, 234 Squadron at St Eval also lost their first pilot. Pilot Officer Geoffrey Gout from Kent crashed his Spitfire on a routine patrol and was killed. This was the first of several accidents for 234. As Plymouth fell under regular attack, their daylight convoy patrol had been added to by the need for patrol during the hours of darkness. Patrolling Plymouth was relatively simple; landing back at St Eval at night was much more tricky. There was often tension in the control tower between the flying control officer and the duty pilot, the latter of whom was positioned there to advise the control officer but had no executive authority. If there was an air raid alert, the flying control officer would usually switch off all the lights on the airfield, leaving pilots on night patrol in complete darkness. Also, the airfield beacon was some way to the south of the airfield, out of range of radio. The trip to Plymouth and back, the patrol and then the landing via the beacon left pilots extremely short of fuel, so a swift, first-time landing was essential. Failure to achieve this seems likely to have been the cause of Geoffrey Gout's fatal accident.

The other pilots could not allow Gout's death to affect their own flying, so they shut it out of their minds. Indeed, Gout's flying clothing card, which had a list of all his gear on it, was closely inspected. Pilots themselves had to pay to replace missing items, so some members of 234 used the occasion to ensure that anything they lacked tied up with the details on the dead man's card. 'It sounds callous,' admitted Bob Doe, 'but it was part of our survival mechanism.'

Doe himself was the next target for such treatment. While he was flying another of the long and boring patrols over Plymouth, a thick cloud suddenly descended. 'The only way home was to fly just off the coast where the cloud was thinner, round the tip of Cornwall,' he recalled. 'I was very late arriving back at St Eval.' When he landed, he found his colleagues roaring with laughter. They had already raffled off two of his flying suits.

The pressure of night flying was continuous. As one of the few fully-qualified night pilots, Doe was regularly called out after dark. He would be on call all day, often scrambled three or four times, then he would sleep on a camp bed at dispersal waiting for night-time patrols. One night he had a lucky escape. Exhausted after patrol, he landed so fast that he did not realise that he was heading for a ditch dug by workmen who were laying new concrete runways. He slewed the plane round but one wheel went into the ditch and a wing hit the ground.

Less than a week after Gout's death, Sergeant 'Tommy' Thompson crashed into a Cornish stone wall on the edge of the airfield. Once again, the pilot had been returning home from a routine night flight over Devon. He hit the wall in the early hours of the morning, when there were no lights on the airfield. Thompson was taken to the Royal Cornish Infirmary and was never fit enough to fly again. His Spitfire was a write-off.

Into this difficult situation came two replacements, Polish sergeant pilots by the name of Zigmund Klein and Joseph Szlagowski. The Poles still only spoke a modicum of English, so at first they did not pick up the nuances of the hostility that was undermining the squadron. They were just pleased to be in action at last.

* * *

Cyril Bamberger finally rejoined 610 Squadron at Biggin Hill on 27 July. His logbook records that by then he had completed the General Instrument Flying Course and that his proficiency as a pilot was 'average'. With Ted Manton, an old friend from Cheshire who was also rejoining 610, Bam arrived to find the close-knit band of men from Merseyside in a sorry state. Seven pilots had been lost over France, and two more had been killed since the Battle of Britain had begun, including Squadron Leader Smith, who had crashed on landing at Hawkinge, his plane bursting into flames when he hit an engine-testing shed. Those who remained were already exhausted from the daily round of sorties. They looked ragged and dispirited.

Bam and Manton reported with nine other newly trained pilots from No. 9 Fighter Training School to 610's Commanding Officer, John Ellis, who had taken over from Andrew Smith on an acting basis. Of these group of pilots, only four were to survive the war. Bam and Manton were horrified to discover that 610 had changed from flying Hurricanes to Spitfires, with which neither of them had any experience. It seemed an appalling piece of planning after several years of training, and with their squadron so short of pilots.

'You're no bloody use to me,' bellowed the normally pleasant commanding officer, and Bam and Ted soon found themselves travelling homewards again. This time they were sent to No. 7 Operational Training Unit at Hawarden, near Chester. There Bam gained twenty-five precious hours flying experience on Spitfires. He immediately loved the sleekness and speed of the Spitfire, but received virtually no practice in gunnery or aerial combat in his new aircraft. His logbook records that he had only one experience of firing his guns in the air: he flew out over the Dee estuary, found a sandbank, peppered it with bullets for ten seconds or so, and flew back to base.

Following the early skirmishes, the RAF at last began to reassess its tactics. The Germans flew in pairs, with the senior marksman guided by his wingman or *rottenhund*. Two pairs would fit together into the basic unit of a *schwarm,* or a finger four, which was a formation first used in the Spanish Civil War. The RAF, on the other hand, flew in a restricted V formation, which offered less flexibility in both attack and defence than that used by the Luftwaffe.

Modern aerial warfare required the fighter pilot to be constantly vigilant in his search for the enemy. He could not do this efficiently if he was concentrating on maintaining a tight-knit formation which inevitably restricted vision.

Furthermore, defensive protection in Fighter Command was often supplied by a weaver, or 'tail-end Charlie', at the rear, but it was soon realised that the weaver provided an excellent target for the enemy. Some squadrons recognised the virtues of the German formation and began to fly in pairs, but all too often fresh squadrons who moved into the front line were still using the archaic close-formation tactics.

Those first weeks also enabled each pilot to assess the strengths and weaknesses of both his own and the enemy's machines. On the British side, the slow-moving two-seater Boulton Paul Defiant proved especially vulnerable; six Defiants from one squadron were shot down in a single day in July. The Luftwaffe developed a respect for the single-engined fighters, particularly the swift-climbing Spitfire. Both sides came to acknowledge the importance of proficient gunnery, of armoured protection and of all-round visibility in the modern battle in the air.

Above all for Fighter Command, the early weeks of July had demonstrated what formidable opposition they faced. So far, the weather had been poor. The bright blue skies of August and increasing ferocity of the German attacks would soon show which side had learned most from the first skirmishes.

10

The Battle Warms Up

1–8 August

During July, the Luftwaffe suffered nearly twice as many aircraft losses as the RAF. However, the 145 British planes lost were virtually all fighters, while the Germans had lost only 105 fighters. Fortunately, Beaverbrook was doing a remarkable job in swiftly providing replacements for Fighter Command. His ability to bend the rules and cut through the red tape helped put fighter production up from 141 in February to 496 in July. His civilian repair units were the backbone of the system, responsible for about a third of replacement aircraft at this time.

Less easy to replace were the pilots, particularly those with experience or leadership abilities. Some front-line squadrons had been badly hit, even in the first two weeks. Others were already exhausted by the need for constant readiness. Nonetheless, the RAF managed to reinforce the depleted squadrons, albeit with younger and less well-trained men. Overall the RAF had over two hundred more pilots available in early August than on 1 July, but numbers were still below the level Dowding regarded as essential.

The German leadership saw this phase of the air battle merely as a prelude to the real conflict, during which the German fighters would decisively break through the British defensive system. Their confidence was boosted by woefully inadequate intelligence information. Led by an inept cipher of Goering's called Josef 'Beppo' Schmidt, their intelligence gatherers regularly overestimated the number of losses suffered by the RAF. All too often, Schmidt told his political masters the good news they wanted to hear, rather than providing an accurate assessment. Admittedly, Major Schmidt's initial report, *Studie Blaue* ('Study in Blue'), made a more precise assessment of Fighter Command's aircraft availability than some of the intelligence department's later work, but it nonetheless ignored the significance of radar and the shortage of experienced pilots.

Hitler clung to the hope that the British spirit would collapse and that Churchill would sue for peace. Not until late in July did he begin to accept that he would reluctantly have to go ahead with his invasion plans. Meanwhile, the Luftwaffe had lost the opportunity to destroy the RAF before it could rebuild after France. Though there would have been risks, an early invasion following Dunkirk would have found British defences extremely vulnerable. But Admiral Raeder had insisted that his navy needed air mastery to be established before an invasion could be launched. Now, Raeder and the navy were growing increasingly pessimistic, fearing that, unless Operation Sealion could take place by mid-September 1940, the autumn weather would put the Germans at a serious disadvantage. They had to face a formidable navy and air force. If the large invading forces were to be successfully put ashore, the sea must be calm. Also, if the first wave of invaders were not joined by second and third waves in swift succession, the troops were in danger of being cut off. Raeder suggested postponement until May 1941, but Hitler did not want to give Britain a chance to re-form and re-equip her army. While accepting the possibility of postponement until 1941, he decided first to see what his much-vaunted air force could achieve. On 1 August he issued Directive No.17:

> The German Air Force is to overcome the British Air
> Force with all means at its disposal and as soon as
> possible.

Operation Sealion was set for 15 September, and meanwhile the Germans decided to step up the attack. The new offensive was codenamed *Adlerangriff* (Attack of the Eagles). Its planned launch-day was to be called *Adlertag* (Eagle Day). However on 1 and 2 August, before the Attack of the Eagles had begun, the Luftwaffe dropped thousands of leaflets on southern England outlining, in English, the veiled peace offer Hitler had made on 9 July. The British public treated them as a joke.

It was a strange action so many weeks after Hitler's original speech, and seems to suggest that, even after deciding on an immediate battle for air superiority, the Führer was hoping that the British might still see the folly of resisting German advances.

On 3 August Hitler travelled to Berlin for the launch of his Eagle Day offensive, but it was put back because of bad weather, and he returned to the Berghof.

The postponement of Eagle Day and a dramatic reduction in convoys by the British in response to Luftwaffe pressure meant that early August was relatively quiet. For the RAF, any delay was important while it hurried to complete the post-Dunkirk rebuilding of its fighter force.

While Hitler was making up his mind, 234 Squadron at St Eval was celebrating the marriage, on 1 August, of its popular Australian flight commander, Pat Hughes. Hughes's bride was Kay Brodrick, whom he had met while stationed at Leconfield. 'He reminded me then, and always did,' said Kay, 'of Errol Flynn, with his good looks, moustache and smart uniform.'

Joseph Szlagowski and Zig Klein, the newly arrived Poles, had already sensed that it was Pat Hughes rather than the remote squadron leader, Dickie Barnett, who commanded the respect of the pilots. Despite their limited command of English, 'Slug' and 'Zig' soon settled in. With his warm smile and open manner, Joseph Szlagowski soon became popular with his British colleagues. Bob Doe recalls, 'He must have been twenty-three or twenty-four, which at that time was quite an old man. He'd had a lot of experience. He was very gentle but solid. The right sort of person to have in the squadron.'

On one occasion, Sergeant 'Budge' Harker, who shared the same mess as Slug and Zig, was confined to camp indefinitely by Squadron Leader Barnett for a serious error while landing. Slug and Zig cut through the wire mesh, got Harker out and took him to the pub. As a result, Harker got alcohol poisoning and slept on a stretcher in dispersal for the next two days.

On the night of 6 August, Joseph Szlagowski flew his first flight with 234. It was a routine patrol, but the list of landing accidents was added to when Flying Officer Pat Horton, a New Zealander who had already proved himself a first-rate pilot, crashed on returning, writing off yet another Spitfire but escaping unhurt.

Next day, Flying Officer Igglesden was mysteriously removed from flying duties. On the same day, Flight Lieutenant Thielman relinquished command of 'A' flight and was posted as 'non-effective sick'. Thielman's asthma made it difficult for him to fly at heights, but also, his relations with the squadron leader had grown more tense as pressure increasingly fell on him and Hughes as the two flight commanders. As one 234 pilot put it, 'Thielman was older than the rest of us; nearer thirty, it seemed like. The Battle of Britain was not for older people who thought too much. If you were young and full of bravado, this was for you.' Whatever the reason for the two departures, they indicated just how bad morale had become – and 234 were not yet on the front line.

On 8 August, 234 Squadron and all RAF units listened silently to the memorable order of the day: 'The Battle of Britain is about to begin. Members of the Royal Air Force, the fate of generations lies in your hands.'

That same day, Sergeant Szlagowski's name was added to the growing list of accident victims. On his way home from a patrol, in daylight this time, he encountered thick fog. With only two gallons in his tank, he bellowed in the best English he could manage into the RT. Pat Hughes told him to keep calm. Then Slug's engine stopped, and the plane began to bank away: 'It must have been a miracle, but a hole suddenly appeared, a big circle in the fog.' Szlagowski glided down and landed quite smoothly in a small field. Unfortunately, the propeller blade was vertical and hit a lump in the ground. The nose of the Spitfire went down and the plane slowly flopped over: 'It was a good job I had run out of petrol, otherwise the plane would have been in flames and I wouldn't be here now.'

The cockpit door had shut tight in the crash and, lying on his back, Szlagowski could not open it. Then he spotted a young boy, aged about eleven or twelve, and gestured for help. The boy ran off, to return with a big stone with which he smashed a hole in the cockpit for the Pole to crawl through. Soon afterwards the police arrived and the shaken pilot was transported back to St Eval.

At the airfield, Zig Klein was delighted to see his fellow countryman back safely. It had been a salutary experience for Szlagowski, but it made him all the more determined to fly against the Germans.

A couple of days later, Szlagowski went back to the village of Pensilva where he had crashed to thank the schoolboy, called Sam, and his parents. He never saw Sam again, but kept a photograph of him for good luck.

On the day Joseph Szlagowski nearly killed himself at Pensilva, Geoff Myers saw the start of the disastrous fortunes suffered by 257 Squadron. The squadron had scarcely flown since Sharp had taken over; now it was to find itself in the thick of the fighting.

8 August was the worst day so far for the RAF in the Battle of Britain. Twenty-one planes were destroyed; in the previous five days together, only twenty-three had been hit. By nightfall, three of 257's pilots were dead.

This was not an early attempt at Eagle Day by the Germans. Rather, the British, having lately halted Channel convoys as a result of Luftwaffe pressure, had surprisingly decided to run a big convoy, CW9, codenamed Peewit, consisting of more than twenty merchant ships, from the Thames estuary to Cornwall. The German orders were to wipe it out.

For 257 Squadron, their first day at the centre of the conflict was ill-starred from the beginning. Squadron Leader Harkness stayed in his room, saying it was his day off. The rest of the squadron left late. One pilot, Jimmy Cochrane, a Canadian who was killed later in the war, did not wake until 9.00 a.m., when someone called him a second time; he had been up drinking until 4.00 a.m.

From France, the Germans sent up fifty-seven Ju 87 Stuka bombers with the aim of destroying convoy CW9 near the Isle of Wight. They were escorted by fifty fighters. The first British plane to reach the enemy was piloted by Lieutenant Noel Hall, commanding 'B' flight of 257. For the next twenty minutes the sky was dark with planes in combat. Some of the pilots from 257 wondered what was going on; never before had they encountered such ferocity.

The day left only four of convoy CW9's merchant ships undamaged. The sea was awash with life rafts and bits of boats. Nearly 70,000 tons of shipping had been destroyed. In defending their target, the RAF had lost nineteen planes. Five pilots from 145 Squadron at Westhampnett had lost their lives – though the squadron had the consolation of probably having accounted for eleven enemy planes and damaging six more. In contrast, as they limped home, 257 had only one victory to think about: an Me 109 shot down by Pilot Officer Grundy off St Catherine's Point. In return, they had seen three men killed – Flying Officer D'Arcy-Irvine, Flight Lieutenant Noel Hall and Sergeant Smith. One of these deaths, that of D'Arcy-Irvine, affected Geoff Myers particularly sharply. He wrote in his notebook to his wife:

D'Arcy-Irvine, always ready with a new scheme to improve the squadron, always keen. One of the best. Just before he went, he had worked out a new method of camouflage for Hurricanes. His idea was to merge the blue with the greyish and pink effects to mix up with the sky; also to paint the sides of the leading edges of the wings and darken the middle portion to give the effect of a tailplane, and make the German gunner think that the Hurricane was flying the other way round.

The rest of the squadron were equally shattered. The late-rising Jimmy Cochrane felt guilty about his drinking and his failure to get out of bed on time – though he had later caught up with his colleagues and shown his determination by staying with the action until the very end. He too was particularly upset about D'Arcy-Irvine. He told Myers what had happened:

'Poor D'Arcy boy. He yelled out to me over the RT, "There's a Gerry on your tail," and they must have got him just at that moment. I swung round, got on the tail of the Gerry and beetled off after him. I'm buggered if he didn't go splosh in the drink without me firing a shot at him. But poor old D'Arcy boy! And to think he warned me just before they shot him down! That shook me.'

It fell to Geoff Myers, as intelligence officer, to inform the relatives of the pilots who had been shot down. He was kept busy during the night of 8 August. When he wrote to inform D'Arcy-Irvine's parents, he tried to draw a heroic picture of the dead pilot, but, as he later recorded in private:

... all the time I could see him grinning over my
shoulder. I could hear him saying, 'Looks all right that
sob stuff but a fat lot of use it is to anyone. Damn silly
waste of a pilot, and then you write pretty letters about
it. Well, I suppose you're trying to do your job.'

For 257, the blow stemmed not only from the fact that three
popular colleagues were dead, but also from the manner of
their going. One of the deaths had been particularly avoid-
able. In the absence of Harkness, twenty-four-year-old Noel
Hall had been leading the squadron that day. From the south
coast, they had been ordered right up into the enemy near the
Isle of Wight, but for some reason Lancelot Mitchell, acting
commander in charge of 'B' flight, had left Hall and dashed
off with his section towards France, leaving Hall's flight adrift.
Mitchell was a sensitive, almost poetic man, perhaps not of the
usual mould from which fighter pilots are made, but nonetheless an enthusiastic and brave flyer. Myers commented:

I still don't know what happened to Mitchell that day.
After flying off at a tangent like this, Mitchell realised
what he had done and tried to link up again with the
squadron but failed to find them. Seeing that Hall had
not yet returned, he took off to look for him. When
he came back, Mitchell looked at me blankly. 'I saw
nothing,' he said, 'just the rest of our convoy, which
the Germans had bombed. Two ships on fire and a raft
with dead men on it. No sign of Hall or D'Arcy-Irvine
or Sergeant Smith.'

Other pilots were angry at what had happened. One of them,
Arnaud, a small man with a light brown moustache and a

rather haunted look, refused to talk to Mitchell for a week after Hall had been shot down. 'Hall would have been our flight commander if Mitchell had not been yellow,' he kept saying. No one else really shared this view. Perhaps Mitchell had suffered from a brainstorm and had just flown off in the wrong direction. It was easily done in the sky, particularly in a squadron that was confused and without leadership. When Fighter Command asked for a supplementary report about how Hall and Mitchell had become separated, Geoff Myers tried to create a loophole for Mitchell, claiming difficulties in catching the vector over the RT. But Squadron Leader Harkness would have none of it. Myers wrote:

> 'It's just bloody rot,' he shouted at Mitchell, in front
> of all the young pilots. 'You simply made off like a
> damned fool instead of following your leader.'

Lancelot Mitchell was distressed enough as it was. That night, Myers went to see him in his room to offer comfort and help:

> Mitchell said, 'I never let poor Hall down before. I'll
> admit it was my fault. Somehow I just followed the
> vector instead of sticking behind him.' He looked
> haggard. 'This is a dog's life. I sometimes think
> I shouldn't have been a pilot at all.'

11

Disaster

11–12 August

The fateful journey of CW9 served as a hectic and dangerous prelude to Eagle Day, now planned for 13 August. As Kesselring tried to draw the fighter squadrons based in southern England into the air, the two sides met in large-scale conflicts that signalled an end to the early probing and skirmishes. The tempo of the battle had increased significantly.

Geoffrey Page at twenty was, in Battle of Britain terms, already a veteran. In the previous month he had seen several of those close to him die, among them 'Minny' Ereminski, the White Russian who had first introduced him to 56 Squadron and Michael Maw, a close friend since September 1939, when the two had met at the Aircrew Receiving Centre in Hastings.

On 11 August, 56 Squadron suffered a most unpleasant incident. Sergeant Pilot Ronnie Baker was flying his Hurricane on a convoy patrol at lunchtime when a solitary Spitfire from 74 Squadron, apparently mistaking him for a German, attacked and shot him down. Sergeant Baker bailed out successfully but, by the time the rescue launch in the Thames estuary had pulled him out of the water, he was dead.

That day, 11 August, saw the loss of thirty-two British planes – the highest daily total of the battle so far.

At Coquelles, Ulrich Steinhilper and his squadron sensed that the real battle was about to begin. They had admired the qualities of the Spitfire, and were impressed by the speed with which the radar-controlled RAF could get its fighters into the sky, but they remained supremely confident. If Luftwaffe intelligence reports were to be believed, the British were almost on their last legs. In common with many German pilots stationed on the airfields strung out along the French coast, Steinhilper's one nagging doubt was the Channel. It took only a few minutes to cross and the airfield at Coquelles was mercifully close, but even in summer if a pilot was shot down or had to ditch, it did not take long for him to drown. The Luftwaffe were no longer allowed to carry pistols because pilots had used them to commit suicide after ditching.

On 11 August, this nervousness about the Channel was compounded when a Heinkel 59 ambulance seaplane was destroyed by Blenheims of 604 Squadron under the protection of Spitfires. The crew survived, but the shooting of an ambulance plane on the sea infuriated the German pilots. Dowding had reasoned that, even with their red crosses, ambulance planes were legitimate targets, because they enabled German pilots to fly against Britain again. It was no longer a gentlemen's war.

In the world outside North Weald and Biggin Hill, life in Britain still seemed disconcertingly normal. On 12 August, twenty-seven people wrote to *The Times* to report the fine quality of the cuckoo song that year. Grouse shooting began in earnest. Londoners queued in the West End to see Robert Donat in *The Devil's Disciple*.

But in Fighter Command the thoughts were only of war, and the few pleasures grabbed between the dangers. At 56 Squadron the tragic death of Sergeant Baker before he could be rescued from the water had turned Geoffrey Page's thoughts towards the sea. In three weeks in July, two hundred and twenty men had been killed or were missing at sea, yet the British still had only eighteen high-speed rescue launches – just two more than in 1936. Page knew that one day it might be his turn, but in the frenzied activity of war he had little time to think about death. He lived for the moment and, in a way, he was happy – flying planes by day, heading up to the West End in a battered old car by night, drinking too much, and sleeping too little. If life were going to be short, why not live it to the full? The comradeship was marvellous; united as the men were by a common bond, every experience, every emotion, was distilled to its essence.

Superficially at least, Geoffrey Page was a quintessential Battle of Britain pilot. Appearance: blond, handsome and dashing. Education: public school and London University. Vocabulary: 'wizard' and 'good show'. Interests: wine, women and aeroplanes. Expectations: limited. 'The art was to cheat the Reaper and merely blunt his Scythe a little,' he recalled. 'After all, it was only a game and he was bound to win, but it was fun while it lasted.'*

Yet for all his bravado, all his jolly friendships, all the compulsive drinking and womanising, sometimes the real horror of what he was caught up in would come home to the young man and unsettle him. One such occasion was the morning of 12 August, when Page was alone with his thoughts in one of

*Geoffrey Page, *Tale of a Guinea Pig,* Pelham, 1981.

those quiet moments before daybreak. Pilot Officer Page sat down and wrote to a friend:

> I sometimes wonder … if the whole war isn't a ghastly nightmare from which we'll wake up soon; I know all of this sounds nonsense, but I'm slightly tight and it's only an hour to dawn … to me it will mean just another day of butchery … it makes me feel sick. Where are we going?

Perhaps it was a premonition of the day ahead. When 12 August dawned, it was, like so much of that golden summer, sunny and bright, with a clear blue sky. The Germans had planned *Adlertag* for the following day. As a prelude their aim on the 12th, they were to knock out the RAF radar stations, particularly the giant radio aerials of Sussex and Kent. They were then to take advantage of the lack of radar to hit fighter stations. This task was entrusted to the precision team of Experimental Group 210, led by Walter Rübensdörffer, who carried out a series of brilliant and incisive attacks on Kent. Before the RAF had fully realised what was happening, 210 had hit three radar stations, although the giant aerials were left intact.

By 8.00 a.m., Ulrich Steinhilper's *Gruppe* had already lost two pilots over New Romney in Kent. Lieutenant Gelhalsis and another pilot were shot down and killed in combat with Bam's 610 Squadron. In return, 610 had lost one aircraft, and had four damaged, but no pilots had been killed. This was the first time that JG 52 had lost two pilots in one day.

By lunchtime, 257 Squadron had also lost another man, one of their youngest and least experienced. John Chomley was a former sergeant pilot. Recently commissioned, he had spent most of his life with his family in southern Rhodesia.

Fresh-faced, with a friendly smile and soft brown hair, he was only twenty when he died. As a new pilot it had fallen to Chomley to ferry Geoff Myers in the squadron's little Magister to collect combat reports. The two men became good friends. On one such journey, Myers was carrying a replacement oxygen panel which obscured his view. Then he fell asleep. Suddenly, he was woken up by shouting on the intercom: 'Bandits ahead!' As he peered in panic out of the plane, he saw friendly Hurricanes fly by and heard John Chomley roar with laughter. As he flew home that night, the amiable Rhodesian dived low over a Sussex village, where a girlfriend lived. He let off a few shots as he swooped down, just clearing the trees, in order to impress her. Two days later, 12 August, following the German morning raids on the radar aerials, over seventy Ju 88 bombers unleashed a huge barrage on Portsmouth, smashing large areas of the dockyards and the town. Ninety-six people died in the air raid. John Chomley, flying one of the fifty-odd planes sent at the last minute to counter the threat, was shot down and killed. Another 257 pilot, the Hon. David Coke, was shot down in the same action and lost a finger. The son of the Earl of Leicester, David Coke was a well-liked figure in the squadron whose pronounced stammer disappeared magically in the air. The Portsmouth raid put him out of action until much later the Battle of Britain.

As 257 pilots were shot out of the skies, Hugh Beresford increasingly carried the burden of responsibility. Geoff Myers wrote:

> Beresford had a nervous flicker in his eyes which
> might have made a man doubt of his personal courage
> if he did not know him. There was no doubt about

Beresford for the pilots in his section though. He knew the risks but he did the job properly every time.

The story of 257 in the early weeks of the Battle of Britain is one of confusion, low morale, poor leadership and startling losses. 'My experience of the air Battle of Britain,' said Pilot Officer Charles Frizzell of 257, 'before a car crash put me out of it, was that we were losing. I looked at the claims in the newspapers, and the discrepancy between the portrait painted there and what was happening in my own squadron was enormous.'

After an early lunch at North Weald on 12 August, 56 Squadron moved on to their forward airfield at Rochford near Southend to relieve their sister squadron. Rochford was a grass airfield whose only dispersal facility was a bell tent containing a single telephone. Geoffrey Page remembers being very tired that day: 'My muscles felt drained of energy and, although the spirit was willing, the flesh was very, very weak.' That afternoon the young pilot officer slept on the sweet-smelling grass. He was woken up for tea, and then, the solitary telephone rang.

'Scramble. . . seventy plus approaching Manston Angels fifteen,' bellowed the telephone orderly. Manston airfield in Kent was under attack. Page's weariness disappeared as his aching body began to pump adrenalin, and the ten Hurricanes lifted steadily into the air. Odds of seven to one, no better or worse than usual, he remembered thinking. It was 5.20 p.m.

Page flew on the right-hand side of Flight Commander Jumbo Gracie; Barry Sutton was on the left-hand side. The ten planes from 56 climbed but, when they were still at a slow and vulnerable speed, they saw what looked like a swarm of midges ahead. Barry Sutton was acutely conscious of the flight commander's determination. 'He was a "press-on" chap whose one idea was to destroy as many Germans as he could. He wasn't very scientific about it, but he was desperately brave and he led Geoffrey and myself into a fruitless chase. We just had not got enough height.'

Page also felt that the flight commander's decision to get into the action quickly was unwise. In fact, the 'midges' were sixty Dornier 215 bombers escorted by thirty Messerschmitt 109s. On the starboard side, Page was nearest to the bombers. Habit prompted him to lock his sliding hood in the open position – for a hurried exit, if need be.

The distance between the Hurricanes and the German bombers was closing, while the Me 109s hovered high above. As the Hurricanes reached the same height as the Dorniers, they picked up speed and began to overtake them like racing cars speeding past family saloons. There was even time for a brief glance at the bomber pilots.

As the Hurricanes moved in on the leading bomber, they ran the gauntlet of the German rear guns. Pilot Officer Page looked behind and then above; from as far away as six hundred yards, he began to fire on one of the leading Dorniers.

One minute the sky between the two sides was clear. The next it was full of streams of white tracer from the cannon shells loosed off by the rear gunners. Suddenly Page was only thirty yards away from the leading German. In a desperate race to destroy before he himself was destroyed, he fired his Brownings at the port engine of one of the bombers. Objects like electric light bulbs flashed past him. There was an explosion, followed by two more bangs, which split his eardrums. A gaping hole suddenly appeared in the starboard wing. Page couldn't believe that he'd been hit. 'There was a tremendous explosion on my right only about ten yards away,' said Barry Sutton, 'and such a sheet of flames came out of his aeroplane that I thought he must be dead already. I was quite convinced there was no way he could have got out of that.'

The smallest of the Hurricane's three fuel tanks, the one behind the engine, was the only one that was not self-sealing. Suddenly that tank exploded like a bomb. Unfortunately for Geoffrey Page, it was situated just above his lap.

Page's fear turned to terror as flames engulfed the cockpit like a fireball, spreading rapidly towards the draught from the open hood. He screamed. A few minutes earlier, he had pushed his goggles up for better vision and removed his gloves to get a firmer feel of the controls. Now, as he looked down, he saw the bare skin of his hands, which were gripping the throttle and control column, shrivel like burned paper in a blast furnace. Page felt that the life was, almost literally, draining out of him: 'They say the temperature goes from 5° to 350° Centigrade – which is fairly hot, like a cooking oven – in about seven seconds. It's as if someone was putting an enormous blow-torch on you – it was a crossroads in my life.'

Many fighter pilots feared burning more than death. Most of them had seen fires in the air and had rehearsed in their minds what to do if it happened to them. Occasionally the radio was still on when the flames and the screams began, and some had even heard a pilot being fried.

For a moment, a strange peace and calm enveloped the burning plane. Page had accepted that he was going to die, and nature was now protecting him from the fear of death. Yet, in the middle of the inferno, he was able instinctively to put into practice the life-saving routine that had been drummed into him. With his tortured right hand, he groped through the searing flame for the release pin of the Sutton Harness. As the fire licked round him, he cried out in agony, 'Dear God, save me, save me, dear God.' Then, from habit, he half rolled his plane and tumbled out of the furnace. There was a snap as the plugged-in oxygen tube and radio communication line disentangled and jerked his head. Then he felt fresh air streaming across his burning face, and somersaulted head over heels through space.

Perhaps because he had been so close to death, the terror disappeared like the burning Hurricane behind Geoffrey Page. As he fell through the sky, he summoned up all his strength to try and pull the ripcord on his left-hand side, by edging his burned right hand across his body. Agonisingly, as it touched the chromium ring, his mutilated hand bounced away, unable to get a firm hold. In despair, Page recalled the RAF expression 'It don't mean a thing if you don't pull the ring.' Just one more try, he thought, as he stretched his damaged hand out once more. The pain drove through him, but this time he succeeded. Almost magically, the silken canopy billowed open with a thump. The young pilot looked up and found, to his relief, that his parachute had not been damaged by the inferno. He began to drift slowly down towards the sea. It would be ten or fifteen minutes before he hit the water, he thought, and now, feeling extremely cold, he noticed that his trousers had been blown completely off, as well as one shoe. There were a few small burns on his legs.

Suddenly there was a glint of summer sun on wings as two fighters sped into view. Page had heard rumours of pilots being cut to ribbons by German bullets while parachuting gently to the ground. Seeing that the two planes were Hurricanes, he breathed a sigh of relief. In the extraordinary silence he could hear the battle continuing in the distance. Then he noticed a stench – the distinctive smell of burned flesh, his burned flesh. He had an almost irresistible urge to vomit.

When he landed at Manston, Barry Sutton, whose plane had also been hit, told everyone that Geoffrey Page was dead. 'No. 2 bought it, No. 2 bought it,' he kept saying.

Having escaped from his blazing plane, Geoffrey Page was still far from safe. The English Channel had swallowed up scores of pilots from both sides who had been forced to bail out. Sixty per cent of all air fatalities occurred over the sea.

As he floated down from ten thousand feet, Page had no time to think about the cold statistics of pilots dying in the uninviting waters beneath. Common sense told him that, to survive in the Channel, he needed to land as close to the coastline as possible. From his parachute, the Kent coast appeared to be six or even ten miles away. He could see only a dark and empty expanse of water. Peering down again, he laughed at the thought of what he must look like, half-naked and dangling from a parachute; slowly easing off the one remaining shoe with the toes of the other foot, he watched it spin helplessly down towards the water.

As the parachute swayed from side to side, Page started to shiver uncontrollably, teeth chattering as the shock from the injuries took its toll. By now his face was swelling and beginning to impair his vision. But he was aware enough to realise that, if he did not release his parachute within seconds of landing, the great white canopy would drag him down into the deep. Around his stomach area was a small metal release box with a circular metal disc attached that had to be turned and then banged to release the parachute. Page's mutilated fingers just could not manage it, so he hit the water while still dangling from his parachute. In the sea, the smell of his burned flesh seemed more sickening, and he watched, part horrified, part fascinated, as strips of his own skin began to float around him.

The water felt icy on his badly shocked body, but the cold also helped clear his mind and, with quite extraordinary courage, Page continued his fight for survival. Flesh flaked from his fingers, blood poured from raw tissues and salt water stung his burned face, but, kicking madly in the water, he managed to turn the vital metal disc from his release button and bang it in order to free himself from the white silk tentacles.

Relieved to find that the parachute had not dragged him down to his grave, Page trod water and tried to inflate his life jacket, but the inferno had burned a hole in its rubber bladder. He had two alternatives: to drown or to swim for his life. Fortunately a strong swimmer, he struck out for the distant Kent coastline. Every stroke was agony. As the salt dried on the raw tissue of his face, what had been a sting escalated into a searing pain. The strap of his flying helmet cut deeply into his chin, but the flames had welded the buckle and leather together and it was impossible to wrench it off.

Then he remembered the slim silver brandy flask given him by his mother. In great pain he undid his tunic and inch by inch his mutilated fingers worked their way towards the breast pocket. With one final effort he undid the last copper button and, easing the flask up between his wrists, began to undo the top with his teeth. At that point a wave washed over him; the flask slipped inexorably between his wrists and disappeared into the sea. For a brief while Page broke down and cried. Then, with his flesh aching and swelling so much around his eyes that he couldn't see the sun, he struck out for shore again, knowing that he could keep going only for a few more minutes.

By now, the burned airman had been in the water half an hour. As he had almost resigned himself to death, he saw a thin plume of smoke ahead drifting up from a funnel. He thrashed around and waved his arms with all the energy his aching body could muster, but it seemed that the ship had missed him, that everything had been in vain. Then a small motor boat with two British merchant seamen aboard chugged into view.

As Page struggled to stay afloat, one of the men shouted, 'What are you? Jerry or one of us?' His answer was inaudible as a mouthful of water drowned the reply. With the struggling pilot growing rapidly weaker, the boat circled for a second time. The sailors probably had good reason to let a German drown. 'Are you a Jerry, mate?' they asked again. The swimming airman shouted back, 'You stupid pair of fucking bastards, pull me out.' As they hauled his limp body onto the boat, one sailor said, 'The minute you swore, mate, we knew you was an RAF officer.'

The sodden uniform was slashed away from the burned flesh and Page's naked body wrapped in a blanket. On the old tramp steamer, he was taken down into the warmth of the galley, where sips of hot tea brought life back to his body. Using pink lint, the captain cut out fingerless gloves for the survivor's raw hands, and tied another strip of lint across his forehead.

The Margate lifeboat arrived. Page's body was placed on a stretcher, where he lay quietly smoking a Woodbine. Although he had more feeling in his limbs, Page was suffering from intense pain and he soon lapsed into semi-consciousness. Close to Margate, he was gently lifted out of the lifeboat and taken ashore. On the neat little harbour, which was fringed by the golden beach and dotted with people enjoying the late evening sun, Page was astonished to see through his aching eyes a man in a top hat and chain. It was the Mayor of Margate out to greet the injured pilot.

Page has dim memories of an ambulance ride, the imposing façade of the Royal Sea Bathing Hospital and long hospital corridors. Much of what followed was like a dream. In the operating theatre he regained full consciousness and asked a doctor if he could have a mirror. The request was refused but, as he lay there on the surgeon's table, Page caught sight of himself in the reflector mirrors of the overhanging light. It was a ghastly sight. What had once been the face of a handsome twenty-year-old was now a hideous mass of swollen, burned flesh. Geoffrey Page lapsed back into oblivion and the operation began.

12

EAGLE DAY AND BEYOND

13–15 August

For the Germans, *Adlertag* began badly. A postponement was called for by Goering himself when a pre-dawn reconnaissance flight reported that the weather was getting worse but, although the order reached the fighters, a group of seventy-four Dornier bombers had set out from Geoff Myers's old base at Arras at 5.00 a.m. They had not been given the correct crystals for their radio wavelengths, so attempts to recall them failed. Furthermore, two of the three crucial radar stations the Luftwaffe had hit the day before had quickly been repaired, leaving only Ventnor on the Isle of Wight ineffective.

Over the French coast, the Dorniers' escort of fighters returned home, leaving the bombers, led by Johannes Fink, to fly on unprotected. In a classic example of German intelligence failure, the Dorniers were planning to destroy RAF Eastchurch on the Isle of Sheppey: Eastchurch, like other airfields on the German target list, was thought to be a base for fighters, but in fact had not housed fighters regularly for ten years.

Fink's Dorniers hit Eastchurch, successfully damaging hangars and runways and destroying five Blenheims. But without an escort they were vulnerable; ten were damaged or destroyed, and twenty men were either killed or listed missing. Back at Arras, an angry Fink telephoned Kesselring to complain about the mix-up which had led to such a heavy toll. Kesselring travelled from Calais to Arras to apologise personally.

Before dawn on 13 August, in the hospital at Margate, Geoffrey Page awoke from a dream about his squadron, with a strange pain in his arm, and the stickiness of sweat all over his body. He could just distinguish the vague outline of a woman in white standing by his hospital bed. The white shape gently lifted the injured man's head from the pillow and held a glass of lemon drink to his parched lips. Page looked straight at the nurse. For a split second he caught a look of horror flash across her pretty face. He lay back on the bed, hating that moment. He hated the nurse for that look.

Soon afterwards the sharp prick of a needle stabbed him out of his semi-daze. The awkwardness in the sister's voice was clear enough as she said, 'I'm sorry to trouble you, Pilot Officer Page, but I'm afraid I've got to get one or two particulars from you. I should like to know,' she continued, growing more embarrassed, 'the address of your next of kin, and your religion.' The sound of a chuckle emerged from Page's swollen lips. 'I'm going to disappoint you, Sister. I'm going to live.'

It was not until late afternoon that the Luftwaffe began to see some of the success *Adlertag* had been designed to bring. More than a hundred 109s cleared the way for bombers to smash

Detling airfield near Maidstone without opposition. Twenty-two aircraft on the ground had been destroyed. Sixty-seven of the staff at Detling were killed, but it was a hollow victory. Once again, Luftwaffe intelligence had been inaccurate. Like Eastchurch, Detling was a coastal command base with no Hurricanes or Spitfires on its roster.

Although the Luftwaffe claimed more victories than the RAF on *Adlertag*, forty-seven of the British planes destroyed had been on the ground, and, apart from one fighter plane, the aircraft had not been at the heart of the RAF's defensive system. Despite their nearly 1500 sorties, *Adlertag* had been a failure for the Germans. Nevertheless, the day had brought a lesson for the RAF too. It had been a defensive victory, but the ease with which the Germans had slid through the British defences must have concerned Fighter Command hierarchy. If German intelligence had been better and Biggin Hill had been hit as effectively as Detling, the RAF would have suffered a major catastrophe.

In the short but unhappy history of 234 Squadron in the Battle of Britain, 13 August was a red-letter day. Bob Doe and the other pilots were now well aware of the weaknesses in the squadron. The newly arrived Polish pilots, Szlagowski and Klein, were the only men who did not seem to understand the confusion and difficulties 234 faced. Through their eyes, compared to the swift destruction of the Polish air force in 1939, the RAF appeared to be doing well.

The intense activity of 11 and 12 August had led Dowding to move three of his most ravaged squadrons out of the front line. 234 Squadron were ordered to move up to Middle

Wallop, near Southampton, as a replacement. On 11 August, Quintin Brand, the air officer commanding No. 10 Group, had visited the squadron at St Eval. Two days later, on Eagle Day, Squadron Leader Barnett, MBE, relinquished his command. Most of 234 were pleased at this development, among them Sergeant Budge Harker: 'He was a hopeless CO. He did all his flying in the hangar. I was delighted to see the back of him.' Some felt it was simply a case of what the RAF call LMF (lack of moral fibre). Others were more charitable, feeling that an 'old school' leader such as Barnett was not really equipped to lead from the front in war. 'Looking back,' said Bob Doe, 'I understand how it happened. You start thinking about other responsibilities. Your family and everything else.'

The combination of Squadron Leader Barnett's departure so soon after a flight lieutenant and a flying officer had been posted away and the news that 234 was to be pushed into the front line was inevitably unsettling. In the absence of a new squadron leader, the pilots turned to Pat Hughes for leadership. Joseph Szlagowski found him tough but friendly: 'He knew a lot and taught us all how to fight.' Unlike Barnett, Hughes was willing to lead his men in the air as well as on the ground.

The transfer from St Eval to Middle Wallop on 14 August almost led to further casualties. Bill Hornby remembers clearly: 'The move to Middle Wallop was a shambles. The day dawned with a thick wet mist. It was quite impossible to fly. As the morning went on, the mist broke. The squadron took off in good weather but everyone … forgot that the mist was rolling west to east and the squadron would catch it up.' Indeed, before reaching Middle Wallop, the squadron, flying in tight formation, hit the mist. 'Dark shapes loomed everywhere and it was a miracle that there were no collisions,' remembers Hornby.

The previous day, Middle Wallop had been attacked by enemy bombers that had failed to find their target. On 14 August the Luftwaffe were not so unlucky. At 4.45 p.m., the newly arrived Spitfires from 234 were being refuelled when Middle Wallop was attacked by Heinkel Ills and Junkers 88s, flying like huge birds low over the airfield. Three Blenheims and several Spitfires were written off as they dropped their load.

Joseph Szlagowski saw the Germans coming and ran into a field, aiming for shelter in a nearby wood. As incendiaries crashed behind him, he dived onto the ground. At that moment, the wood ahead of him went up in flames. An ammunition dump was hidden in it.

Bob Doe was on a lorry taking some of the 234 pilots the four hundred yards to the mess. Halfway up the road they heard bombs exploding. They turned around to see the huge doors blown off one of the hangars. 'It was like an accordion collapsing,' remembers Szlagowski. The effect of the blast was devastating. Three airmen were killed and two wounded as they bravely tried to close the thirteen-ton steel doors to protect the aircraft inside. One airman's foot was blown off, another lost his arm at the shoulder.

Middle Wallop's only consolation that day was that 609 Squadron had given chase to a Heinkel III, killing three senior Luftwaffe men, including the group captain leading the formation and its navigator. As a result, the two remaining bombers hit the old airfield at Netheravon instead of Middle Wallop. Nonetheless, it was a fearful start to 234's life at their new base, and had come at a strikingly bad moment for an already ragged squadron. Wallop seemed an appropriate name for their new home.

In London, 257 Squadron were still licking their wounds from the week before, and had not yet been posted to reinforce one of the coastal stations. Their morale was not helped when, on 15 August, Pilot Officer Charles Frizzell, one of their most skilful pilots, bailed out over London when his engine caught fire. He landed just off the Edgware Road, his Hurricane finally crashing at Harrow-on-the-Hill.

If the exhausted RAF pilots were having doubts as to the ultimate success of their battle, the Luftwaffe pilots across the Channel were beginning to question the tactics of their leaders. Intelligence reports told them of destroyed airfields and broken-backed squadrons, but they had seen for themselves the chaos of *Adlertag*. Within 3/JG 52 Ulrich Steinhilper participated in increasingly intense debates about aerial tactics with Helmut Kuhle, the leader. Kuhle was a popular man, but as a Spanish veteran he felt that pilots should put survival first. Never take a risk in attacking unless you are certain of success, was his maxim. He believed that, by concentrating on survival, the Luftwaffe pilot could grow more experienced and more deadly. Younger and more headstrong pilots such as Steinhilper felt that the opposition had to be finished off. The Luftwaffe was clearly superior in the volume of planes available and was foolish to allow the British to hold on long enough to regroup further and delay invasion plans.

15 August, called Black Thursday by the Luftwaffe, was to add further fuel to this debate. As Goering met the hierarchy

at Karinhall for a post-mortem on *Adlertag,* the rest of the air force were left directionless. Some of the discussion at Karinhall centred on the role of the Stuka dive-bomber, so effective in the *Blitzkrieg* but so vulnerable in the Battle of Britain. Goering now proposed that every Stuka formation be escorted by close formations of precious fighters. Betraying little understanding of the tactics and technology of modern aerial warfare, Goering also announced the abandonment of attacks on the radar stations which provided the vital early warning of attacks to a hard-pressed Fighter Command.

Meanwhile, the German pilots attempted to attack northern airfields with Air Fleet 5 based in Scandinavia. Once again, German intelligence had failed to recognise that the rotation system used by Dowding meant that several battle-hardened squadrons sent to rest in the north were available to take on Air Fleet 5. The seventy-two Heinkels lacked an escort of 109s. Although they inflicted damage on towns such as Driffield and Bridlington, the unescorted Heinkels were badly exposed, and nearly one out of every five aircraft was hit.

Part of a fleet of a hundred and thirty 109s detailed to protect a huge strength of eighty-eight Dornier 'Flying Pencil' bombers in the afternoon, Ulrich Steinhilper was more fortunate. The small band of RAF fighters in the area could do little. The Dorniers dropped three hundred bombs on Rochester, badly disrupting production for months at the Short Brothers' Stirling bomber factory and killing several dogs at the nearby greyhound track.

About an hour and a half after the Germans had hit Rochester to the west, 234 was in action for the first time from Middle Wallop as they attempted to prevent Stuka dive-bombers hitting Portland. The squadron was scrambled to intercept the Stukas' escort of eighty 109s and 110s.

As the order to scramble came, the shy twenty-one-year-old Bob Doe felt sick in the pit of his stomach: 'I was convinced I would be killed on that first sortie. I knew I was the worst pilot in the squadron. I'd passed my Wings exam by one per cent. I was nobody. I had an awful inferiority complex anyway, and I knew that I was no good as a pilot, but I was determined to try.' As soon as he was airborne the nervousness engendered by being at readiness all day slipped away.

The odds were heavily against Bob Doe, Joseph Szlagowski and their colleagues, but their cause was not helped by the use of archaic flying tactics. Nearly five weeks after the official start of the air battle, 234 flew into their first action using Fighter Command's traditional V sections of three aircraft in close formation, which was, as Bob Doe said, 'the one thing we should not have done; we were vulnerable to attack from above'. As they headed for the enemy in their stiff and inflexible vie of three, 234 made a second mistake by moving up and down the sun. Suddenly they found themselves in the middle of hostile aircraft. Doe was flying number two and broke away to chase a Messerschmitt 110: 'Not knowing what to do, I followed. I had a go at it and it went down into the sea.' Doe followed the German plane in its descent. 'I was surprised, to be quite blunt. It crashed into the sea and I was very chuffed. As I pulled up another aeroplane went straight across; out of sheer instinct, I fired and that also went into the sea.' To his astonishment, Doe had casually shot down two in his first day's combat.

As expected, Pat Hughes had led 234 from the front and shot down two Me 110s himself. The rest of the squadron had not been so lucky. Budge Harker was hit in the tail and staggered back the twenty-five miles to Middle Wallop without having fired his guns. '15 August was an eye-opener. We were all very shaky by the end of the day,' he said. Joseph Szlagowski was also slightly hit, but managed to limp back. Harker and Szlagowski awaited news of their colleagues. Three of them, Pilot Officers Hight, Hardy and Parker, were all missing. Cecil Hight, a popular twenty-two-year-old from Stratford, New Zealand, was the leader of yellow section 'A' flight. One of the other pilots had suggested that Hight had not been well enough to fly because of a hangover, but Hight had insisted.

* * *

Just after six o'clock, Ulrich Steinhilper and the rest of JG 52 headed for England again, still flushed with the success of their earlier escort of Dornier 17s. This time, the job was to accompany the specialist bombing teams of Experimental Group 210, who had put the Kent radar stations out of action three days before, on a mission to hit the RAF fighter station at Kenley. The operation was a disaster. Somehow Experimental Group 210 missed their rendezvous with JG 52 over France. Confused, Steinhilper and his colleagues landed back at Coquelles, relieved to have finished their duties on such an intense day. Experimental Group 210 flew on unprotected to inflict heavy damage on an airfield; they did not realise until later that, instead of their target, they had hit the strategically insignificant Croydon. In making their escape, the group lost seven aircraft, and thirteen crew were either killed or missing. Among the dead was their brilliant Swiss-born leader, Walter Rubensdörffer.

Once again, the Luftwaffe had paid a high price for attacking inessential targets, though only a handful of their nine losses that day (two and a half times the RAF losses) were Me 109s. But the day was not over yet.

An hour after JG 52's abortive rendezvous with the ill-fated Experimental Group 210, one of 234's missing pilots, Cecil Hight, landed at Middle Wallop. His colleagues saw his Spitfire come in erratically, almost hitting a wooden fence as it turned left at the end of the runway. Hight switched off the engine and Gregory Kirkorian, the intelligence officer, ran out towards the plane. He saw that Hight had a huge bloody hole right through his chest. The young New Zealander slumped into Kirkorian's arms and died a few minutes later.

The squadron waited in vain for the return of Pilot Officers Hardy and Parker. The squadron record describes them as 'unaccounted for'. Their fate is one of the most intriguing puzzles of the Battle of Britain. Richard Hardy was flying as Red I, with 'Bush' Parker as Red II, and 'Morty' Mortimer-Rose as Red III in one of four sections. Mortimer-Rose's combat report for 15 August states that, when the squadron leader gave the orders to attack, 'Red section was somewhat behind at the time. Red I and II (Hardy and Parker) appeared to lose the enemy in the haze.' Despite losing Red I and II, Mortimer-Rose himself was undeterred and, although what was left of Red Section was 'well behind', he chased an Me 110 and shot it down.

Subsequently, Parker was seen by another former 234 pilot in a German prisoner-of-war camp, but the events leading up to his capture are shrouded in mystery. Francis K. Mason, in

Battle over Britain, states that Hardy 'was hit by machine-gun far out to sea and force-landed near Cherbourg'.* Yet, if his plane had been hit over the Channel (and the combat reports indicate that the action took place twenty-five miles south-west of Swanage), would it not have been more natural for Hardy to land in Britain rather than fly a long way south to be taken certain prisoner?

The 234 Squadron newsletter contains reference to the 'Hardy incident'. Some pilots talk about Hardy landing in France 'in mysterious circumstances'. Intelligence Officer Gregory Kirkorian says 'there's nothing in it'. A German diary entry of a former member of the 3/JG 53, who were in combat with 234 that day, indicates that Hardy did not put up much of a fight and preferred to go towards France rather than the British coast when chased by Oberleutnant George Claus. The diary entry reads:

> Claus brought a Spitfire to Cherbourg. He caught him
> in mid-Channel. The Tommy ran away to the south.
> Claus corrected each of his turns with small salvos
> of tracers. So he conducted him to Cherbourg. The
> Tommy lowered landing-gear, our 2 cm flak gave him
> a hit too, then he landed and came to a stop.

Oberleutnant Claus was presumably in a position to have shot down and killed Hardy, who did not seem to be resisting par-ticularly strongly, on the long way back from Cherbourg, but Claus seems to have thought that 'arresting' Hardy was a more humane or sporting alternative.

*McWhirter Twins, 1979.

Whatever the motives behind Hardy's landing in France, the net result of 15 August for 234 Squadron was that virtually a quarter of their strength had been destroyed in one go.

A few days later, Cecil Hight was buried at Christchurch in Hampshire, draped with a New Zealand flag donated by Christchurch, New Zealand. The funeral cortège was led by pilots from 234. At the close of the service three volleys were fired, followed by a salute from his fellow pilots. For men like Joseph Szlagowski and Bob Doe, the death of Cecil Hight had little impact. They just could not afford the death of a friend to intrude too much. Doe said, 'I think we'd been so indoctrinated to it that when it happened we were expecting it.'

13

MORE LOSSES

16–26 August

At their new base at Middle Wallop, 234 Squadron were still hoping that 16 August would see the return of Hardy and Parker, but there was no sign of the missing pilots by early evening when the depleted squadron was scrambled for the third time that day.

Once again, their job was to intercept a big raid, this time over Portsmouth. Despite their recent disasters, the pilots' confidence had grown a little. Now at least they knew what to expect. During the battle, Pat Hughes shot down two Me 109s, and Bob Doe, Pat Horton and Zig Klein accounted for one each. They landed at Middle Wallop elated, Szlagowski and Klein babbling away together excitedly in Polish. But the squadron had paid a price for its success. Keith Dewhurst and Francis O'Connor both lost their Spitfires; Dewhurst managed to parachute out safely and O'Connor landed in the sea where he was picked up by the navy, but during the incident he suffered a knee injury, which put him in Haslar Naval Hospital for two months.

Despite his third success in two days, Bob Doe was lucky to be alive. A stray bullet from a flying-boat hit his propeller.

A Me 109 spotted Doe's damaged Spitfire, and was sitting on his tail waiting to destroy the vulnerable aircraft, when Pat Hughes picked him off. Doe knew nothing about it.

17 August saw a short lull before the intense action of the 18th, which became known as the 'Hardest Day', when both the RAF and the Luftwaffe lost more planes than on any other day during the conflict.

'Beppo' Schmidt's departmental assessment of the RAF fighter strength issued on the 17th was, not for the first time, woefully inaccurate. He drew a portrait of a command desperately weakened and ready to be finished off. In eight days, Fighter Command had lost nearly eighty pilots and had twenty-seven seriously wounded. The leadership was indeed worried – they now transferred thirty pilots from other commands onto a brief fighter conversion course – but the Command was not yet in the parlous state Luftwaffe intelligence claimed. The Luftwaffe had calculated that, by 16 August, they had destroyed over ninety fighters; the real figure was closer to twenty-five with others damaged.

Inspired by this false picture, the Luftwaffe leadership resolved to drive their bombers, particularly the Stukas, deep into British defences. At 2.35 p.m. on the 18th, Stukas, escorted by Me 109s, made raids along the south coast, but ran into a heavy defensive group of Hurricanes and Spitfires. It was 234 Squadron's job to hold off the escorting fighters while others shot down the dive-bombers.

By now, Bob Doe had become used to the sky being full of aircraft, so he was surprised to spot a lone Messerschmitt a few hundred feet from the sea; he chased it a little way, then fired. 'I thought, well that's it, so I pulled up alongside him to see what I'd been shooting at. This was the only occasion I actually saw the enemy. He was a big blond man in a sky-blue flying suit and he just sat in the cockpit, apparently hit.' Slowly, the blond German pilot turned and looked at Bob Doe. For a moment Doe thought of waving. Then the Messerschmitt crashed into the sea. Doe could not afford to hang around, so he circled away, not knowing what happened in the water.

Sixteen dive-bombers were destroyed in the action, and 234 had considerable success against the Messerschmitts. Apart from Bob Doe, Hughes, Mortimer-Rose and Harker all claimed enemy aircraft destroyed. So did the new squadron leader, 'Spike' O'Brien, who had only joined the squadron the previous day.

Back in Margate Hospital, Geoffrey Page's burns were so severe that his chances of recovery were regarded as remote. Burns units were learning fast, but they were still relatively unsophisticated; if more than a third of the body was burned, death was certain. More than half of the skin on Page's hands was covered in burns.

Page drifted in and out of consciousness, woken usually by the thump of the anti-aircraft guns right outside his window. Every time they were fired his whole body would jerk, causing stabs of intense pain. When his sister Daphne arrived, Page's suspicions that something was very badly wrong with his face increased. However hard his sister tried to hide her feelings, he noticed the occasional look of revulsion in her eyes. Soon after the visit, he was told he was being moved to London, because German attacks on nearby RAF Manston were increasing Margate's vulnerability.

For the five-hour journey to the Royal Masonic Hospital at Hammersmith, Page was laid on the lower of two stretcher racks. It was a nightmare. Every bump in the road was agony, despite liberal helpings of morphine. Yet the two giggly Fanny drivers seemed to have no idea where Hammersmith was or of the terrible suffering that their meanderings were causing the man in the bottom stretcher. On arrival, Page thought he had never felt such severe pain, particularly in his arms. When the porter treated him like a carcass of meat, he finally lost his cool and let out a horrendous scream. The noise echoed round the ward. Then all he could remember as he slid into a twilight world of drugged sleep were flashes of pain interspersed with vivid images of a burning aircraft.

One day, for no apparent reason, Page drifted back into the real world. The haze that had surrounded people and objects dissolved, and their outlines sharpened. Instinctively, the nurse sensed the change. That morning, Skipper, as the patients called her, pulled the heavy curtains back for the first time and sunshine flooded into the room.

Skipper was tender and kind, but firm too. Slowly, she built up her charge's strength until he was permitted a visit from three friends from 56 Squadron. Page was anxious for news of his colleagues. The three visitors were very jokey, full of rather boisterous camaraderie, but Page could sense that underneath they were tense and ill at ease. He could see the strain in their eyes, the tiredness on their faces. As they told him about the deaths of mutual friends, his colleagues tried not to upset the wounded pilot.

When they had gone back to the war, he sat quietly for a few minutes. Then he sobbed helplessly for a long time. Was it for his friends now dead? Or was he feeling sorry for himself, no longer part of his squadron? Or was it just the shock after such horrific injuries? Whatever its cause, Geoffrey Page felt cleansed when the crying was over.

With Skipper's help, he inched his way forward and began to think of only one thing – flying again. But there were numerous obstacles ahead. One day Skipper arrived with a new assistant, a beautiful Red Cross nurse. As soon as she looked at the burned lump that had once been a handsome twenty-year-old pilot, she recoiled in horror, unable to hide her feelings. For the first time, he acknowledged how much he had physically changed. His eyes followed the stare on the nurse's face down to his arms. They were a putrified mass of pus-filled boils, a result of the condition of his blood. The hands from the wrists to the fingertips were jet black and shrunken. Soon after the crash, tannic acid had been smothered on his raw face, hands and back in Margate Hospital. The acid was designed to coagulate any blood that was oozing from the burns and to lessen the risk of death from shock, by reducing the pain. 'That black stuff's only the tannic acid. It's not the colour of your skin,' said Skipper, interrupting the patient's grim thoughts. His relief was not shared by the Red Cross nurse, who scuttled out of the room. He looked down again at his ghastly arms and hands. Fearful about the condition of his face, he demanded a mirror from Skipper. No, she insisted. He asked firmly, almost coldly, again and again. 'You will be allowed to look in a mirror, Pilot Officer Page, when I see fit to permit it and not before,' she said with equal firmness.

The mirror was over the washbasin. It was two steps away from the bed. As soon as Skipper had disappeared, Page thought, Right, you miserable bitch. I'll look in the mirror if it kills me. It took five minutes of throbbing pain in his hands just to pull the sheets back. After agonizingly swinging his legs back so they dangled over the side of the bed, he prepared for the big drop onto the floor. His knees buckled as he hit the surface, and he was forced to rest before moving slowly across the room. Sweating with fear, aching from just those few steps, he stared at last into the mirror. A gargoyle stared back, its face swollen and ugly, and three times its normal size. Weak from the effort, Geoffrey Page collapsed on the floor, his body crashing against the washbasin.

By mid-August the Luftwaffe High Command believed that the vast bulk of Fighter Command was out of action. The RAF had, they thought, been reduced to only about three hundred serviceable Spitfires, Hurricanes and Defiants to defend Britain. When the small number of remaining planes were dealt with, the invasion could follow.

At this stage of the aerial conflict, the officers of the Luftwaffe wings strung out along the Channel coast not only believed the errors of their own intelligence gatherers, but also had sensed from the daily engagements that the enemy was weak and already fatigued by the constant fighting. They did not realise that the airfields they had seen badly hit, such as Eastchurch and Detling, were largely irrelevant to the activities of Fighter Command. Even Manston, which, as the nearest airfield to Calais, was frequently hit on the way home to France, was of little strategic importance. True, it was a useful refuelling airfield, but it was the sector stations, with their communications networks, that were crucial.

On 18 August, 3/JG 52 were told that planes were refuelling at Manston, and were diverted to attack it. The Messerschmitts turned and flew low over the airfield. Ulrich Steinhilper was going so low that he had more or less to jump over a refuelling tanker. The ground crews were taken by surprise and caught out in the open. As Steinhilper drew level with the petrol bowser, he noticed a man holding a petrol hose between the bowser and a fighter. He sprayed the airfield with bullets and the man with the hosepipe fell to the ground. Fifteen other airmen were injured. As they pulled away, 3/JG 52 were elated by what appeared to have been a spectacular raid, but Steinhilper's jubilation was tempered by what he had done to the man filling the aircraft: 'It was probably the only time I knew I had hit a fellow human being when I pulled the trigger. I didn't like to think of it then, and I don't like to think of it now.'

For ten days following John Chomley's death on 12 August, 257 Squadron were relatively quiet. Two pilots had their planes damaged but were unhurt. Sergeant Pilot Jock Girdwood was shot down and hurt his foot, but that was the sum consequence of their involvement in the battle. The waiting increased tension, and Geoff Myers could not help but be affected by the mood, especially as the younger men turned to him for support. Yet, when questioning the pilots about their precious few claims to success, he had to be firm and precise. It was good for flagging morale to report enemy planes destroyed, but bad for Dowding to plan his strategy on the basis of inaccurate intelligence reports:

> When they came back, some I knew had done their
> stuff, others were shooting a line. Sometimes it

sounded like cricket. I carefully used to check up on how much ammunition had been fired to see how it tallied with how long the pilot said he had shot. It can't have been pleasant for them, to have me doing it.

In public, Myers had to keep his thoughts to himself, but alone in his room at night, he worried about his children.

I get sudden terrors when I think about you and the babies, but I will not let them get the better of me. You would be ashamed of me. They have not interned you, Darling. 1 hope you are able to bear up – we are fighting for hope and as long as we are fighting, hope cannot be destroyed.

During the day, much of Myers's time was occupied with the problems caused by the squadron leader's behaviour. Even more cheerful pilots such as Alan Henderson were fed up with it. To Henderson, Harkness seemed always to lead them away from action, and scarcely anyone could understand the squadron leader's technique on the radio transmitter. Incompetence was one thing, thought Myers; perhaps Harkness was doing his best, but the squadron leader's arrogance, his refusal to accept that anyone he dis-agreed with could be correct, was much more difficult to forgive. The morale of his men swiftly dropped. 'Some of the sergeants were openly talking about running away,' said Alan Henderson. 'I tried to cheer them up.' Henderson admits he was sometimes scared too. 'Anyone who says he was not frightened in the Battle of Britain is either a liar or an idiot. One of the best reasons for choosing to be a fighter pilot was that you were only shit-scared for forty minutes at a time.

The other was that we were kings of everything. Girls were flinging themselves at you all the time.'

Another of 257 pilots, David Hunt, had been married only a few weeks and to be near him, his wife Terry took lodgings at Northolt. Most days Hunt worked from the early hours until late at night, so it was important to the Hunts to snatch what time together they could. Terry Hunt never met Squadron Leader Sharp but she sensed the squadron's lack of respect for him. Sharp had been against the Hunts' marriage – 'because you'll soon be popping babies out,' he told them.

On 19 August, 257 moved from London to Martlesham Heath in Suffolk, seven miles east of Ipswich. It was a flat, well-drained site, ideal for an aerodrome. From Martlesham, the squadron patrolled the east coast, often meeting heavy contingents of German bombers with fighter escorts on their way to London.

On the evening of their arrival at Martlesham, David Hunt held a small party to celebrate his twenty-third birthday. It was a pleasant occasion and the pilots were more relaxed than usual. For once they seemed able to avoid talking about the war.

Terry Hunt later wrote:

> There were eight pilots at the party, and Geoff, the intelligence officer . . . After three weeks, no one was left in commission. David and I made a list. It was too complete to be shocking. It was perfect in its completeness.*

*Esther Terry Wright, *Pilot's Wife's Tale,* Bodley Head, 1942.

One of the men present that night was twenty-four-year-old Pilot Officer Gerard Maffett from Bray in Berkshire, a stocky young man with a kind and sunny disposition, who performed the prodigious feat of guzzling a quart of beer in eight and a half seconds. A few days later, Maffett wrote to his parents:[†]

My Dear Mum and Dad,

. . . We start at 04.30 hours and go on until 21.30 hours with about thirty-five minutes off for each meal. Last Tuesday I had a cup of cocoa at 04.00 and breakfast at 11.15, a plate of soup at 14.00 and dinner at 20.00 hours. Actually it was a very bad day and now things are much better, although we still get up before 04.00 hours.

The other day . . . I was lucky enough to have a crack at the leader of a sub-formation of Heinkel IIIs. I think it was probably rather unpleasant for them as I was above them and I fired from a position where they could not fire at me. I think the leader was damaged. The third and last attack was in the middle of the main formation and I picked out a Dornier 215. I attacked him from above and dived down on him. The intelligence people have given me the aircraft as shot down as there was quite a glow in the fuselage as I dived away. I suggested that the glow might have been the sun, but they think he was destroyed . . . the Hurricane certainly is a grand aircraft.

Love to you both,
Gerry

[†]Letter quoted in *The Battle of Britain Then and Now*, Battle of Britain Prints International, London 1980.

Even during this quiet period, 234 continued to fly from Middle Wallop. Their new leader, Spike O'Brien, wrote to his wife, 'They seem a grand crowd of chaps in this squadron and very flat out.' On 21 August Bob Doe added to his successes when he spotted a Junkers 88 hopping in and out of the clouds near Winchester. Doe and Squadron Leader O'Brien shot it down together. It crashed into a field. 'Every occupant had at least five bullet holes in his helmet,' recalled Doe. 'I must have been bloodthirsty then.'

In that operation, Doe's plane was hit by a bullet through the main spine, so he flew it gently to Hamble, where it was fixed by the civilians from Supermarine. For Doe it was a pleasant break. One of the men took him to the pub, then home, where his wife cooked him lunch: 'I had a strong feeling that everyone in Britain was in it together. It was comforting to have that support.'

After three seemingly never-ending weeks at No. 7 Operational Training Unit at Hawarden where he was learning to fly Spitfires, Cyril Bamberger returned south to his squadron with his friend Ted Manton. As he heard the news from the front line, Bam had become increasingly frustrated at being out of the action. But when he rejoined 610 at Biggin Hill, he soon realised that the battle so far had not been all fun: he noticed how much more drained and tense his colleagues looked; and some familiar faces were missing.

21 August saw Bam's first day of action since he had begun flying. 610 were airborne before 8.00 a.m., with the aim of intercepting the enemy off the coast, but the squadron was soon split up, and the enemy was never engaged except by

a couple of individual pilots. Throughout his first experience of war in the air, Bam felt hopelessly lost. One minute the sky was full of aircraft, the next the planes all seemed to be flying in twos and threes. Where they were going and what they were doing was not at all clear. As he went to bed that night, Bam thought that the days to follow could only bring an improvement.

In the morning of 24 August one of Bam's fellow sergeants, Ronnie Hamlyn, was about to be reprimanded by the group captain for a bad landing when the order came to scramble. Hamlyn made his excuses and left. In the air, Bam still felt uncertain and lost, but Ronnie Hamlyn managed to shoot down a fighter and a bomber. In the afternoon, as Hamlyn was about to receive his reprimand for the second time, there was another call to scramble. In two further intensive actions in a day of fierce and prolonged activity for 610, the errant Sergeant Hamlyn shot down three more enemy fighters. 610 lost one Spitfire in each action; none of the pilots were killed, but all three were wounded.

Bam wondered at Ronnie Hamlyn's achievements. He knew that his fellow sergeant was an experienced pilot, a veteran of Dunkirk, but if Bam had a chance of any action, he always seemed to arrive too late.

That night, an apparently insignificant raid was launched on England that was to prove an important turning point in the conflict.

By this time, even Goering was coming to realise that, despite intelligence reports, the Luftwaffe were not sweeping all before them. If an invasion were to be launched before the uncertain autumn weather set in, now was the moment to make a decisive thrust against Fighter Command's defences. The Luftwaffe plan was to launch big raids on the key sector airfields that circled London, such as Biggin Hill and Debden, and also to hit the aircraft factories which threatened to replenish Fighter Command's supplies. More fighters were moved to airfields near Calais, alongside Ulrich Steinhilper's base at Coquelles, for huge escort formations were needed to protect the bombers.

Hitler had issued strict orders that London itself was not to be bombed, but on 24 August a German attack damaged the City of London instead of the docks. In the first hit on central London since 1918, the Church of St Giles, Cripplegate, was bombed, rather than the docks at Thames Haven. As part of the fighter escort, Steinhilper realised immediately that a serious error had been made.

The attack provoked Churchill into sending, the next night, a reprisal raid of Hampden bombers to Berlin; the bombs affected civilians as well as hitting the planned military target of the Siemens – Halske factory. It was something that Hitler had promised would never happen. The physical damage was irrelevant: the capital of Germany had been bombed for the first time; Germans were no longer safe in their own beds. The process of disillusionment for Hitler's people was beginning. The indignity of the Berlin raids was also a catalyst for Goering's future mistaken decision to blitz London instead of continuing his policy of attrition on the airfields.

On 26 August Bob Doe was in the thick of the action again, chasing an Me 109 towards the Channel Islands. When he finally caught and hit it, it seemed to explode in one go. On the same day, Pat Hughes destroyed another two Me 109s, and Pat Horton, Bill Hornby and Mortimer-Rose were all successful too.

The transformation from the shambles of the first days at Middle Wallop was startling. Pat Hughes was an inspiration and Squadron Leader O'Brien had been an important steadying influence. Pat Horton, the New Zealander, had grown into an excellent pilot; so had 'Budge' Harker, one of the sergeant pilots. But it was Bob Doe who had changed most. The underconfident young man who had been slow to go solo and barely scraped through his Wings exams had matured into a highly proficient fighter pilot. The early lack of leadership in 234 had suited Doe's determination to fly his own way. Yet that success brought its dangers. Doe's increasing self-confidence began to grow into a belief that he was infallible – and, in the Battle of Britain, no one was infallible.

At noon on 26 August, 610 Squadron were in action from their-forward base at Hawkinge. They were involved in a battle with eight Me 109s on a bombing escort over Folkestone. The 109s had made the short journey across the Channel from Coquelles, and were the remnants of Ulrich Steinhilper's sister squadron in JG 52, No.1.

At the end of the action four 109s and one Do 17 were destroyed. On the other side, Sergeant Else was seriously wounded when he bailed out over Hawkinge. Frank Webster, a likeable publican's son from the Isle of Wight, also had his Spitfire severely damaged in the combat. As he bravely tried to land his smoking plane back at base, he crashed and was killed.

For both Ulrich Steinhilper and Cyril Bamberger it had been an unhappy day. Four of Steinhilper's fellow pilots at Coquelles were missing. Bamberger's squadron had lost another sergeant, and an officer had been killed.

Also on the 26th, the Luftwaffe mounted a huge raid with forty Dorniers on Hornchurch and Debden, the forward base of 257 Squadron. Again, they got it wrong: the 109 escorts were inadequate and were committed to protecting the 110s which, with their poor acceleration, were vulnerable to the Spitfire. Goering had seen the 110s as the ideal plane to escort bombers; now he was having to utilize his valuable 109s to protect the much-vaunted 110s. The Dorniers were badly hit but a few had managed to reach Debden, where three released their load, hitting several buildings and damaging one plane. Three airmen were killed in the raid.

Geoff Myers wrote in his notebook for his wife:

> Jones didn't understand what we were fighting for. He was one of four RAF clerks who were blown to bits when a bomb dropped on Debden. He knew nothing about the war, regarded it as the weather, as something that happened.
>
> Bolton this morning over breakfast couldn't think of anything better to say than to describe in detail how he dug out the bits of Jones and the other men who were blown to pieces . . . he relished describing the whole thing. 'We couldn't find one of the heads at all,' he said as a grand finale.

14

UNDER THREAT

Late August and early September

On arriving at Biggin Hill, Cyril Bamberger had put his gear on the first floor of the accommodation block. He never saw it again: 'I used to sleep at the dispersal hut. We were fed there quite frequently. All I can remember of my few days at Biggin Hill was that hut, and constantly being scrambled. Although I slowly learned to be scared at Biggin Hill, I never reached the point where I did not want to be scrambled. I just wanted to be a fighter pilot and a good one.'

Except for the odd night at the forward base further into Kent at Hawkinge, Bam seemed to be either in the air or at Biggin Hill dispersal. Perhaps the officers with cars were more mobile, but Bam can remember going out of the airfield only once: 'We went to a pub in Bromley. It made me mad, made me really want to spit. We had suffered very heavy casualties but here was the civilian population quietly drinking as *if* there wasn't a war going on.'

Even the deaths seemed unreal to Bam, as he tried to comprehend what was happening both to him and his squadron. On 28 August, Pilot Officer K. H. Cox was shot down and killed. Cox had joined 610 the same day as Bam. It was not until the next day that the full extent of the danger came home to Bam, when Ted Manton, his friend from Cheshire whom he'd known since 1936, met the same fate.*

At about four o'clock on the 29th, on his fourth sortie of the day, Bam was flying in formation when he suddenly saw a Spitfire hit by an Me 110 and explode. Back at base, he discovered it had been Manton in the Spitfire; the former postman had, after more than a year's training, been a Battle of Britain pilot for little over a week. His death, which made Bam angry rather than frightened, sunk in only slowly. Bam began to realise that flying in war was not a game, but he was still too busy trying to understand what was going on: 'I wasn't really scared – yet – and that's very dangerous.'

Bam's ignorance stemmed from the fact that no one told him anything: 'We never had a single briefing. No one said, "You are all in II Group, this goes from here to here." I never saw a map of the Channel; no one showed me where the enemy forces were. It was just my job to get the plane up and see what happened. Maybe all this was talked about in the officers' mess – it certainly wasn't among the sergeants. I had no idea we were in the Battle of Britain.'

Bam soon came to see that the classic image of fighter pilots was not wholly accurate: 'The impression the public had of scores of enthusiastic pilots was wrong. If we scrambled, we knew our heads were on the block. We were relieved if the weather was bad and we were stood down.'

---

*There is some confusion about the date of Manton's death. According to his headstone and burial records, it was the 28th, but the squadron record book gives the 29th.

To make matters worse, the Luftwaffe, now almost all grouped along the Pas de Calais, were at last striking at the heart of the RAF's defensive system, focusing their attacks on such key Fighter Command targets as Biggin Hill, Hornchurch and Debden. At Biggin Hill the exhausted ground crew and pilots now had to take on the responsibility of keeping the airfield operational and clear of debris, as well as flying. The day after Ted Manton's death, the airfield was nearly taken out of the war by a huge evening air raid by nine low-flying Junkers 88s, during which scarcely a building was left undamaged. A direct hit on a personnel shelter killed thirty-nine people and wounded twenty-six. Digging out bodies from the ruined shelter – including those of three of 610's regular ground crew – took most of that night and the next day.

On 31 August, battered and depleted, 610 were moved out of the front line to Acklington in Northumberland for rest and re-equipping. 'The day we moved out, the CO was told there was enemy aircraft some distance away, but heading in our direction,' said Bam. 'He said no, we're not going up. We were glad to be leaving, we'd been so badly hit.'

Pilot Officer Deacon Elliott of 72 Squadron, which flew down from Acklington to relieve 610, wrote:

> We landed at Biggin Hill at 15.30. As we flew in, No. 610 – or what was left of them – flew out; they seemed in a hell of a hurry and we were soon to find out why. Within minutes we were to take off on our first mission in what we now all knew as the Battle of Britain. I saw at least two dispersed aircraft burning from direct hits with incendiary bombs. Bomb craters everywhere.[*]

---

[*]Marcel Julian, *The Battle of Britain,* Jonathan Cape, 1967.

To add to the carnage of the previous day, a further seven people were killed and another pilot was seriously wounded.

On this last day of August, the Luftwaffe maintained relentless pressure on the RAF, and when radar reported an estimated two hundred German planes airborne and heading towards Britain from the Calais area, Keith Park ordered thirteen squadrons from seven airfields near London into the air. For 257's Alan Henderson and Gerry Maffett, the manoeuvre was to bring disaster and death.

Henderson, although reliable and hard-working, was something of a playboy, always keen to shoot up to London in the hope of meeting some pretty girls. Also, at times, he took an over-casual approach to his job. For example, rather than running to his plane like everyone else when the order to scramble came, it was his habit to stroll. 'If I ran, I got out of breath,' he said. Left behind on this occasion, he swiftly set about catching up with his colleagues, but, alone at twenty thousand feet, he sighted enemy planes. He singled out a target and fired. The next thing Henderson knew was that his own small fuel tank had been hit: 'The cockpit was full of flames. I've never been so terrified in my life. There was a smell of cordite. With a superhuman effort, I opened the canopy and jumped out.' The parachute seemed to take a long time to open and, when it did so, the jerk was so fierce that it dislocated his shoulder. As he drifted helplessly out to sea, Henderson began to think he would drown. Fortunately, a motorboat already carrying several German pilots soon pulled him out of the icy water. (To Henderson's astonishment, one of the men who had come to his rescue was his peacetime stockbroker.) At the end of the day Alan Henderson was still alive but his active participation in the Battle of Britain was over.

Gerry Maffett was not so lucky, though quite what happened to him is unclear. In the combat 257's twelve Hurricanes had been outnumbered more than four to one by 110s. Maffett was hit and his Hurricane R4 903 crashed into the foreshore at Walton on the Naze. It was generally concluded that his parachute had failed to open and that he died on landing. However, some 257 pilots who survived that day, such as Alan Henderson, believed that in the panic Gerry Maffett had jumped out without his parachute.

By now, Squadron Leader Harkness seemed unable to restore morale and, both in the sky and on the ground, was less and less in evidence. Geoff Myers noted that Hugh Beresford had begun to talk all the time about his squadron leader:

> Beresford would come back to the subject most on his mind. 'Why does Harkness just go into his tent after a Blitz and read *Men Only* instead of talking things over with the other fellows? Why doesn't he attempt to lead them? Why does he even refuse to get on with all the administrative work that a CO must do? He might at least make up a bit by going on some of the dull convoy patrols. But he simply disappears into his tent and goes to sleep while the boys are wearing themselves out. When they make mistakes he just bawls them out with bursts of short-tempered abuse like a turkey.'

Although 31 August saw heavy Luftwaffe losses, there were signs that the German war of attrition was paying off, and the regular bombing of key airfields had left the back-up staff feeling particularly vulnerable. At RAF Manston, for example, which was the closest airfield to Calais, many airmen resolutely refused to come out of their shelters, while locals stripped the buildings that had been hit of tools and spares. Overall, however, Fighter Command had withstood the German pressure well. Despite the loss of life and damage to buildings, Biggin Hill was kept operational. When the Germans began hitting radar stations again, they were only out of action for a few hours. The aircraft factories and Beaverbrook's civilian units were so active that Dowding was able to fill the vital gaps in his fighter forces, though he realised that he had to husband his fragile resources carefully. Virtually every day Fighter Command was losing fewer planes and pilots than the Luftwaffe, but it was not always on the ratio needed to maintain an even balance: two or three Germans to every British pilot. Despite pressure to commit bigger defensive forces to the battle, Dowding knew that Fighter Command's job was to survive and, unwilling to lose any more pilots in the sea, he decided that the defensive line had to be redrawn. Fighter Command, helped by radar, were now instructed to wait until the enemy had crossed the Channel before engaging in combat.

For Bob Doe and Joseph Szlagowski's squadron at Middle Wallop, free of their former poor leadership, their success rate was now higher than their losses. But for 257 the problems would not go away. Hugh Beresford created difficulties for the newly-wed David and Terry Hunt by forbidding David to leave camp. Writing soon afterwards, Terry said, 'Beresford has tried to wreck our married life by keeping David in like a child.' Perhaps it was frustration at being apart from his own wife or his burden of responsibility that made Beresford inflexible for, when she met him, Terry Hunt found 'Bloody'

Beresford, as she called him, quite charming. Geoff Myers talked to Beresford and helped to ease the visiting restrictions for the newly-weds. Terry wrote:

> In the evenings I would wait for David at the gate.
> Tonight I had mother with me. We looked at the
> immense sky, and the cage the searchlights made,
> closing us in almost. Two bombs fell somewhere near.
> I was a bit excited. I left a note on the door for David
> and went down to the shelter.

Apart from personnel troubles, 257 continued to find it difficult to stem their losses. The next to go was Pilot Officer Robespierre Bonseigneur. It had never ceased to amaze 'Bonny', a twenty-two-year-old French Canadian with the rough, rustic looks of a backwoodsman, that the standard of living in wartime Britain was higher than in the peacetime depression of Quebec. Bonny was a loner but well liked.

On Tuesday 3 September, fifty-four Dorniers escorted by about eighty 110s flew up to the Thames estuary at breakfast time. They turned north near Southend and shattered North Weald airfield with two hundred bombs, killing four people and damaging several buildings. Scrambled too late by their masters, the RAF only intercepted the Germans on their way home. Francis Mason wrote of the incident:

> As the bombers strove to reach the coast the escorting
> 110s performed magnificently; although they lost
> heavily they took a surprisingly heavy toll of British
> fighters.[*]

---

[*]Francis K. Mason, *Battle Over Britain,* McWhirter Twins, 1979.

Among them were four planes from 257. Pilot Officer Gundry's plane was damaged but he landed unhurt at base. Sergeant Nutter's Hurricane was also damaged and he was slightly wounded. Bonseigneur was shot down at Ingatestone and bailed out, but was killed. Bonny's death particularly upset young Carl Capon, who had been with him when it happened. Geoff Myers wrote:

> He said to me, 'We could do nothing against those planes that kept swooping down on us. They were flashing about the sky above us at twenty-five thousand feet. There must have been hundreds of them. And Bonseigneur, the fool, just climbed up there into them, followed by me alone. Well it was too damned silly. He was asking for it. Now he's gone and what's left of the Squadron.' The strain was too much for him.

That lunchtime, Terry Hunt rang Martlesham Heath to speak to her husband. An airman casually answered and said: ''E's one of the ones who've come down.' By persistence she discovered that David had come down by parachute and had been burned; he was in hospital in Billericay, Essex. At the hospital a tall imposing doctor in a navy flannel suit with white stripes told Mrs Hunt that her husband's eyebrows had been burned off. Later, Terry wrote:

> David was lying on the bed. The newness of the accident was a sensation in the room. He himself was something brand new and very real. I saw him just for a moment, his face and arms purple with fresh dye and very swollen. I thought he had no eyes; and I thought they had not told me that but had left me to find out

quietly for myself; and curiously, how wise they were. Behind all this was David. I saw then, as I cannot see now, how we should manage his blindness. The visiting surgeon said we would know in thirty-six hours if David was going to live.[*]

Afterwards the official report told the full tale of David Hunt's crash:

> . . . flame came through the instrument panel, filling the cockpit and burning my hands, legs and face. The reserve fuel tank had exploded and I had neither gloves nor goggles, which I had pushed over my forehead in order to get a better view. I then tried to open the hood but found it jammed. Using both hands on one side I managed at last to pull the hood open, undid my button harness, grabbed my helmet off and plunged out of the starboard side of the plane . . . my hands were all bloody like I was feeling and they were covered with projecting tissue; that was the skin; and all that was left of my sleeve was a charred ribbon of ranks.

For David Hunt's young wife his accident was a harsh jolt to the sense of unreality that had dominated her first few months of marriage. Looking back, Terry Hunt remembered:

> It was a queer, golden time. The world seemed full of lights. They were golden boys too. You met people once, or twice, and then they were dead. Now they seem such little boys, such boys.[*]

[*]Esther Terry Wright, *Pilot's Wife's Tale*, Bodley Head, 1942.
[*]*Pilot's Wife's Tale.*

With Bonseigneur gone and Hunt on the danger list, the embattled squadron had lost two more good pilots. Morale was low, but it hadn't yet hit rock-bottom.

After Hall's death on 8 August, Lancelot Mitchell had been made acting flight lieutenant in charge of 'B' Flight. This improved his confidence enormously and he began to believe he was an excellent pilot, showing off with acrobatics and hedge-hopping. But Geoff Myers, now sharing a room with Mitchell, perceived the stress beneath the confident façade:

> The life of perpetual readiness, the strain of air battles and the heavy odds had begun to tell on Mitchell. He had become fidgety and his big, brown eyes would not come to rest. We've all been through hell since the Squadron was formed a few weeks ago. We've all grown old. We've changed. It's grim.

On 3 September, Fighter Command and the Luftwaffe each lost sixteen planes. A better ratio was needed for Fighter Command to survive. Although it was the 110s that had done particularly well on the 3rd, overall the Me 109, increasingly flying at higher altitudes around twenty-five thousand feet, was showing its efficacy as a first-class fighter aircraft. As usual, German intelligence underestimated British aircraft availability, but fighting had grown so intense that II Group was now in danger of being neutralised.

On 4 September in Berlin, Hitler indicated that he was still interested in invasion. 'In England they're filled with curiosity and keep asking, "Why doesn't he come?"' he said. 'Be calm. He's coming. He's coming.'

On that same day, Joseph Szlagowski was at last able to chalk up a success. Sixty-five Me 110s were engaged over Surrey and, to his delight, Szlagowski managed to shoot one down. He hardly had time to gather his thoughts before going on to attack a Dornier 17. As a German parachuted out of the burning plane, Szlagowski saw that his parachute was alight and flames were burning through the silk. By the time the pilot hit the sea near Hove with great force, only the straps remained. In Szlagowski's case, the desire for revenge that had been eating up all the refugees from Poland dissolved with that German pilot into the sea.

4 September saw a record for 234 Squadron: they suffered no casualties but shot down fifteen enemy planes and damaged seven. Apart from Szlagowski's successes, Pat Hughes and Bob Doe destroyed three each.

The squadron's run of victory continued over the next couple of days. On the 6th, eight Me 109s (plus two probables) were destroyed and three Dorniers damaged. Hughes and Doe had destroyed one each, and Squadron Leader O'Brien two, but Pilot Officer Gordon was killed, their first casualty for three weeks. Pat Horton almost met the same fate, but was rescued by a naval launch from Weymouth. That night, Pat Hughes went to see Gregory Kirkorian in a depressed and unsettled state. He told the intelligence officer that spots kept appearing before his eyes when he was flying. Kirkorian tried to reassure him and pretend that it was because he drank too much.

Meanwhile, at 257 Squadron, Geoff Myers recorded Hugh Beresford's increasingly tense behaviour:

> As the days of adversity piled up, he became a bit
> fidgety on the ground, but he remained brave and
> cool-headed in the air. Sometimes he would ask me

if there was going to be a Blitz four or five times in
a quarter of an hour. The strain under which he was
living penetrated my system, and I could do nothing
for him. It was tough.

Beresford was the only pilot who could have pulled the
squadron together. Alan Henderson remembered him as
a gentleman: 'He was a very nice chap. Not a line shooter,
friendly with a sense of humour.' None of his fellow pilots
doubted his courage and determination but, as Myers noted,
he continued to be obsessed by the leadership vacuum:

> 'Sharp makes me tired,' [Beresford said]. 'I just can't
> stand the way he frigs about in the air every time
> there's a Blitz on. We all shout at him that he's not
> following the vectors given by the Controller, but it
> makes no difference. He just goes the wrong way then
> circles round and round in the air until the section
> leaders peel off and leave him. This afternoon he saw
> all the bombs crashing below us in the oil tanks in the
> estuary. But do you think it made any difference to
> him? No, he just went on circling at 18,000 feet. He
> didn't seem to hear or see anything.'

The pressures were showing on the others too – on Carl Capon,
for example, one of the keenest pilots in the squadron and held
in high esteem by Myers: 'He was my own personal hero. He
was so pure. He knew his job and he was going to stick to it.
He'd never leave anyone in the lurch.' And, despite the profound tension, Capon never hesitated or flinched:

> Poor Capon will go crackers if we don't look out. He's
> just twenty, and to look at him with his innocent,

earnest blue eyes, his open face and wide forehead under that light, wavy hair, you would think he was not yet eighteen. He would follow his leader anywhere in the sky and never let him down whatever the odds against them. Tonight he couldn't stop writhing as he sat on the table with his hands. There are too many of them. We just couldn't do a thing. They sailed down the Thames estuary in perfect formation. And we did nothing. They just bombed us and went back. Just count up the Squadron now and think for yourself. On the 8th of August we were 26, and now what's left of us? Nine?

On the other side of the Channel, the Luftwaffe were showing signs of exhaustion. They would undoubtedly have felt better had they known that Fighter Command was now very vulnerable, but their own experiences of fierce conflict in crowded skies had destroyed their credence in intelligence reports.

At 3/JG 52, Kuhle gave firm leadership at squadron level, but the group commander, not an inexperienced combat flyer, was rarely seen in the air. There was open talk of *Kanale Krankheit* ('Channel illness'), as pilots turned back more often than was normal, claiming engine or radio failures. One senior pilot's alleged appendicitis, requiring hospital treatment, was viewed with suspicion by his younger colleagues. Nor was sympathy forthcoming when another senior man, who had been decorated in Spain, was also hospitalised.

On one occasion, when Ulrich Steinhilper was flying in a formation of over two hundred aircraft, fighters escorting bombers, he heard amid the terrible noise and chaos on the radio a very panicky voice say, 'There's a Spitfire behind me.'

Major Adolf Galland, who was then Group Commander of 3/ JG 26, brusquely cut in, 'Then jump out of your plane, you bedwetter.' The radios went silent. The nervous pilot had been publicly humiliated.

Tension was fomented by constant reminders of the Me 109's short range, which gave only a few minutes combat time over London or the airfields close by. As Galland himself pointed out in *The First and the Last*,* additional fuel tanks that could be discarded after use, as used later in the war, would have enormously increased the potential for penetration into Britain. As for morale, Galland said:

> Failure to achieve any noticeable success and obvious misjudgements of the situation by the Command and unjustified accusations had a most demoralising effect on us fighter pilots, who were already overtaxed by physical and mental strain. We saw one comrade after another, old and tested brothers in combat, vanish from our ranks. Not a day passed without a place remaining empty at the mess table.

Even with his additional responsibilities as communications officer, Steinhilper missed only two missions while he was at Coquelles. The first was when Kuhle told him to escort a *Gefreiter* (aircraftsman) flying erratically over the Channel back to Calais. On the second occasion, Steinhilper went into Calais with Kuhle and Waller on such a foggy day that flying seemed just a remote possibility. But as the three sat in a bar, the fog began to break up, forcing the pilots to return to the airfield immediately. Waller and Kuhle did not even bother to

---

*Adolf Galland, *The First and the Last,* Methuen, 1955

finish their whiskies, but Steinhilper downed his to the bottom of the glass and finished off his colleagues' too. He was not drunk, but his concentration was weaker than it should have been; as he taxied away, he skidded across the potato field, causing damage to his undercarriage. The mission left without him and Steinhilper felt so guilty that he offered the airmen in the maintenance tent a crate of champagne to work through the night so that he could fly next day.

Even the solid Albert Waller, the farmer's son from outside Hamburg who had trained with Steinhilper, began to show his nerves. He had already been hit once and had been forced to bail out, so he had a good idea of what might happen in the future. One evening Waller was teased by the other pilots. Usually it took him a few minutes to see a joke and this time, before the penny had dropped, Waller jumped up, grabbed his pistol and ran off into the woods. Kuhle and Steinhilper chased after him in vain. Back in their tent, waiting for the sound of the shot, they anxiously analysed Waller's behaviour, agreeing that for the past few days he had been exaggeratedly stiff and formal. An hour later, however, Waller returned. Kuhle and Steinhilper discussed whether he needed to see a psychiatrist, but in the end Kuhle simply talked to him quietly and firmly. Waller seemed to relax immediately and the incident was never repeated.

Although Steinhilper felt sick in the pit of his stomach every time he sat in the cockpit of his Me 109 before take-off, he was prepared to die for his country. He saw colleagues who had been given three years' training shot down one by one and replaced by young men who had been in training for a year or sometimes less, but continued to display a steely determination.

Soon after Waller's display of nerves, 3/JG 52 were on bomber escort duties when they were attacked by Spitfires from 72 Squadron based at Croydon and Albert Waller's 109 was hit. Steinhilper held his breath until he saw his friend's blond-headed body tumbling through the blue sky; Waller safely pulled the parachute cord and drifted down towards the Kent countryside below. For a moment Steinhilper considered Waller's fate, but enemy aircraft were still active and a slip in concentration could be fatal. Depressed, he headed back towards France.

15

Turning Point

4–7 September

In the first week of September aircraft losses on both sides were about even, but the RAF had lost exclusively fighters, while German losses were a mixture of fighters and bombers. Misled again by faulty intelligence about remaining British fighter strength, Goering was now convinced that Britain could be finished off, and Hitler was beginning to lose patience waiting for the aerial supremacy that he had been promised weeks ago.

On 4 September, Goering had decided to change tactics again and bomb London. The RAF had survived the intense recent conflict but the British defensive line had grown thinner. As Keith Park at Noll Group noted:

> By about September 5th, the results of [these] attacks had appreciably reduced the defensive potential of the British Fighter Force . . . With the almost total disloca-tion of the defensive organisation, the direction of the Squadrons called up into action became an extremely delicate matter.

Goering had been a poor choice by Hitler to run the air force. It was not simply that his self-indulgent and luxurious lifestyle dismayed the pilots who were working hard at great risk to win supremacy in the air – or that he had accused his fighter pilots of lack of determination. Goering had little to no strategic or tactical experience or acumen, and his technical knowledge about modern warfare also left much to be desired – with the result that his expectations for the Luftwaffe were ludicrously overoptimistic.

At a tactical conference, Hugo Sperrle, Commander of Air Fleet III, cautioned Goering against his change of tactics. Sperrle, who had commanded the Condor Legion in Spain, did not believe that the RAF were only a few days away from defeat. Moreover, he understood that, without long-range heavy bombers, the Luftwaffe's planned strategic bombing of London faced only limited success. Unfortunately for Sperrle, however, Albert Kesselring – who, as commander of Air Fleet II, was nearer the centre of the action – disagreed. Perhaps he was merely telling Goering and, through him, Hitler what he thought they wanted to hear, but Kesselring argued that Fighter Command had been liquidated and that attacks on London would be the final blow. Although Sperrle insisted that attacks on key airfields should continue, Goering agreed with Kesselring. After the war, Hugh Dowding commented:

> I could hardly believe that the Germans would have made such a mistake. From then on it was gradually borne in upon me that it was a supernatural inter-vention at that particular time, and that that was really the crucial day.[*]

[*]Robert Wright, *Dowding and the Battle of Britain,* Macdonald, 1969.

As 7 September dawned clear and bright, Goering, who had moved up to the Pas de Calais to direct operations himself, was aboard his luxurious personal train, *Asia* (complete with bedrooms, a command post and cinema) preparing to put his plans into action. 'The sky of London will be black with aeroplanes,' he had promised.

Goering's abandonment of the free-chase and airfield-attack tactics meant that the increasingly effective 109s were reduced to an escort role, leaving them shackled to their bombers and vulnerable both to attack and fuel shortages As Gunther Rail of JG 52 wrote:[†]

> We really wasted our fighters. We didn't have enough
> to begin with, and we used them in the wrong way, for
> direct close escort. We were tied to the bombers flying
> slowly – sometimes with flaps down over England. We
> couldn't use our altitude advantage, nor our superiority
> in a dive. Of course, the Spitfire had a marvellous rate
> of turn and when we were tied to the bombers and had
> to dog-fight them – that turn was very important.

To a crumpled 257 Squadron, whether they were being hit on the ground at Debden or were defending London against bombers made little difference. Any aerial combat was a nightmare. The night before Goering switched tactics, Lancelot Mitchell, the flight commander whose ebullience had given way to obvious tension and fear, did not want to go to bed. He sat in the ante-room until the early hours of the morning writing letters to his mother and sister, and to his girlfriend

[†]Len Deighton, *Battle of Britain,* Jonathan Cape, 1980.

Margery, who was in the Women's Auxiliary air force. Hugh Beresford had also looked fidgety that evening. He asked Geoff Myers, 'Do you think there'll be a blitz tomorrow? I'm sure there'll be a blitz. Look at the weather.' He repeated the question several times in the next fifteen minutes.

In the late afternoon of the 7th Goering launched a devastating attack on the British capital. Ulrich Steinhilper was just one of a fleet of nearly a thousand fighters and bombers headed for London along a twenty-mile front; the formation was a mile and a half high.

The scramble at 4.25 p.m. was 257's fourth of the day. They were physically exhausted and morale remained weak. With Hugh Beresford commanding 'A' flight and Lancelot Mitchell in charge of 'B', the squadron headed down the coast. The air was smooth and the sky blue, with just a little high cirrus cloud. Over the Thames estuary they intercepted a group of fifty escorted bombers heading for London. Then Beresford warned that four Messerschmitt 109s were attacking out of the sun. That was the last anyone heard of him. No one saw him shot. Hugh Beresford simply disappeared.

If the squadron did not see Beresford's Hurricane hit, there were witnesses to its last moments in the air. Ashley Reeve of Sittingbourne in Kent was one of a group of men laying a pipeline on the mudflats of the Isle of Sheppey. A small wiry man with a pleasant smile, Reeve remembered the crash vividly: 'We heard a lot of enemy aircraft, then we heard machine-gunning. We looked back towards Eastchurch and saw about thirty-six British planes. There was a lot more noise from machine-gunning. Then we saw one plane in a sort of dive. The engine was cutting, spluttering, then it picked up for a second time, roared to life and then literally disappeared into the ground."* And there it stayed for nearly forty years.

Back at Martlesham, Geoff Myers realised that it was not just Hugh Beresford who had gone. The second flight commander, Lancelot Mitchell, had disappeared too. Myers found the loss of his roommate hard to take:

> I slept alone last night. Mitchell has gone. I can't believe that he's missing. There are his pyjamas on the bed. His violin on the table. He played to me only two nights ago. As he played he said, 'I don't mind the noise, do you, Geoff? Sorry, a string's missing. I know I'm not much good at it, but somehow . . .' Now Mitchell can't be a flight lieutenant. It was his burning desire. He had been expecting promotion last week. After that he was going to marry his Margery.

Two hours after Beresford and Mitchell were killed, 234 engaged a large formation of enemy fighters and bombers. At 6.25 p.m. Squadron Leader O'Brien, who had received a DFC at Buckingham Palace only four days earlier, was shot down over St Mary Cray in Kent. 234 Adjutant 'Bish' Owens wrote to Mrs O'Brien:

> By his heroic work and brilliant leadership he brought his Squadron to a unique position during his short command . . . In the dangerous work of leading his Squadron he was always there.

Five minutes after O'Brien's death, Pat Hughes shot down a Dornier 17. He must have been close because, apparently, the

---

*BBC TV, *Forty Minutes*: 'Missing'.

Dornier blew up with such force that it destroyed Hughes and his Spitfire.

During the period when Middle Wallop had been threatened by bombs, Pat's wife Kay had gone to stay at her mother's in Hull. When Kay drove back down to Middle Wallop on 7 September, pilots from 234 were waiting outside. 'I knew then that Pat was missing,' she said. 'That evening I learned he had been killed. Until then I had never really known what true grief was. I had never cried so much in my life. I wept until I could cry no more.'*

Pat Hughes had been married for thirty-eight days. At a time when the already low morale could have collapsed completely, he had pulled the squadron round. Since Squadron Leader Barnett's departure, 234 had shot down sixty-three enemy planes. Hughes himself had shot down fifteen and damaged others in just twenty-five days. As Gregory Kirkorian put it, 'Pat Hughes was the real hero of 234 Squadron. When he came to see me the night before he died, saying he had spots in front of his eyes, it was already too late. How could pilots cope with tension? In a way I felt responsible for Pat's death.'

As intelligence officer at 257, Geoff Myers was responsible for informing the next of kin, including Lancelot Mitchell's fiancée, Margery. Mitchell had used to talk about her late into the night. 'I don't think she'll let me down. She's the most wonderful woman in the world. Don't smile, Geoff, I know that's been said before.' Myers, who had met Margery at Hendon, wrote:

Hull Daily Mail.

There was something about Mitchell that attracted
women, and they really intended to get married,
I think. They had been telling everyone in the mess
that the wedding was for the next month. Now
Margery will wait awhile for another man.

Mitchell's mother at first found the news impossible to take.
No one had been able to find and identify his Hurricane, and
this gave her some hope to cling to; her son's photograph was
even taken to a medium, who reported that Lancelot was
safe – 'but it will be weeks before you hear from him'. It was
the intelligence officer's job to dash such hopes.

Nineteen-year-old Pat Beresford had been married to Hugh
for only eleven months. Of her grief, Myers wrote:

Hugh Beresford. Another hero gone. Mrs Beresford
rang up last night. She was in tears. The Adjutant tried
to soothe her over the telephone. He didn't quite know
what he was saying, spoke about boats that might have
picked Beresford up at sea. We told her not to give
up hope, but she knew. She asked if she could fetch
his clothes. 'She sounds sweet,' the Adjutant said. He
was almost in tears himself. He had a double whisky
after that.

While Mrs O'Brien, Mrs Hughes, Mrs Beresford and Mrs
Mitchell mourned the loss of their husbands and sons, the
East End of London was cruelly ablaze. That day, more than
1200 German aircraft, half of them bombers, had flown over
the capital. From east London, the whole city appeared alight.
Every fireman in the south of England was pushed into dock-
land to fight huge fires in the warehouses on the waterfront.

One blaze at the Surrey Docks was reputedly the most savage single fire ever seen in Britain. The attack had been the most powerful mass bombing raid on a city in history.

Goering was delighted with his day's work. Four hundred and forty-eight civilians were dead; east London was an inferno. The bombers had caught British defences unawares, destroying or damaging about forty British aircraft and killing nineteen RAF pilots. If Fighter Command was as low in aircraft as German intelligence claimed, they would not be able to survive much longer. 'I personally have taken over the leadership of the attacks against England,' said an elated Goering, 'and for the first time we have struck at England's heart. . . this is an historic hour.' The expected victory proved elusive, however: 7 September was the first of nearly sixty consecutive nights of raids on London. That date, as Francis Mason has suggested, marked 'the irretrievable turning point of the Battle of Britain'.

Eventually, as the long nights of regular bombing progressed, euphoria at seeing the Thames ablaze died away, and the Luftwaffe began to pay a heavy price for their leader's change of tactics. London was well defended and the potential combat time over the city was so brief that any failure to rendezvous with the bombers or any diversion from the shortest route left the German fighter pilots desperately short of fuel. All too many pilots were forced to bail out or crash-land in the sea. Goering had unwittingly taken the pressure off both the RAF pilots and the airmen in the front line – and, at a crucial time, given Dowding a further opportunity to husband his limited human and mechanical resources. By enabling Fighter Command to make good some of the damage created by the

August battles, Goering had started, as Francis Mason put it, 'the down-hill progress which would, in time, place Germany in the predicament she most feared: war on two fronts'.*

*Francis K. Mason, *Battle Over Britain,* McWhirter Twins, 1979.

16

THE TIDE REALLY TURNS

Mid-September

As the bombing of London grew worse, Geoffrey Page was told that the patients at the Royal Masonic Hospital in Hammersmith were to be evacuated to the country. Soon afterwards he received a visitor. In his late thirties, squat, with dark hair, horn-rimmed spectacles and a friendly smile, the man at first glance resembled the film comedian Harold Lloyd.

Although Page did not know it at the time, this stranger – New Zealander Archibald McIndoe, consultant plastic surgeon at Queen Victoria Hospital, East Grinstead, one of three maxillo-facial units set up for injured servicemen – would be the man to put his life back on course.

McIndoe crisply asked the injured pilot some rudimentary questions. Which plane? Which tank was hit? How long in the water? How long before receiving tannic acid treatment? 'Were you wearing gloves?' asked McIndoe. 'No,' replied the pilot. 'Clot,' said the surgeon, smiling; and he was right – gloves would have protected the hands against burns. 'See you again, young fellow,' said McIndoe, and was gone.

McIndoe was furious about the tannic-acid treatment – a standard procedure recommended by the authorities, but known by McIndoe to be ultimately damaging. As he walked away from the hospital, the surgeon from New Zealand was well aware how badly crippled Geoffrey Page's hands were going to be.

Next day, as the evacuation of the hospital began, Page said goodbye to his favourite nurse, Skipper. 'You'll get better more quickly in the country and you can have a nice long convalescence,' she said. 'Convalescence be damned. I've got to get back to flying as soon as possible,' he retorted. Skipper laughed. 'Silly boy, you'll never fly again.'

On the way to RAF Halton, Page tested out public reaction to his new Mr Hyde features. He and two other burns victims asked the ambulance driver to stop at a pub. When the three men walked in like a terrible apparition, the regulars, interrupted in a game of darts, were visibly shaken. The newcomers ordered pints; as Page couldn't lift his glass, the beer had to be poured down his throat. Two pints each was more than enough for men in such a weak condition, and the three arrived at their destination much the worse for wear.

At Halton, Pilot Officer Page's hands hurt more than ever. The surgeon, Wing Commander Stanford Cade, explained that the only answer was to remove the tannic-acid covering; the acid was useful for first-degree burns, but for serious third-degree burns like his, it caused the skin to thicken and the fingers to curl. After the acid had been removed, Page woke up from the anaesthetic to see that his hands were no longer coal black but pink, and as thin as tissue paper. They were so sensitive that even a gentle draught across the room caused a sharp burst of pain.

The true consequences of the tannic-acid treatment only began to emerge in the following few weeks. Slowly, relentlessly, Page's tendons contracted, curling the fingers downwards until they actually touched the palms and would not move. The thin skin hardened to the texture of a rhino's hide, at the same time welding the fingers together so they were no longer separate digits. In an attempt to soften the skin, the patient daily endured the agonizing process of hot-wax baths. Gradually, it became obvious that the attempt was failing, as the skin hardened even more. The only answer was a skin graft.

Page was dispatched to Archibald McIndoe's unit at a trim cottage hospital on the edge of East Grinstead, where he was put in Kindersley Ward, a small twelve-bedded room, divided by glass partitions into three sections.

At Margate, the Royal Masonic and Halton, the patients had been receiving treatment for anything from sprained ankles to third-degree burns. Now Geoffrey Page was face to face with pilots just like himself, some even more hideous and damaged. Among those who introduced themselves were Toby Tollemache, Roy Lane and, standing at the foot of the bed, Richard Hillary, who two years later was to write his classic book *The Last Enemy*. Now Hillary looked monstrous. There were two large bloody red circles of raw skin around his eyes. Each circle had horizontal slits in it, with an eye peeping out. His hands were wrapped in lint covers. He had just had a new pair of eyelids grafted on. Courageous and heroic, but also embittered and cynical, the voice from behind the mask called out, 'Another bloody cripple. Welcome to the home of the aged and the infirm.'

McIndoe's worst cases were treated in Ward 3, one of the temporary huts outside the main building. Here Page met the most severely burned patient at the hospital – indeed, the most severely burned wartime pilot to live: Godfrey Edmonds. A twenty-six-year-old South African, Edmonds had crashed at night on his first solo flight in his Hampden bomber. He had fried for several minutes before being rescued. On admittance to East Grinstead, he appeared scarcely human. Another patient of McIndoe's remembered hobbling on crutches from Kindersley to Ward 3 and meeting Edmonds: 'I had never seen anyone so badly burned. I was terrified. He looked literally like Frankenstein. His face was a grotesque mask. His hands were burned. His ears were just stubs and holes, he had no lips, just a hole for his mouth. There were no eyelids, just two holes in the face. With his lipless mouth he picked up a chair and said, "Have a seat, old boy." ' The uncomplaining spirit of men such as Godfrey Edmonds raised morale and served as an inspiration. And, as Geoffrey Page waited for his long, painful round of skin-grafting operations to begin, he looked around the ward and realised that, although his injuries had been terrible, there were others whose condition was even worse.

On 11 September, four days after the deaths of Squadron Leader O'Brien and Flight Lieutenant Hughes, an exhausted and leaderless 234 were moved out of the front line back to St Eval. 'Only about three pilots and five aircraft from our original squadron had survived to return to St Eval,' said Budge Harker. 'I was quite twitchy myself by then.'

'Morty' Mortimer-Rose and Keith Dewhurst acted as officers commanding 'A' and 'B' flights while the squadron waited for replacements, their relaxation disturbed only by an occasional local patrol. By the end of their first week, twelve replacement pilots had arrived. Soon afterwards, Minden Blake moved from 238 Squadron, also based at St Eval, to become acting squadron leader of 234. Blake was a New Zealander who combined the skills of a one-time university physics lecturer with an outstanding athletic ability which had made him the New Zealand Universities' gymnastics champion. It was Blake's job to heal the squadron's wounds and to instruct and integrate the crop of fresh pilots, many of whom had received extremely limited training. To withstand the intensity of the current German raids, Dowding needed all the pilot replacements he could get, even if their experience of Hurricanes or Spitfires was rudimentary.

On 12 September, five days after the deaths of Beresford and Mitchell, 257 Squadron also had a change of leadership: Squadron Leader Sharp was moved to a training school. By then, eleven of the original twenty pilots were dead. A missed rendezvous in the air, yet another mistake by 257, had finally cost Sharp his post. Geoff Myers was pleased, but upset:

> I had a painful day today. What I had been working for, for weeks, happened, and I knew that it would cut me up when the day came.
>
> Harkness told me, 'I'm to hand over the Squadron to Stanford Tuck.'
>
> I couldn't say anything. Under his command the Squadron had been going to pieces. I had done my best to have him moved.

Sharp gave me an appealing look as if to say 'it's not my fault'. My eyes did not reply.

Tall, thin-faced and immaculate, with slicked-back hair and a Caesar Romero moustache, Bob Stanford Tuck seemed to most outsiders a dandy; he smoked cigarettes in a long holder and behaved like someone who owned the world. But there was no mistaking his courage and skill both as a pilot and as a shot. To a demoralized squadron, a leader with his drive and panache would either inspire them or crush their self-confidence.

Stanford Tuck remembers 257 as a lifeless, argumentative group of men, keen to blame their troubles on the decisions of the RAF hierarchy and numbed by the grim experiences of the last few weeks. He tried to listen sympathetically to their problems but made no comment, quietly taking note of the fear and bitterness.

By the time he arrived at 257, Stanford Tuck was already a legend. Myers wrote:

> He soon told me of all the aircraft he had shot down.
> Something like eighteen. Most of his claims seemed a
> bit hazy to me, but that did not matter. The very sight
> of him seemed to give confidence to the boys.

An amazing series of escapes had earned him the nickname 'the Immortal Tuck', and with his prewar-filmstar good looks he had a reputation as a man who enjoyed his private life with as much energy and flamboyance as his flying. Yet, for all his arrogance, Stanford Tuck, one of the two or three most famous aces of the Battle of Britain, was an extremely meticulous pilot. His high success rate in combat depended not only on a combination of boldness and good fortune but also on carefulness.

Before flying he would spend hours checking his plane, and his guns in particular. He had a thirst for knowledge about aerial tactics, and if a piece of new technology became available, he would take the first opportunity to discuss it with the manufacturers.

On his first night at Martlesham, Stanford Tuck talked long into the night with Geoff Myers, who confided his doubts about welding the dispirited squadron into a coherent fighting unit, where every man had implicit trust in the pilots flying alongside him. Tuck called the squadron 'a miserable shower of bloody deadbeats. Not worth a bag of nuts.'* Although they were now back at full strength with fourteen pilots and fourteen Hurricanes, two of the sergeants, infected by the atmosphere of fear and mistrust, were bad 'twitch' cases, regularly reporting sick rather than flying. One had been hit a few weeks earlier by a 110; his legs were lacerated with shrapnel. The other was a new recruit who had never fought the enemy – nor, having observed the listless and edgy men around him, did he want to. None of the officers was past dodging a tricky situation if he could manage it.

But the Germans would not wait for Bob Stanford Tuck. The bombing of London continued.

The mass raids on London had seen the start of a period of losses much heavier than JG 52 and the rest of the Luftwaffe had sustained so far, and morale was under increasing strain. On one occasion Ulrich Steinhilper flew on seven different missions: 'When you looked at yourself you didn't see a young

---

*Larry Forrester, *Fly for Your Life,* Frederick Muller, 1956.

man any more. You were nervous enough to have shaky hands. Every second or third day another one was gone.' For every mission flown, the pilots were given special rations of two eggs and a round box of chocolates – scant consolation in the circumstances.

One day, when JG 52 were escorting a group of Ju 88 bombers to London with orders to follow the bombers even if they were short of fuel, the Ju 88s lost their target, and JG 52 were caught in a protracted dogfight. On the way home the pilots' red warning lamps began to light up one by one. To conserve fuel, Steinhilper flew very low over the rough seas; unable to reach his own airfield, he landed at Boulogne. Exactly how many of the other fighter pilots on that raid ditched in the sea is uncertain. By Steinhilper's calculations it could have been as many as nineteen – most of whom drowned. This was the kind of disaster the Luftwaffe were now encountering.

Divorced from the day-to-day experiences of the pilots stationed along the French coast, the High Command were taking more and more unrealistic decisions; and, as they saw increasing numbers of their colleagues drown before the rescue boats could reach them, the German pilots' fear of the sea grew – talk of Channel sickness was more regular and widespread.

Meanwhile, feelings in Britain about the German pilots hardened, though Geoff Myers, as always, saw the common humanity in war:

It is satisfactory to write combat reports which are clear cut. The thing can be treated like a sporting game, but you must forget that the score is in the points of death. If you start thinking about that you feel the gloom floating heavily about a German pilots' mess. A good comrade, a good fighter, who won't return for the promised night out in Amiens or Abbeville. Perhaps he was a decent man. He was probably brave. Most German pilots are brave, like our own.

When he rang up one day to see if a rescue launch had gone to look for some Germans shot down in the sea, Myers had a furious row with the operations officer. 'We would have been better to have let them all drown,' said the officer. 'They don't deserve any consideration, having dropped bombs on the civilians of Lowestoft.'

Expectations in the German hierarchy had been growing that Hitler would give the order to launch a British invasion on 11 September, with the sailing planned for the 20th and the landing the following day – giving the navy time to complete its mine-laying programme satisfactorily – but in the event the decision was postponed.

Although an invasion was not paramount in Hitler's mind, he seemed certain that Britain's morale would not stand up to the pressure much longer. Fighter Command was still hanging on, but Hitler reasoned that the regular and constant assaults on London would eventually create huge panic. The German navy knew that they still did not have the necessary air superiority – but all the time the weather was deteriorating, with the forecast for late September particularly unpromising. On the 14th, Hitler agreed that 'in spite of all our successes, the prerequisite conditions for Operation Sealion have not yet been realised'; the decision was further postponed for three days. A new possible date of 27 September presented the risk of unsuitable tides as well as bad weather. The directive postponing Sealion also called for further attacks 'against military and other vital installations'. The bombing of residential areas was left as the ultimate option.

Meanwhile, there was a resurgence of confidence in the RAF, as they prepared for what was to be the climax of the air battle on 15 September, two days before Hitler was due to make his decision about invasion. 15 September, which has ever since been officially designated Battle of Britain day, was to see the Germans, in Churchill's words, 'cut to rags and tatters'.

Stanford Tuck had used the few quiet days before the 15th to reorganize 257 Squadron. He tried to teach them more flexible and up-to-date flying formations, and to instil pride and discipline in the lacklustre 'Burma' boys. He was lucky that the new flight lieutenant, Pete Brothers, proved to be quick and reliable.

Ironically, 257's first scramble on 15 September took place in the absence of Stanford Tuck, who had been called to Debden for a conference. Myers waited anxiously as his pilots struggled back. They were not without their problems: two of them complained about sustaining shots from their own anti-aircraft gunners. A third, Sergeant Squire, returning from his first sortie, descended from his plane with a worried expression. Myers recorded:

> 'I don't quite know what happened,' he said. 'I expect I'll get my nerve next time.' I did not press him. It was his first encounter with the enemy and obviously something had gone wrong. 'Come and sit down, old man,' I said. 'Don't worry, lots of chaps get queer turns

at the beginning.' When he felt a bit reassured, he said, 'I passed clean out at fourteen thousand feet. No, it wasn't a black-out or anything like that. The sight of all those bombers just made me feel queer and I fainted. It's a poor show and I find it difficult to explain.' I quickly put in my word: 'You needn't worry about that sort of thing, old chap.' The first time the boys went up in a Blitz they all felt a bit queer.

As the tired pilots lay in two rows of beds at the dispersal unit, with Pete Brothers and Carl Capon still not back, the call 'Scramble angels fifteen over Duxford' went up. Stanford Tuck had just arrived back from Debden. He immediately grabbed a Mae West and took Sergeant Squire's place.

As the Hurricanes roared up into the clear, windless sky, one plane was left on the ground. Myers went over to speak to its nineteen-year-old pilot. 'I seem to miss all the big shows,' the young man said. 'It is a damned shame! Something seems to happen to me every time there's a Blitz. This is the fourth I've missed in succession.' He spoke with little conviction, and Myers's thoughts were obvious. 'I don't like letting the other boys down,' the pilot went on. 'Nobody enjoys the Blitzes, I'm quite sure, and I don't mind telling you that I'm shit scared of them and that all the others are too. Some of them pretend that they're not, but deep down you'll find they're all shit scared like me. Fear's biological like everything else.'

The first pilot back from the second Blitz was West, who had been sick all down his uniform just as he was entering the enemy formation. Myers later wrote:

West was no coward. He was a typical brave young lad.
But he was new to air fighting and did not know the
dangers of a half-digested meal at fifteen thousand feet.

Slowly the rest drifted back, except for Stanford Tuck – and
there was still no word from Brothers or Capon. The squadron
was buzzing with excitement: eight German planes had been
'destroyed' or 'nearly destroyed'; three had been damaged. The
Canadian Jimmy Cochrane had shot down a Heinkel III with
two other pilots: 'I watched the pilot bring the plane down
in the mud just off Boothness Point. It was a luscious sight!
We circled around the parachutes. I bet they went through
a few uncomfortable moments when we flew round them.
They must have wondered whether we'd machine gun them as
they've been doing to our boys, the bastards.'

But the elation was checked by the knowledge that three
men were missing; the memory was fresh of eight days earlier,
when both 257's flight commanders had died. Was this to be a
hollow victory after all?

The pilots were drinking tea when the news came through
that Stanford Tuck had refuelled elsewhere. Soon afterwards
Pete Brothers's plane, slightly damaged, limped back in. By
this time, Capon had been virtually written off, but then he
too landed. Myers recorded:

Terrific excitement in the mess. Everybody back
without a scratch. The Squadron's luck had turned.
That evening we all went out to celebrate.

Ironically, having survived the intense battles of the day, the
squadron met disaster on the way back from the celebrations.
One of their cars ran into a concrete defence block in the road,

then Pete Brothers's car went into the back of the first one. Charles Frizzell and Jimmy Cochrane were badly hurt, and were out of the war for some months. Geoff Myers, less seriously injured but still out of action for a few weeks, wrote in a letter to his wife:

> What would you have said, darling, if years later you
> would have learnt that I had been killed in a car crash
> after a night out at two bars? You would probably
> have guessed that I had made an effort to be sociable
> with the boys and not to damp the enthusiasm of that
> night. Yes, darling, I was doing my job.

The squadron's triumph enhanced Stanford Tuck's reputation:

> The Tuck legend rapidly grew. Twenty-seven swastikas
> were photographed on his plane . . . an over-
> enthusiastic flight rigger had included the 'probables'
> and 'damaged' in the swastika score. [Tuck's official list
> of victims was fourteen.] Tuck was photographed and
> filmed. He was described as the great ace of the war.

The claims that day for the RAF as a whole were as inflated as the number of swastikas the flight rigger had painted on Tuck's plane:

> It was a great day for the whole RAF, the biggest
> bag of the war. One hundred and eighty-five planes
> claimed shot down. I had expected a record, from
> what the pilots told me, but the figure fairly took my
> breath away.

Psychologically, the estimated number of successes and the apparently clear-cut nature of the victory on 15 September gave hope and confidence to both the tired and bedraggled older pilots and the inexperienced new recruits.

Later, official German records reported only fifty-six planes lost – fewer than 30 per cent of those claimed by over-enthusiastic RAF pilots, but still twice as many as the losses suffered by the Luftwaffe.

Ulrich Steinhilper was relieved to land safely that day (though he later discovered that his good friend Hans Berthol, a lieutenant in 1/JG 52, was missing over Kent), and in the evening he and other remaining pilots in 3/JG 52 discussed their vulnerable position. They knew from personal experience that the RAF had not suffered the heavy losses their leaders had claimed so far in the battle, and that the continuing failure to launch Operation Sealion meant that the daylight raids were leading to nothing.

On 17 September, Hitler postponed Operation Sealion indefinitely because, according to the German Naval War Diary, 'The enemy air force is still by no means defeated. On the contrary it shows increasing activity. The weather situation as a whole does not permit us to expect a period of calm . . .' An invasion as late as 27 September had anyway never been a realistic proposition; Hitler had left such a possibility open simply to apply pressure on the enemy. On the 19th the wind-down of invasion shipping began.

Although Fighter Command had survived to win the crucial defensive air battle, the struggle would not be over for several more weeks. German attacks on Britain continued, and

Dowding knew he could not afford to have good pilots out of the front line for too long.

Bob Doe, who had been resting at St Eval, soon found himself back at Middle Wallop with 238 Squadron. He was soon followed by Joseph Szlagowski and Zig Klein, who were moved to 152 Squadron, also based at Middle Wallop. From Acklington, Cyril Bamberger returned to Port Sunlight on leave, but he had only been home for a day when a telegram arrived notifying him of transferral to 41 Squadron at Hornchurch in Essex. Like 610, 41 Squadron had been at the sharp end of the battle. 'It was there at Hornchurch that I began to see things clearly, to form my own opinions, to have views on my own ability and those around me,' said Bam. 'That might seem premature, even presumptuous, but you had to know what was right or wrong when your life was at stake.'

17

The Risks Continue

The last week of September

The progress of autumn saw a decrease in aerial activity to, primarily, one or two fighter sweeps each day, and in late September the Luftwaffe began to focus its attacks on the British aircraft industry – a tactic that could have been more profitably employed earlier in the battle. On the 25th, British reconnaissance revealed that the number of invasion barges in the French Channel ports had dropped by 40 per cent – a reduction that was also noticed by 3/JG 52 at Coquelles. It had become clear to both sides that the invasion would not now take place, and for 3/JG 52 the bombing sorties over London which had so depleted their squadron seemed more senseless than ever.

By the end of the month the evening debates within 3/JG 52 about the Luftwaffe tactics had grown more tense. Faith in Hitler himself never seemed to waver, but the pilots increasingly questioned the quality of advice he was receiving from Goering. Helmut Kuhle, who discussed with Steinhilper the stupidity of flying in regular waves, had always put great emphasis on survival. Now that Operation Sealion had been postponed, he felt even more keenly that the prime responsibility of his pilots was to live to fight another day.

Despite the losses in his Gruppe, Ulrich Steinhilper was still full of bravado and youthful enthusiasm, and, on account of his complete lack of fear and his steely determination, he emerged as one of the best respected pilots left in 3/JG 52. He argued fiercely but politely with Kuhle about tactics. Steinhilper believed that, if the Me 109s were freed from the shackles of being bomber escorts, their attack capability would be more than a match for the RAF. Intelligence suggested that the RAF's reserves were limited; all-out attack could finish them off. Ulrich himself hated the escort role; it made him feel a sitting duck. At least in attack the pilot was in control of his own destiny.

On 30 September, Steinhilper had a chance to put his theories to the test: Kuhle was ill, and he was designated to lead the squadron. Taking off at about 9.40 a.m., they spotted near Tonbridge a circle of Hurricanes and Spitfires below them. Kuhle would probably have held back and waited for the optimum moment, but Steinhilper ambitiously forged ahead, and soon himself picked off one of the enemy fighters. The next moment, he turned to see Hans Wolf, a jolly easygoing sergeant who was one of the most popular pilots in the squadron, on fire beside him. The action had gone disastrously wrong. Wolf bailed out safely and was taken prisoner, but Steinhilper felt responsible; when he landed back at Calais, Kuhle criticized him vehemently. Wolf was one of four pilots lost by the *Gruppe* that day. Steinhilper was so troubled by the incident that he wrote a guilty letter to his father about it. His father, in reply, tried to reassure his son that he was doing his best in the service of his country.

At Hornchurch, Cyril Bamberger was keen to get back into action, particularly as his earlier stay in the front line at Biggin Hill had been so brief. But Bam lacked self-confidence and he knew that he would have to be skilful and alert to survive – let alone to score successes against the enemy.

On the day Bam arrived, 17 September, 41 Squadron had four Spitfires shot down. No pilots were hurt, and three of the aircraft were repaired – nonetheless, it was not the perfect situation for an inexperienced pilot such as Bam to walk into. A few days later he was even more depressed on hearing that Doug Corfe, his old friend from Hooton Park who had been one of the other lucky applicants for training as a sergeant pilot, had been shot down. Corfe, now with 66 Squadron, had survived, but was in hospital injured.

To the newcomer, 41 seemed altogether more professional and battle-hardened than 610. Yet, again, there were no briefings, and Bam spent a lot of time wondering what was happening. The divisions within the squadron seemed just as sharp as in 610, even though no one had a Rolls-Royce parked outside the officers' mess. 'The senior officers were like gods,' he said. 'There was also a hard core of regular sergeant pilots, and even they thought they were above the likes of me. 41 was full of professionals; it was a bit of an insult to have replacements like me with no experience landed on them.' Although there was mixing in the dispersal hut, it did not stretch much beyond that: 'If after a sortie an aircraft had to be taxied into maintenance, a sergeant would have to do the job, even if he'd flown four times that day and there were officers available who'd been sitting around all day.' 41 included some able and likable men – it was led by Norman Ryder, whom Bam described as 'a good pilot and a fine man. I could never criticize him' – but some of the other officers, even the senior ones, gave Bam very little confidence: 'There were several I had no respect for. Take Murray; he was dreadful. If I had to fly number two behind him, I was terrified, literally terrified.' For all that, Bam soon won a reputation as a honest and reliable pilot who, despite his inexperience, never shirked his duties. One colleague said, 'He was such a sincere and trustworthy person that it was difficult not to like him, even if he was a little shy.'

For a month Bam struggled to survive: 'There was always an air of unreality both in the air and on the ground. After one sortie I was shouted at and told off for coming indoors with my boots on. The fact that we were at war hadn't really got through to everyone.' When he was flying in formation and the order to 'break' came, the pilots would split off and all too often, it seemed to him, his plane was left alone in the sky. So much of the time, too, he was simply trying to gain height in order to keep up: 'We were always vectored towards the enemy – maybe if we had waited for five minutes before going, we wouldn't always have been scrambling for height. I always had a feeling that, as a result, we were in a defensive rather than an offensive position.'

It did not take long before Bam's youthful naivety gave way to a firm understanding of the frailties both of himself and of those around him: 'I had no sense that we were winning. As an individual I thought I was losing. The leader, the man at the sharp end, went on because it was his job. The rest of us blindly followed – ninety-nine per cent of us would have turned back given a chance. Only a fool wants to be killed.'

Two experiences soon after his arrival sharpened Bam's instinct for self-preservation. After a skirmish with a group of Messerschmitts, he heard a funny noise as he came in to land – he had obviously been hit without realizing it. His ailerons were drooping and, as he touched down, they broke. If it had happened a fraction earlier, the Spitfire would have turned over and crashed.

Even more disturbing was an extraordinary mission less than a week after Bam had joined 41. He had already completed two patrols when, under the leadership of J. N. Mackenzie, a very good pilot officer from New Zealand, he was ordered to fly from Hornchurch to 41's forward base at Hawkinge near Folkestone, from where he and three other pilots were to escort an Avro Anson trainer plane over the Channel to France and then up the coastline. Bam could never discover the purpose of this almost suicidal exercise – gun-spotting, perhaps; more likely, the Avro's job was to observe where long-range British artillery shell was landing. It was quite clear, however, that the Germans would not allow a slow aircraft like an Anson and its Spitfire escort to cruise up and down the French coast at will. 'I'd never heard of anything so stupid in my life,' said Bam. 'Only one thing could happen: we'd be attacked and picked off. Whoever devised these crazy tactics wanted poleaxing . . . but I was too new to the squadron to argue.' One of the other pilots simply disappeared after he heard the orders: 'Later, we heard he had a mysterious bout of engine trouble. But the real reason was obvious. There was a lot of disappearing in situations like that.'

The three remaining Spitfires, their pilots grim-faced and nervous, took off with the Anson and headed towards the French coast. Just before Calais, the inevitable happened: about two dozen Me 109s suddenly appeared from nowhere. The Anson pilot sensibly dropped down and headed for home, flying just above the water. Bam turned his Spitfire and followed the Anson down. He had never flown so low before, and he had heard of pilots losing their sense of where the sea began and flying straight into it. The pursuing aircraft had to face the same problem, however – and, even worse, they had to take their eyes off the sea to fire, which could prove fatal. A few feet above the Channel, his propellers almost touching the water, Bam flew carefully but swiftly back to Hawkinge. Four or five times on the way he caught a glimpse of the Anson just above the sea. Bam, Mackenzie and the third Spitfire pilot all reached home safely. The Anson just managed to reach Britain, but landed on its belly, killing two of the crew: 'I was so angry when I heard. They were brave men killed quite needlessly for someone's hare-brained scheme.' Nonetheless, there is evidence to suggest that such sorties by antiquated Ansons were regular events.

Bam's near-miss crystallised his views about the stupidity of some of those on whose decisions his life depended. With characteristic honesty, he said, 'I realised then that the officers, the public schoolboys, did not have a monopoly on brains. That Anson trip somehow summed up the disorganisation of the Battle of Britain. Later in the war, when things were more professional, we would have had a debriefing after such an incident and said what we thought.'

Back at Hawkinge after the trip to France – his third trip that day – Bam was told to return to Hornchurch, from where he set out on a final patrol, lasting one hour twenty minutes, making a total of five hours twenty minutes of operational flying in one day – during all of which time he was vulnerable.

Throughout the Battle of Britain 41 lost forty-eight planes and had ten pilots killed. From his early days with the squadron Bam made a subconscious decision to preserve his own life; not that he would let anyone down, but he wasn't going to look for trouble: 'It seemed a mystery to me how frequently I found myself alone in the sky surrounded by the enemy, and when I came down others claimed they had shot down planes and I had hardly seen a thing. It sapped my own confidence.'

Bam was not the only one taking it carefully: 'Sometimes if I was in heavy cloud there seemed to be more planes – of both sides – hovering in there, than those out in the clear.' Even Norman Ryder, the highly respected squadron leader, was not above giving a thought to self-preservation rather than taking on the enemy at all costs. One day Bamberger was flying as Ryder's number two. As they climbed, Bam found himself caught in a circle of Me 110s. No other Spitfires were to be seen: 'There was tracer flying about. I saw lots of black crosses. I shut my guns off, turned over on my back and spun on down, losing them. Suddenly, over London, I saw a Spitfire. It was Norman Ryder. The old bugger had had the wisdom to get the hell out of it. Discretion was the better part of valour. Because of inexperience I'd left it later, but had managed the same thing. On the ground Ryder just praised me for sticking with him.'

Bam liked flying number two, particularly to Ryder, who respected and trusted him: 'If I was two, it meant there were another ten behind they had to get before they got you.' Sometimes, however, they used the archaic formation of two 'weavers', one below and one above, to spot the enemy: 'It was the worst job. I hated it. The whole thing was stupid. I did it a lot. You were constantly exposed, and were much more likely to run out of petrol. I had no idea what it achieved.'

Back in the front line at Middle Wallop, Bob Doe was brim-full of confidence from his successes following the early disasters in 234. Though things did not go well at 238 at first. Shortly after Doe's arrival, the squadron's first Czech pilot, Sergeant Horsky, who had been there only a fortnight, was killed in combat with Me 109s over the Solent. 238 lost three pilots in a defensive action against a huge Luftwaffe formation. Sergeant Little and Pilot Officer David Harrison were both shot down and killed. Sergeant Eric Bann died when his parachute failed to open. Bann's loss was particularly unfortunate. The intelligence officer noted that 'he was held in high esteem, able, reliable and very popular. Had taken a particular interest in the Polish pilots. Very kind.' Bob Doe was concerned about losing four men in such swift succession, but by now he had become very hardened to wartime death, and he had scarcely known his four dead colleagues.

At the end of September, 238 were transferred to their satellite airfield at Chilbolton, which had until recently been arable fields. The record notes:

> In this way, the 238th Squadron of the line entered the depths of the Hampshire countryside to a common . . .
> so as to bring to mind the lines:
> Royal the pagent closes
> Let by the last of the sun

Opal, and ash of roses
Cinammon, amber and dun.

Bob Doe did not have much time for poetry. Late that afternoon he was busy shooting down a Heinkel III south of
Portland; its five-man crew were reported missing.

September's summary for the squadron stated:

> This month was one of very heavy fighting. 7 pilots,
> 14 aircraft were lost by enemy attack. 5 aircraft were
> damaged beyond Squadron repair. Details of the Daily
> Slate signals . . . make sad reading, but add another
> page of excellent accomplishment to that of August.

* * *

As they sat outside on sunny autumn days at the Queen Victoria
Hospital in East Grinstead, Geoffrey Page and the other burns
victims brought there by Archibald McIndoe heard the sound
of fighting overhead and watched the Spitfires and Hurricanes
returning home.

Page was coming to accept that, as McIndoe had predicted,
repairing his damaged body was going to be a long job. Flying
fighter planes seemed a distant prospect, as he began an initial
series of skin grafts that were to take two years to complete.
The first graft involved scraping the thick scar tissue from his
hands and replacing it with a paper-thin layer of skin taken
from the inside of his thigh. Afterwards, his thigh hurt almost
more than his hand; for five days he was in constant agony,
unable to sleep at night.

When McIndoe arrived to inspect the graft, he explained
what he had done: 'This skin graft is sewn into position – in

your case about sixty to seventy inches – and long ends of thread are left hanging at regular intervals from quite a few of these stitches. After that, a dry sponge is cut and placed to fit over the grafted area. The trailing ends of the stitches are then brought back over the back of the sponge, and knotted together. The sponge is then moistened which in turn causes it to swell, but as the thread restrains it, it can only exert pressure against the hand, facing the new skin against the raw surface. That way the two surfaces join together.'

'He stitched every face,' said one of his assistants, 'as if it were the Bayeux Tapestry.'

Slowly McIndoe nicked the stitches with scissors, easing the pressure that had been causing Page so much pain and making his fingertips turn blue through lack of circulation. Carefully, he lifted the blood-stained sponge. Underneath the hand was disgusting, a swollen lump of raw, putrified flesh, oozing with pus. But the surgeon seemed quite cheerful: 'Luckier than I thought. That's about a fifty per cent take, I should think. Now we've got to get you fit enough for the next lot.'

His first graft completed, Geoffrey Page began to be drawn more into hospital routine. For men used to the discipline and rigours of service life, it was an extraordinary place. For a start, there was no division among the ranks; a sergeant pilot could be in the next bed to an air marshal. In most hospitals, officers would have expected to have their own rooms, but McIndoe had realised that officers on their own did not recover as swiftly as those in combined wards. Apart from their bodily injuries, the young men were not sick, so they could still enjoy themselves in a high-spirited way, and gain confidence by sharing their problems. By going out to the town, or up to London in groups, they could conquer together the fear of how the world outside Ward 3 would react to their new faces and bodies.

In all burns units a sense of humour was essential. One young pilot was so badly burned that he had to be helped on to a bedpan by two nurses, one of whom wore a rather obvious wig of golden curls. On this particular occasion, as the patient was being moved off the pan for cleaning up, the other nurse stretched forward for the foal (a gold-coloured substance used instead of lavatory paper). 'She found some resistance,' her sister remembered. 'She went on pulling and found she'd pulled the woman's wig and was about to wipe his bottom with a foal with a Red Cross hat on it. He laughed so much he had to have morphia. We thought he'd die of that. Still it was a turning point.'*

McIndoe allowed far greater freedom than was permitted in any other hospital in Britain. For example, at the end of Ward 3 was a big barrel of beer that was never empty; visits could last much longer than the usual hour. The nurses were carefully chosen for their sympathy and understanding; they treated patients not as cripples but as ordinary active young men. Often the patients would return from a night in East Grinstead and settle down with the nurses for a couple of drinks and some slices of toast and dripping. Good-looking nurses were chosen to encourage those who were disfigured; job applications had to be accompanied by a photograph. There was an unwritten rule amongst the patients that anyone who was very ill should be left alone, but the moment he was better they would probably throw beer over him. The operating table was the 'slab',

*BBC Radio, 'A Fine Blue Day'.

being burned was 'fried', and an operation was 'going under the knife'. Any self-pity was soon dispelled.

The atmosphere, said Geoffrey Page, was 'a cross between Emergency Ward Ten, the Bull's Head and a French brothel'. Edward Blacksell, who worked with McIndoe, described the ward as 'a very jolly sixth-form room or undergraduate common room just before Christmas. This was quite deliberate. There were no rules and regulations. If you felt like having a drink, you had a drink. If you felt like chatting up the nurses, you were encouraged to do so.'* Anyone who abused such lavish freedoms was soon brought into line by his fellow patients. Much of the ward atmosphere was created by McIndoe himself. He would laugh with them and drink with them, and yet he somehow stood above it all as well. His Guinea Pigs had every confidence in him, and he would always carefully explain what he was going to do to them. He cared deeply about his broken airmen, putting them back together with love and care. To some of them he was a god, slicing through red tape, fighting for their rights, and bringing life back to charred limbs.

*Peter Williams and Ted Harrison, *McIndoe's Army,* Pelham, 1979.

18

THE FINAL DAYS

After the intensity of September, October was an anti-climax, but the exhaustion and battle-weariness of the pilots who had been fighting since July and the inexperience of the rapidly trained new pilots who had been pushed in to the front line meant that danger was ever-present. As the month progressed and Operation Sealion began to seem like a distant dream, more and more German planes were removed from daylight raids. The daylight war had been lost, but Goering wanted his weary and depleted squadrons to maintain the pressure. Therefore more than two hundred 109s and 110s were converted to fighter-bombers.

In September the Luftwaffe had lost many senior officers and hundreds of aircraft, yet they were still a powerful force, capable of launching huge raids against London and other major cities. The next stage of the aerial conflict was to be night bombing.

On the morning of 1 October, the first day on which the Germans had made full use of their fighters in a bombing role, Bob Doe scored yet another success, shooting down an Me 110 south of Poole and killing two Germans.

That same afternoon, Cyril Bamberger, on his second patrol of the day, was vectored southwards to intercept a formation of 109s. Bam remembers sporadic combat with the enemy in and out of the clouds. As usual, he felt uncertain and flew cautiously. Everyone returned safely from the sortie except for George Bennions, the Yorkshireman whom Bam had grown to admire for his sensitivity as well as his shooting skill. Bennions had been caught alone in the midst of the 109s: 'The bullets thudded into the plane. I think a shell must have exploded in my cockpit. It was just as if my brain had exploded and I had been punched in the eye. There was a screaming in my ears.' Bennions tumbled out of his aircraft over Sussex. The shell had blinded him in one eye and caused severe burns. He was taken to join Geoffrey Page in McIndoe's unit at the Queen Victoria Hospital.

Pressure on the East Grinstead hospital was increasing steadily as burned men flooded in. McIndoe worked throughout the crisis with dedication, care and skill, spending long hours in surgery. By now, he had moved on to Page's face, which was marked with burns from the helmet-line down to where his silk scarf had been. There was a particularly vivid mark where his chin strap had sat. The scorching heat of the fire had caused a general contraction about Page's eyes, with the result that the top and bottom eyelids could not meet for sleep. Although he could still blink a little, 'when I woke up in the morning there was no lubrication and it felt like someone had shoved a bucket of sand in my eyes.' New eyelids were needed, decided McIndoe, but the operation meant that the patient would be blind for three weeks. This was a lonely time for Page, during which the nurses had to do everything for him; the first time they cut up his food, the blind pilot officer succeeded only in stabbing himself with his fork.

Geoff Myers had three weeks of convalescence from the car accident on Battle of Britain day which gave him time to recollect and evaluate his recent trials. For that brief respite Myers was no longer engulfed by the hard work and daily highs and lows of the battle. Since July, every experience, joyful or tragic, had been magnified in intensity. Now, away from the battlefront, he was able to think more and more about the fate of his family in occupied France.

Back with his squadron, he felt the nightmare of separation growing darker, more permanent:

> Darling, I do hope you will see me again. I long to see
> you and my little ones. But if I am no longer here when
> the war is over, even if you are overtaken by disaster, keep
> your confidence in eternal things. We had seven won-
> derful years together, my love. We may have no more
> on earth. You may never see my letters. And yet we are
> bound up in each other in the scheme of things eternal.

The only communication he had received from his family since his return to England was a coded message reading: 'Conditions are good.' At least his wife and children were alive, but if he ever saw them again would they all be changed irrevocably by distance and war?

> If I survive the war, it may be that you, my little chil-
> dren, will find a very different Daddy from that of
> your imagination, and you may be disappointed. We
> would have to start again like new friends. If only they
> leave you alone.

As Myers uncertainly eased himself back into squadron life, he noticed that things had changed. It was partly that the

Germans had altered their tactics, almost abandoning daytime rounds but still sweeping over in large numbers at night; also, the personnel were different – the pilots he had known from the early days were more experienced now, but the air battle had been in progress for a long time and some of them were very tired and battle-weary. The new arrivals were young men, but – in contrast to men like Hugh Beresford, who had had considerable experience and training – some of the young boys had been trained for only a few weeks. At the beginning of the war, a fighter pilot had been required to complete two years' training before qualifying for combat.

On 4 October Joseph Szlagowski was successful with his new squadron, 152 (Hyderabad), at Warmwell, a satellite airfield for Middle Wallop. While intercepting enemy fighters near Southampton, planes from 152 separated in heavy cloud and Szlagowski found himself on top of an Me 110. After a traditional dogfight, he hit the Messerschmitt with a burst of cannon fire and sent it into the sea. Szlagowski's personal logbook and Francis K. Mason's *Battle Over Britain* both record this victory but it is not in the squadron record book. Mason also records against Szlagowski's name that day that he destroyed a Do 17 bomber, but other sources are not so certain about the details of Do 17 losses on the 4th.

It is certain, however, that 152 were scrambled to intercept a big group of enemy aircraft. As the squadron climbed, Szlagowski could see huge black clouds in the distance; as he drew closer, he realised that they were advancing bombers. He attacked one of the bombers with a sharp round of cannon fire, splitting it in half. One of the crew was left in the gap between the two halves. Szlagowski was close enough to see him stretch his arms up to try and cut something. For what seemed an eternity the man clung to the wreckage as it drifted down, before he was thrown free, and, unable to open his parachute, headed towards the ground. It was a moment Szlagowski has never forgotten: 'I thought of trying to rescue him. I thought to myself, Oh God, if I only could catch him on a wing and bring him down gently. I will never forget it. I will always see that fellow coming down without his parachute open.'

The first week of October brought unexpected success for Cyril Bamberger. On the 5th, 41 left Hornchurch at 11.05 a.m. and headed for the Kent coast. Over Dungeness the squadron met a formation of yellow-nosed Me 109s. Bam was credited with shooting down Lieutenant Alfred Zweis of 1/JG 53 at noon. Today Bam cannot recall the incident, even though it was the only plane he shot down in the whole Battle of Britain: 'Mostly something splashed across the sights, very momentarily; you snatched a shot. The only way to be certain was to get close behind and watch – but that was too risky. I wanted to get out. Maybe I shot more down, I honestly don't know.' He noticed that some pilots would swarm round the intelligence officer, an elderly peer, making sure he took in what they said: 'I was always too tired, I just wanted to slump in a chair.'

Meanwhile, Bob Doe was informed that he had received a DFC – as the squadron records put it, 'for downing twelve skyrats'. Among his former colleagues in 234, Pat Hughes had (posthumously) won a DFC and Sergeant 'Budge' Harker a DFM (sergeants were awarded different medals from officers). For Doe, the crowning glory of the DFC brought problems. Already dangerously overconfident, he was made more so by the medal: 'I flew from that moment onwards with my chest stuck right out.'

He did not have to wait long to celebrate. 7 October, a bright sunny day with wisps of feathery cloud, saw heavy activity that also brought Joseph Szlagowski and 152 into conflict with 110s. Doe was part of the defensive force in the same action. For the loss of one Hurricane, 238 shot down four enemy aircraft, including a Ju 88 destroyed by Doe.

Three days later, the remarkable success of RFT Doe, DFC, the shy young man from Surrey who had been convinced that he was such a lousy pilot that he would be killed on his first sortie, came to an end.

On 10 October, 235 were scrambled over Dorset in bad weather. The squadron was soon split up; on his own, Bob Doe came up through thick cloud underneath some enemy fighters, who immediately attacked him from behind and in front simultaneously. One bullet hit him through the shoulder, one passed through his wristwatch into his hand. Cannon shell cut his Achilles' tendon. He had already automatically bashed the stick forward in an effort to go downwards and escape his difficulties. All Doe's weight was on his sutton harness and, in the panic, he tore the harness as he fell out through the hood, pulling the parachute – but, to his great relief, the parachute opened. Then he began to assess the impact of his injuries: 'My shoulder felt as if it had been hit by a sledgehammer, and as I had been shot through one of my legs, I couldn't land on them.' In addition, the parachute had been hit in the cockpit by a cannon shell and two gores were missing. The injured pilot spun downwards towards Brownsea Island at Poole much more rapidly than was safe. Terrified of the effect of hitting the ground, he tried to steer his injured leg out of the way. He landed on his bottom, bending his spine slightly and knocking himself out.

When Doe came round, his head was in a rose bush and he felt wet and smelly: he had landed in a sewage quagmire, which had provided just the soft landing he needed. Within minutes a workman arrived and stood over him with an iron bar, asking him to identify himself. Bob Doe swore luridly to convince the navvy that he was in the RAF, and then he was taken to hospital.

That night, Geoff Myers wrote in his notebook:

> Tonight I happened to look into the mirror and saw an old man. He had a scar on his forehead, wrinkles below it and sad, tired eyes. His hair was still dark and he had a trimmed moustache, but both might have been grey.
>
> Not a cheerful companion, I thought; he should pull himself together, not let the gloom get the better of him. He should be stronger and think of the future and be confident. He should be brave.

The morale of 3/JG 52 at Coquelles was low. For Ulrich Steinhilper, even success had begun to taste sour. In early October, he escorted a young *Gefreiter* (aircraftsman) on a training flight just off the coast; he had been airborne for about forty minutes when he was informed on the radio that a Blenheim was bombing a convoy in the Channel. Steinhilper broke away but could not find the bomber. To help him, the anti-aircraft guns let off three shots in the direction of the plane. At the end of these three clear little points Steinhilper could see a tiny black dot. He very quickly headed towards it at full throttle. As the faster Me 109 drew close, the Blenheim disappeared in clouds on its way home. The German was cursing his luck when the Blenheim reappeared, flying in a curve towards France. After first overshooting him, Steinhilper shot the Blenheim twice; within a minute the RAF plane was in the water and tiny figures could be seen below scrambling into a dinghy. In the distance Steinhilper noticed the rescue boat from Dunkirk heading for the site of the crash. When what looked like two survivors had transferred safely from the dinghy to the rescue boat, he wheeled his Messerschmitt round and headed for home.

Next day, Steinhilper was telephoned and asked if he wanted to see the Blenheim crew. He declined the offer: 'I didn't want to be reminded that one of them was dead. I know it would have given me sleepless nights, which is no good if you want to survive a war.'

By this time Goering had produced a new plan which outlined five aims for the Luftwaffe, including control of the Channel and coast, the breaking of civilian morale and the progressive weakening of the enemy.

RAF attacks had already destroyed two hundred and fourteen barges and twenty-one of the transporters to be used for the German invasion. Across the whole front this was a serious but not a devastating loss. On 12 October the Germans began to dismantle much of the rest of their invasion fleet.

While finally putting into practice the decision of a month earlier, Hitler kept open the vague possibility of an invasion in the spring or early summer of 1941; preparations continued – 'solely for the purpose of maintaining political and military pressure on England'.

Although the abandonment of Sealion and the end of autumn weather meant that there were several quiet days in the second half of October, there were still bursts of intense activity. On the 27th, for example, more than a thousand sorties were flown by Fighter Command – more than at the height of August. The action, however, had an order, a certainty, about it that had been absent in August.

By mid-October, Ulrich Steinhilper had five stripes on the tail of his Messerschmitt, yet he recognized that the Luftwaffe were the ones under pressure. At night the few remaining pilots in his squadron asked themselves when they would be withdrawn and they still continually questioned the tactics of flying in waves over London. After such decimation as they had suffered, no one could understand how the Luftwaffe's fighter division could ever be rebuilt, and as they observed the progressive removal of invasion transport from the French Channel harbours the Luftwaffe pilots' confidence in High Command tactics grew steadily weaker.

Steinhilper estimated that, by now, he had flown over one hundred and ten missions. Kuhle, the sensible old squadron commander, had survived, but, apart from him, only about five other pilots of the thirty-six who had begun the air battle over Britain were still with JG 52 as the battle entered its dog-days.

Bob Doe, confined to hospital in Poole, and Geoffrey Page, undergoing an endless series of skin grafts in East Grinstead, were among the few who did not welcome the arrival of winter. For both of them, the Battle of Britain was clearly over. Doe knew he would be flying again in a few weeks but the crash had dented his self-confidence.

Despite his success in early October, Cyril Bamberger scarcely had any more confidence at the end of the battle than he had possessed at the beginning. His impression of continual chaos when 41 was airborne was intensified when two more pilots were killed in an accident in the middle of the month. Climbing up to engage a group of Me 109s over Kent, Sergeant Carter and Flying Officer O'Neill collided. Both bailed out: Carter was successful, but O'Neill's parachute failed to open and he plunged into the ground below. Six minutes later, nineteen-year-old Pilot Officer John Lecky was shot down in combat; he bailed out but was killed. Born in Yokohama, Japan, where his father was a language officer with the British embassy, Lecky had been with the squadron only a short while. The previous day he had been thrilled to shoot down an enemy aircraft; now, on his very next flight, his third with 41, his life as a fighter pilot had been swiftly extinguished.

Twenty-three-year-old Sergeant Philip Lloyd met the same fate a few days later when he was shot down in a surprise attack at 9.00 a.m. Lloyd had joined 41 after only two weeks of married life with a girl he had known since childhood. He had flown successfully through the early weeks of September when 41 had been badly hit, only to be killed just as the air Battle of Britain was drawing to a close. Sergeant Lloyd's body was later washed up on the shore near Herne Bay in Kent. He was buried at the Church of the Holy Innocents in Epping Forest, the very place where he had been married a few weeks earlier.

Although he still felt ill at ease in the air, Bam was becoming hardened to death – out of necessity: 'Someone would say, old so and so bought it, and that was it. We almost made jokes about it. I am a very sentimental and affectionate person, but the war taught me to feel nothing when someone died. If you saw a plane coming down you would scream to the pilot to bail out. Something could be done – but once they're dead, they're dead.' Nor did the prospect of killing Germans worry Bam. To him it was just a matter of knocking another machine out of the sky – not that at Hornchurch he had had much of a chance to reach that stage.

In mid-October 41 Squadron was asked for volunteers to fight in Malta. Bam was keen to go: it was a chance to travel and combat had to be better organized there than it was in the Battle of Britain, he thought. One other pilot volunteered but, in the eyes of the commanding officer, Bam was more dispensable. So, two weeks before the Battle of Britain was officially over, Cyril Bamberger left 41 Squadron for the sunshine. Looking back, he said, 'I got a DFC and bar for what I did in the Mediterranean in 1943–44. On that basis, I should have had a Victoria Cross for what I went through in the Battle of Britain and then in Malta.'

Geoff Myers thought that Bob Stanford Tuck had done a marvellous job welding 257 Squadron together, primarily by leading from the front, and he had been helped by the arrival of Flight Lieutenant Peter Blatchford.

A dumpy, tough Canadian from Alberta, known to his friends as 'Cowboy', Blatchford won the immediate respect of the entire squadron. He was a man of undoubted courage with his own set of ideals, his own high standards. He was, said Myers, 'thoroughly decent'. But, even with Blatchford's experience and skill to support him, Stanford Tuck still had problems.

In the late afternoon of 22 October two more pilots – Norman Heywood and twenty-year-old Sergeant Bob Fraser – were shot down within four minutes of each other over the Kent coast, while trying to defend British convoys against enemy attack. That day, which had begun foggy, had been quiet by Battle of Britain standards: only three RAF pilots met their deaths – but two of them were from 257. Myers commented:

> One of them, Heywood, a new pilot full of fun, had been shot down by our own anti-aircraft defences at close range.
>
> The death of Sergeant Fraser, the other pilot, was confirmed tonight. I had come to believe that he would outlive the war. He had come back after so many of his fellow pilots had been shot down. He seemed to be so sturdy. Three weeks ago the poor lad knocked out all his front teeth in a car accident. His good-looking features were spoilt by the accident and he was acutely aware of this. He complained the other day that the dentist had not yet finished making his false teeth. Today, I suppose, the teeth were waiting for him.

The squadron's next encounter was with a group of thirty or forty 109s over the Thames estuary. As Stanford Tuck led three other Hurricanes into battle he noticed one of them, flown by a sergeant pilot, peel off. The other outside plane, also piloted by a sergeant, followed suit. Stanford Tuck was furious, but by now he was in the thick of it: he managed to shoot a 109 down himself before his plane was hit by two bursts of fire. The glass reflector plate of the sight was blown to pieces a few inches away from his face, and his canopy was peppered with holes. The Hurricane limped home. When he landed, Tuck sought out the two disappearing pilots and pulled a pistol on them. 'In time of war,' he said to the two white-faced men, 'desertion is as bad as murder. It bloody nearly was today. A bullet apiece – that's all you're worth.'

One pilot shook and made a feeble excuse. Tuck, lowering his pistol, had him arrested immediately, whereupon he was court-martialled and demobbed. A few weeks later he was seen sweeping the stairs in the control tower of another airfield. The other young pilot, who was only nineteen and had suffered leg wounds earlier in the battle, openly admitted his fear. As the first pilot's behaviour had obviously pushed him over the brink, he was given a second chance and developed into a reliable pilot, eventually earning himself a commission.

The four Polish pilots also made problems for Tuck. Their only concern seemed to be shooting down as many enemy planes as possible, and this all-consuming hatred obstructed their integration into the unit of a squadron. Occasionally they would disobey their leaders' commands and pursue their own almost private vendettas. One Pole was grounded after such an incident and, as the squadron took off without him, tears rolled down his cheeks.

On 29 October, the Luftwaffe launched a brilliant dive-bomb attack on North Weald (where 257 had been re-stationed), using a team of the very best pilots led by the veteran Otto Hinze. The Germans' 109s, equipped with three hundred-kilo bombs each and working at the very limit of their range, dropped their load at 4.40 p.m.

As the bombs dropped 257 were taking off. The squadron had scarcely become airborne when the end of the runway seemed to explode into flames. Twenty-two-year-old Sergeant Jock Girdwood, a dogged, able pilot highly respected by Stanford Tuck, took the full brunt of the blast. Above him, Tuck noticed Girdwood upside down; narrowly avoiding a collision, he saw the young Glaswegian smash into the ground in flames. Myers also witnessed the incident:

> I saw a great fire a few hundred yards away from our
> dispersal point. I didn't even know that he was in
> the middle of the fire. A few minutes before he went
> we were joking together. He was Bob Fraser's friend.
> I know he felt his loss, but we don't talk of those
> things. It was like that. Tuck said, 'Can't be helped. It's
> all in a day's work. There's a war on.'

Nineteen people were killed and forty-two injured by the twenty-seven bombs dropped in the raid. Among the casualties was Pilot Officer Francizek Surma, who was hit on take-off but managed to bail out at fifteen hundred feet. He landed in the tree of an inn and the landlord, once he realised that the unexpected visitor was Polish rather than German, gave him two whisky and sodas. For 257, the grim day was only slightly offset by the courage of Cowboy Blatchford, who had been shot once and then almost blown out of the sky by a cannon shot from a 109. Despite a huge hole in his plane and the fact that petrol was pouring out from underneath, he continued fighting and when he landed treated the whole thing as a joke.

As the face and hands of Geoffrey Page slowly changed shape and texture under the knife of Archibald McIndoe, the wounded pilot began to go out more, almost always in a group of other patients. Sometimes the men would pile into a car and head for London, joining other RAF officers at the pub in Shepherd's Market. Failing that, they would frequent the Whitehall in East Grinstead, where the barmaids and customers were used to seeing young airmen with scorched faces and crippled limbs and did not give the airmen that embarrassed look that they still dread. From the beginning, mirrors had been taken down in most of the bars and pubs of the town.

McIndoe was deeply conscious that it was not just the airmen's hands and faces that needed repairing, their confidence and personalities also needed bolstering. He once said to welfare officer Edward Blacksell, 'Imagine how they feel. On Friday night they were dancing in a nightclub with a beautiful girl and by Saturday afternoon they are a burned cinder. A fighter pilot can't help being vain because the girls all swarm round him like a honeypot. He can take his pick. Think what it must be like for that young man to go back into the same circle with his faced burned to bits.'* So McIndoe encouraged his patients to go out into the town and asked the local community not to treat them as 'freaks' but as ordinary young men.

When Geoffrey Page began to notice an improvement in himself, he decided to visit his former friends and colleagues in 56 Squadron. He jumped into his sports car, strapped one hand to the steering wheel and the other hand to the gear lever, and drove up to North Weald. Before he had even unstrapped his hands on arrival at the officers' mess, a group of pilots had gathered around his car. They were delighted to see him but were unsure how to behave. To Taffy Higginson, 'He looked absolutely dreadful. He had no eyes, no eyebrows; just two slits in his horrid ploughed flesh – nothing like the handsome young fellow we'd known before.' Barry Sutton, however, who had seen Page crash in a ball of flame, was amazed that he had survived: 'I'd never seen a close friend so badly burned. It was a terrible sight. But the moment he spoke his voice was cheerful, and I felt that Geoffrey hadn't changed.' The small excited

*Peter Williams and Ted Harrison, *McIndoe's Army*, Pelham, 1979.

crowd took Page into the bar. Before an impromptu drunken party developed, he had time to take in that his friends looked wearier than he had remembered and that several bright new faces were present.

Next morning, rather the worse for wear, Page headed back to East Grinstead. It had been a warm, joyful occasion. He had been delighted with such a friendly welcome back and the visit had underpinned his determination to fly again. Yet, every time he caught a glimpse of his burned face in the car mirror or felt a stab of pain in his hand when he changed gear, Page was reminded that the road ahead was long and hard.

However, Page's obsession with flying gave him a sense of purpose, a reason to persist with the endless round of operations. He even bought himself a small rubber ball, and for hour after hour would squeeze and knead it until his hands were raw with pain. Then, in a vain attempt to get his crooked fingers straight again, he made the nurse strap four splints tightly to his hand. Though they never straightened, his fingers at least became supple enough to tie shoelaces.

Page also began to nurture a growing hatred for the Germans. It was they, he reasoned to himself, who had scarred and disfigured him so severely. It was their actions that prevented him from flying. He resolved to shoot down one German aeroplane for every operation he had to endure.

19

The Prisoner of War

Having survived the ferocious fighting of August and September, Ulrich Steinhilper was acutely conscious that the later days of October could still bring danger. On the morning of the 27th, as fog lay thick on the potato and corn fields around the grass strip at Calais, Steinhilper's squadron leader arrived in his car from Group Command (which was set up in a monastery in the corner of the field) with orders for the squadron to protect a group of fighter bombers – 109s with 250 kg bombs underneath them – on the way to London.

Steinhilper took off at 9.05 a.m., using his trusty old plane, Yellow Two, which had five swastikas on the tail to represent his five victims, because his newer, rather more speedy plane was being serviced. A group of about fifty Messerschmitts, twenty of them adapted to drop bombs, assembled for the day's action. As usual, when flying an escort role, Steinhilper was unhappy at being shackled to the fighter bombers, unable to fly free, and the unearthly quiet that day made him especially nervous.

As they approached London, Steinhilper spotted the RAF in the distance. For a moment, he thought how pretty and peaceful they looked. Then, to his horror, he noticed that his propeller pitch was playing up – probably as a result of water collecting in the grease of the pitch gear in the propeller's nose while Yellow Two had been lying idle for the past few days. It was so cold at the present height that the water had started to freeze. One other German suffering the same difficulty turned back, but Steinhilper flew on, hoping that the propeller pitch would return to normal. As the bombs began to drop, everyone seemed to shout at once into their radios and, in the chaos, the formation, instead of turning right as ordered by the wing commander a few minutes earlier, turned left: Steinhilper, with his faulty machine, was in a highly exposed position. Then a voice shouted down the earphones, 'They're coming, they're coming out of the sun, out of the sun.' About five fighters dived towards Steinhilper's flying partner, Sergeant Shieverhofer; Steinhilper shouted, 'Watch it!' and dived away as fast as he could. For a moment he thought he would be safe in the next layer of heavy cloud, then he felt a shake of his control rudder and a bang on his left-hand side. The 109 still seemed operational, but was losing oil, as its pilot made for safety.

Suddenly Steinhilper found himself in the middle of some Hurricanes flying a loose formation. They had not seen him. To take aim, he took off his oxygen mask; the strong smell told him that he had been hit in the radiator. Hastily abandoning plans to shoot down a Hurricane, he moved back into the clouds, looking anxiously at his oil temperature. With a bit of luck, he thought, he could make it back to the Channel, ditch the plane and get picked up by the rescue services. He called the ground station in Calais to notify the sea rescue services, and was reminded that the squadron's adjutant had drowned in the Channel after an emergency landing – and to be careful.

Steinhilper switched off the engine and started to glide in order to cool the oil. The squadron leader confirmed on the radio that, once they had refuelled, his squadron would search the Channel for him. For a while, the pilot alternated between gliding very low and switching off the ignition, keeping the Calais ground station informed of his position. At 250 metres and gliding, he switched the ignition on. It sounded very rough. Then the engine stopped dead.

The only possibility was to jump. With the 109 going down fast, Steinhilper shouted his intention down the RT and struggled to free himself. Suddenly he managed to pull out his legs and was gone. 'Just like a piece of nothing, I was carried alongside the 109, making fast somersaults. But I pulled in my head and with good luck passed the tail rudders.' He pulled the cord, but as his parachute opened, he caught his left leg and continued to sway and somersault. The leg hurt badly, but he managed to free it and drifted slowly down. 'Just at this moment I could see my brave Yellow Two heading into the soft-looking ground in the middle of a herd of cows, which were running off with raised tails. Its ammunition started to go off right away – a kind of ridiculous salute of honour.'

A few seconds later Steinhilper landed too – one-legged, keeping his injured left leg from hitting the ground too hard. In the distance, he could still hear the explosion of ammunition. He had landed close to a water channel or dyke in a flat field. In one direction was a wood, in the other a pretty village church: 'So now here I stood on English soil. The sky above was dark grey, and light spraying rain came down. I could not believe that a few minutes before I had been floating up there in the brightness of the sun.'

The German pilot felt desolate. Above he could hear the howling engines of his comrades returning safely home. No longer was he master of his own fate. But there was little time for self-pity; he had to make a move. As he tried to walk, a sharp pain ran up his leg. He had started to put down his emergency equipment when a gunshot rang out.

A minute earlier it had been so peaceful. Had someone really been aiming at him? He looked round and noticed a small bridge over the dyke, with a hedge and then a village beyond. Instinctively, he fell to the ground.

Behind the hedge on the other side of the canal, Steinhilper thought he could detect a man with what looked like a bandage around his arm (like all the German fighter pilots, he himself was unarmed), then he made out the movements of a double-barrelled shotgun. It seemed very close, just fifteen or twenty feet away. A voice shouted, 'Get up.' In his broken schoolboy English, the German replied, 'I can't, my leg is hurt.' Slowly the man with the gun stood up. Once again, Steinhilper shouted that he could not walk. The man lowered his rifle, as the German tried to walk up the embankment, only to collapse because his leg hurt so much. The Englishman seemed reassured that his prisoner could not run away; he offered to come across the canal and help. 'I sat thinking about the past and the future,' said Steinhilper. 'My comrades! My parents, would they at some time find out that, after all, everything had gone well, so far?'

In the distance Yellow Two was still exploding, and smoke could be seen drifting from it; all that now remained of the plane was the tail with its distinctive stripes. Steinhilper could see a crowd of people running towards him from the village beyond. For a moment he was worried, mindful that British civilians had occasionally been unwelcoming to German prisoners – although that attitude had been more prevalent earlier in the battle. (Certainly one pilot who had strafed some women in a field had been pitchforked to death by the British when he had been forced to ditch some time later.) The pilot was reassured to see two men in khaki uniforms leading the advancing crowd.

By now, Sam Hood, the home-guard man, had arrived on Steinhilper's side of the canal. The German showed him as identification a badge bearing a wild boar that signified JG 52. Hood asked for the badge as a souvenir, and slipped it quietly into his pocket. He then examined Steinhilper's injured leg and was astonished to find that, underneath his trousers, the Luftwaffe pilot was wearing pyjamas. He laughed as it was explained to him that they were the warmest things to wear. When he found no blood on Steinhilper's leg, he grew more serious, insisting that he try to walk again, but the German was still in pain. His attempt was interrupted by the arrival of the crowd led by the two soldiers. The first one jumped across the dyke, just reached the other side and promptly toppled backwards right into the water. He stumbled out of the dyke soaking wet but roaring with laughter. Then his companion emulated the feat, also falling backwards into the dyke. Steinhilper, Sam Hood and the crowd all laughed, and the tension dissolved. The two soldiers, who were Canadian, were in good spirits despite being soaking wet.

An officer arrived to search Steinhilper but removed only a letter from his girlfriend. Then the two wet Canadian officers carried him over the fields and the Chislet marshes, to the first-aid post. Already a crowd had gathered to take a look at the village's first prisoner; they formed two rows up the drive of the house where the first-aid post was situated. One bystander remarked, 'I thought all Germans would have horns, but he looked quite pleasant and rather handsome. He was fair, and was limping. He was wearing pyjama trousers.'

Already at the first-aid post was the village constable, who, in true *Dad's Army* tradition, had broken his ankle from falling into a dyke while running to apprehend the prisoner. Steinhilper's leg was cleaned and bandaged and he was given a cup of tea. He remembered that only three days earlier an RAF flight lieutenant who had come down in Calais had been taken to the officers' mess for a cognac. Steinhilper had laughed when the English officer had asked him to take his mother's address and let her know he was safe. The Englishman had picked on him because he was certain that he too would soon be shot down, and he promised that, in return for his cognac, the German would get a cup of English tea. Now it was all coming true.

Also present at the first-aid post was a priest who spoke broken German. Although he was being well treated, Steinhilper felt profoundly depressed; he told the priest that perhaps it would be better if he were dead. The priest replied that the war had finished for the pilot; he was now a prisoner, and safe, which was good for a young man. Don't think about dying, the priest said in German, you have a long life ahead of you.

For Ulrich Steinhilper at least, the Battle of Britain was over. Three days later it drew to its official close.

PART THREE

AFTER THE BATTLE

20

THE WAR GOES ON

Although the Germans were still capable of mounting large-scale raids, the RAF had won the Battle of Britain simply by surviving. Dowding's strategy had been proved correct. His rotation of part-time squadrons, his resistance to putting too many squadrons in the air at once and his care not to take the fight to the enemy too readily all helped to avoid Fighter Command's extinction. And Beaverbrook's success at the Air Ministry had allowed the commander-in-chief to replenish his stock of aircraft when necessary.

Not that Dowding and Park always got it right. As the histories of 234 and 257 show, squadron leadership had sometimes been appalling, and in the case of 257 it was only rectified late in the day after an unconscionable number of deaths. The battle-hardened Polish pilots were not used until it was almost too late. The negligence of training before the war had been almost criminal; but even once the battle had begun, training, particularly on gunnery and tactics, was inadequate. Nor did Fighter Command always use its airfield resources to the full, leaving strategically useful airfields such as Eastchurch on the Isle of Sheppey in the hands of other commands.

Yet, for all these faults of detail, Dowding and Park fought a brilliant campaign, without always the greatest support from some of their senior colleagues. Indeed, Leigh-Mallory, commanding No. 12 Group based to the north of London, was instrumental in engineering Dowding and Park's demise. Leigh-Mallory and Squadron Leader Douglas Bader, at Duxford in Cambridgeshire, promoted the Big Wing theory; their plan was to match the big Luftwaffe raids of September 1940 plane for plane by assembling several squadrons at a time. To Dowding and Park, such extravagant use of limited resources was anathema: by the time the Big Wing was assembled, they believed, the Luftwaffe would be through British defences and bombing cities and airfields; the Big Wing would only hit the enemy on their way home. Leigh-Mallory and Bader, however, claimed that they could have the Big Wing airborne and assembled in just a few minutes. The technique was used in 12 Group, north of London, where more time was available to get huge numbers airborne, but Dowding and Park resisted attempts to spread its use to the crucial airfields in 11 Group further south.

The Big Wing debate was a 'running sore' during the final stages of the air battle. When the battle was over and Dowding had hung on, Leigh-Mallory, who had the superficial leadership qualities the quiet Dowding lacked, moved in. Using his political skills and contacts, Leigh-Mallory, supported by Bader, attacked Dowding and Park for their caution at a meeting at the Air Ministry. Soon afterwards, Dowding was given twenty-four hours to clear his desk, Keith Park was switched to Training Command – and Leigh-Mallory took over the control of 11 Group.

By the end of the Battle of Britain, many of the prewar old-school leaders in the RAF had died; the amateur, class-ridden gentlemen's air force was on its way out. An altogether more professional war was about to begin – a war in which the civilian population of the cities on both sides would not be spared.

For the British, invasion had been staved off, but the Germans had not gone home. The focus of their bombing attacks had switched to night-time raids, particularly on British cities. The Luftwaffe reasoned that, if they could not break Fighter Command, perhaps they could bomb Britain into submission – so that, when Hitler had subdued the Russians, he could come back and finish Britain off.

For the much depleted 257 Squadron there was still daytime work to do, with convoy patrols and defensive duties. Victories and defeats continued.

'Cowboy' Blatchford was now at the centre of the action, increasingly taking over many of the more mundane tasks from Stanford Tuck. Geoff Myers wrote at the time:

> Blatchford had hitherto had no glory. Three times
> he had come back from air battles and had made no
> claim. I know others in the squadron who would have
> made out good cases for having at least damaged an
> enemy plane in each action. Blatchford would not
> stoop to that sort of thing, if there was the slightest
> doubt in his mind. His courage was natural.

On 11 November, 257 scrambled from North Weald and headed for the coast on a routine convoy patrol. Tuck was away from the squadron that day, so Blatchford was acting squadron leader; he was warned that enemy aircraft were approaching.

The planes turned out to be Italian bombers escorted by neat, if out-of-date, Fiat CR.42 biplane fighters.

Heading for thick cloud, the squadron broke up the Italian formation, hitting the bombers hard, then the escorting fighters. Having shot a couple of planes, Blatchford ran out of ammunition – so he rammed the Fiat fighter in front of him. He described the incident himself:

> I decided that as I could not shoot him down I would try and knock him out of the sky with my aeroplane. I went kind of haywire. It suddenly occurred to me what a good idea it would be to scare the living daylights out of him. I aimed for the centre of the top mainplane, did a quick dive and pulled out just before crashing into him. I felt a very slight bump, but I never saw him again and somehow I don't think he got back.

Ramming the Italian sliced nine inches off two of his propeller blades, which Blatchford later found were splattered with blood. But that didn't stop the Canadian. With no ammunition, he launched a dummy head-on attack on two more Italians, who turned tail and fled. That day's achievements soon became legend, as Myers recorded:

> For the next few days the wireless, the press and the films were full of the squadron's actions. Our pilots were photographed with bottles of Chianti, crests, Fin hats, daggers and other spoils taken from the Italian planes. Peter Blatchford is to talk on the wireless of his exploits. The speech has been prepared with the aid of a Press Officer.

Myers hoped that Blatchford would get the DFC – and his hope was fulfilled.

Six days later, Blatchford was again leading the squadron in Tuck's absence, on a convoy patrol. South-east of Harwich he spotted a group of 109s. He opened fire on the leading 109 in a head-on attack, but as he levelled out he saw Sergeant Tennison's Hurricane cross right in front of the 109. Although badly damaged, the German hit Tennison's plane and sent him spinning down. Blatchford then finished off the Messerschmitt. Although the day had been a minor success compared to the glory of the Italian job, the squadron was pleased. But Peter Blatchford was deeply troubled by the events, as he confided in Myers afterwards:

'I saw Tennison go down. He did not appear to be crashing but was gliding down in gentle circles with smoke pouring out. I thought he would get away with it. As I was chasing this 109 a Hurricane flew right across his sights and, smoking as he was, he fired at him and got him. That must have been Tennison . . . I'm not a killer, Geoff, I don't like it. I just do it because I've got to.' He hesitated and continued to hold my eyes with his. 'After the Gerry shot Tennison I closed in and got to within fifty yards. Then he suddenly put out his arm and looked at me as if to say "don't fire". But I pressed the button and the Messerschmitt crashed into the sea. He was thrown out and then I saw him for a moment stretched out on the water. Then he disappeared. He must have been dead when he fell out of the plane as it crashed. He was a tough guy, Geoff, a stout fellow. I didn't want to kill him. I've been thinking about it all the time.'

Myers and Blatchford had another drink together, but even that did not relax the solid-looking Canadian. Geoff Myers was deeply concerned about what the war was doing to the behaviour and personality of a transparently honest and brave man:

'Maybe he might have jumped and bailed out, Geoff, if I hadn't shot the second time. Perhaps he would have been picked up by a boat. I was so excited I just pressed the button. My dream is to bring down a great big bomber, with all the men on board, alive, and just have them prisoners. I'm not a killer.'

Next evening, Myers packed up Sergeant Tennison's belongings. With the three other sergeants in 'A' flight having been shot down in the fag end of the battle, the one surviving sergeant had reached the end of the road: Tennison had been his roommate; now he was desperate to move away, but there was little chance of that. Myers remembered that Sergeant Tennison's wife was expecting a baby in two months' time.

On the very day that Tennison met his death, Cyril Bamberger was bobbing on the Mediterranean on his way to Malta. Although the Battle of Britain was over for Bam, the war was only just about to begin. Malta was to be a much more difficult experience.

Bam had sailed from Glasgow in HMS *Argus,* a 1914–18 aircraft carrier. On board were a dozen Hurricanes – on which Bam had received exactly one hour's training just a few days earlier – and their pilots. It was a dilapidated, rather dingy ship, and the six sergeant pilots were billeted in the bows in extremely cramped and uncomfortable conditions.

Their leader was a tall, fair, part Scot, part New Zealander named Flight Lieutenant James MacLachlan. A cheerful, friendly man, MacLachlan was a natural leader and at the same time a rebel too – a combination that attracted Bamberger, who liked him immediately. He seemed much less conscious of class and rank than some of the men Bam had served under before. To Mac it was your skill and character that counted.

Among the other pilots was Jock Norwell, who hailed from Perth in Scotland, an old colleague of Bamberger's from 41 Squadron noted for the dryness of his humour, and Pat Horton, the New Zealander from 234 Squadron at Middle Wallop who had won a reputation as an excellent pilot.

Less than sixty-five miles from Sicily, where the Italians – now involved in the conflict – had several large air bases, Malta was of crucial strategic importance. While Britain controlled it, their ships could avoid the forty-five days' sailing round the Cape. Later, as Rommel began his desert campaign, Malta was a perfect base from which to launch attacks on his convoys to North Africa. Laddie Lucas, who himself flew Spitfires in Malta, wrote:[*]

> History may well say that Hitler's loss of the Malta
> battle – and the High Command's appalling misjudge-
> ment of the island's resilience – was no less crucial to
> his ultimate defeat than his earlier failure to quell the
> strength of Fighter Command in the Battle of Britain.

On its previous two trips ferrying Hurricanes to Malta, the *Argus* had got within four hundred miles of the island before the Hurricanes were flown off. She was a small carrier with

---

[*]Introduction to *The Air Battle of Malta*, Mainstream, 1981.

a ramp on the end, and take-off was difficult; the technique was to hit the ramp hard and almost bounce into the air. Immediately, the aircraft would drop down towards the sea, but there was enough time to pull up again and away. The day before the planned take-off, Flight Lieutenant MacLachlan talked to the pilots. Although there were twelve Hurricanes, there were thirteen pilots, one too many. Bam, with only one hour's experience in Hurricanes, was the obvious candidate not to undertake this tricky exercise: 'It was a bitter blow. I was fed up with being cooped up on that ship.'

Dawn next day, 17 November, broke with a bright blue sky. The Hurricanes took off one by one, each group of six led by a Skua with a navigator on board to guide them towards their destination. The first group took off at 6.15 a.m., the second nearly an hour later. Bam watched nervously as each plane hit the ramp, tottered almost still in the sky, and then pulled up and away: 'That was a hairy moment. I was relieved when they all got off safely.'

After the take-off Bam had his breakfast and retired to his quarters, suddenly spacious without his five colleagues. He felt curiously lonely. That evening he heard the news: of the first flight of seven aircraft, only four had made it to Malta; the entire second flight failed to arrive. All ten missing planes had apparently run out of fuel and crashed, like birds hit by stones, into the sea. All the pilots had been killed, including Pat Horton, who had been one of the few of 234 Squadron's original pilots to have survived the Battle of Britain. Among the handful who landed safely was Flight Lieutenant MacLachlan and Jock Norwell; Dickie Swire had crashed but was rescued. Though hardened to deaths of his colleagues during the battle,

Bam was appalled. As it had turned out, he had been lucky not to go: 'It seemed so needless; they weren't even knocked out of the sky by Germans. As many killed in one flight as some squadrons lost during the whole Battle of Britain.'

In his official secret report at the time, Captain Rushbrooke of the *Argus* concluded that the Hurricanes of the first flight either:

(a) had insufficient fuel for the operation, and that the Air Ministry's endurance figures did not hold good for these six aircraft, or:

(b) most of the pilots made uneconomical use of their mixture control.

According to Cyril Bamberger, the tanks were full, so there should have been enough fuel if the amount required to reach Malta had been correctly calculated. Bam was also emphatic about the pilots: 'Flight Lieutenant MacLachlan, whom I got to know well in Malta, would not have taken off from the *Argus* if he had anticipated a flight lasting three hours. On any long-distance flight, particularly if it was over the sea, it would be against the very nature of any fighter pilot not to economize on petrol.'

The observer in the Skua leading the second flight had been making his first operational flight. This extraordinary lack of experience on a crucial mission had not been helped by the non-arrival of maps of Luqua and Malta – meaning that the observers on the Skuas had to be satisfied with cut-up portions of charts from the ship's ordinary folios. An explanation more plausible than Captain Rushbrooke's excuses can be found in the report of Vice Admiral Somerville to the Secretary to the Admiralty, a few days after the tragedy. He reveals that he selected 'the most westward position' for take-off, apparently forty miles further west than the original intention. The reason was 'the presence of a considerably superior force of Italian vessels in the Lower Tyrrhenian Sea'. It seems likely that, as Bam believes, the ten planes took off too far to the west of Malta: 'Their explanations are not satisfactory. Surely they could have worked that out in advance. To my mind, the navy did not take them close enough.'

After the tragedy, Bam returned to Gibraltar and was allocated to HMS *Manchester,* but at the last minute his passage was switched to HMS *Hotspur.* Again, he was lucky: the *Manchester* went on to Greece and was sunk, but the *Hotspur* arrived safely in Malta. On the island, more chaos and difficulties awaited the Hurricane pilots: 'We seemed to be targets all the time; it was hazardous, extremely shaky,' said Bam. 'Much more dangerous than the Battle of Britain. By now I was a good, experienced pilot, so I was much more aware of the follies and stupidities inflicted upon us by those in charge.'

Although Ulrich Steinhilper was now a prisoner of war and far away from the conflict on the eastern front which his colleagues in 3/JG 52 had become involved in, he still did not feel secure. For the moment everyone was kind and thoughtful towards him, but he knew that at some time the interrogation would have to begin.

At Chislet he was handed over to a major in the infantry, a tall, lean man of about thirty who immediately put the prisoner at ease. Steinhilper was taken to a pleasant manor house in the nearby village of Westbere, where he was kept under guard in a top room. From his window he looked out on a pretty garden and, beyond, the flat Kent countryside he had flown over so often. The damaged leg was very painful and prevented his walking, but it was eased by a hot bath shortly after his arrival, and the major then summoned a doctor who bandaged the leg from the hip to the knee. Later in the day, the major returned from Canterbury with a pair of crutches; Steinhilper was allowed to use them for regular exercise in the garden.

Over the next few days Steinhilper talked to the major, who was open and considerate, as well as he could in his schoolboy English. 'If it wasn't for the war,' the major said one night, 'we would have been good friends.' The prisoner invited the major to come and visit him in Germany when the war was over. That same night, the major phoned London. 'I hope your colleagues aren't in London yet,' he joked, 'or my wife will already be in the shelter.' – 'Good evening, darling,' Steinhilper heard him say, 'we've got an invitation to Germany, free accommodation, for a holiday after the war.'

At first, Steinhilper hoped that he would soon be liberated: 'Death or becoming a prisoner was a close choice. But after a few days you were surprised to find what a normal and good life it was. We were still hoping for the invasion, still hoping to be freed in six weeks or so – I had no idea that it would last six years.'

Only one incident marred his stay in the major's care at Westbere. The rest of the manor house was used as quarters for the officers of what Steinhilper presumed was an infantry battalion. One evening, the officers had a party in the drawing room downstairs. From his pleasant room at the top, the German could hear the laughter and noise. The major came to invite him down; Steinhilper thought the occasion best avoided, but the major persuaded him to join in. It was a mistake. After a couple of beers, one of the lieutenants turned on the German and began to insult him, shouting that Steinhilper was the kind of man who would murder innocent people and shoot children. For a moment, the prisoner tried to reason with him, but the insults grew worse, the incident more ugly. Finally, the major intervened, shunting the lieutenant firmly away with apologies to the German. Up in his room, Steinhilper felt sick: 'I knew then, at that moment, what it was really like to be a prisoner.'

Apart from this incident, the stay at Westbere was too pleasant to last. After less than a week, Steinhilper was driven into the countryside by a captain. (As they sped along the country lanes, he noticed that there were no road signs – in preparation, he presumed, for Operation Sealion.) Eventually, they pulled up at what looked like a set of flat farm buildings surrounded by huge barbed-wire fences. At the guardhouse, the German's crutches were taken away. 'How can I walk?' he protested in broken English, but received no answer. The captain said, 'Sorry for what is going to happen to you. Goodbye,' and drove away.

The atmosphere and conditions here were very different from those at the manor house: 'I had to jump at least three hundred metres on one leg. It was very painful.' In the barn Steinhilper saw rows of individual beds; by each stood a guard with a bayonet. He was given a bed on the second floor among about thirty other German prisoners, who were not allowed to speak to each other or to the guards. Several of the others were lying on their beds with bloody bandages covering their wounds. One or two still seemed to be bleeding badly. One first lieutenant was handcuffed to his guard.

As he limped among the prisoners, Steinhilper was surprised to see Lothar Schieverhofer, his *rottenhund* in 3/JG 52, who had been shot down in the same incident as him. He had not seen Schieverhofer go down and was disappointed to realise that he was also a prisoner. At the same time he was heartened; the two had flown together, nearly died together, and now they were prisoners together. Schieverhofer held his finger to his lips and whispered under his breath, 'They'll know what unit we are in.' Later, during a meal, they were able to talk quietly, and Schieverhofer described what had happened when he had been shot down. Steinhilper also learned that one German pilot whom he knew, Frank von Werra, had already escaped, which explained why the British were so edgy.

That afternoon, Steinhilper was taken to the interrogation room, where several officers, along with soldiers armed with guns and bayonets, were assembled. The prisoner thought that he was going to be shot. Told to remove all clothing, including his wristwatch, he soon stood completely naked in the cold, facing the armed soldiers. A physical check-up followed, then a series of questions in German. Name? Rank? Address? Steinhilper was never threatened, but standing there naked he felt vulnerable and frightened. More questions: the German did not respond. Then he was told to dress.

For the next four days he was interrogated daily. Although he refused to answer questions, he felt a growing sense of helplessness, and wasn't sure how much longer he could continue. At his last interrogation, he was told bitterly, 'We could have kept you in darkness for a month during interrogation; that was what happened to me in the First World War.'

For 152 Squadron, November was generally quiet, so the few dramatic incidents that did occur seemed important. On the 26th, Sergeant Klein was reported missing, and the squadron, particularly his friend Joseph Szlagowski, anxiously awaited his return. Eventually a message was received that he had crash-landed near Torquay having run out of petrol, but was unhurt. The squadron record notes, 'There was great relief when news came that he was safe.'

Zig Klein and Joseph Szlagowski were still inseparable. Their English had improved and their dashing Polish good looks made them attractive to the local girls – Zig had become particularly attached to a young WAAF.

Two days after Zig had crash-landed near Torquay, 152 were scrambled again, this time to intercept enemy aircraft near France. It was misty and the individual pilots in 152 were soon separated. Szlagowski saw no enemy aircraft, and headed back to base. One by one, the squadron came home but, once again, Zig was missing; nothing had been heard of him since take-off. Then Pilot Officer Holmes reported that he had seen a Spitfire spinning three or four times over the sea before disappearing from sight. 'It appears,' said the record, 'that we have lost a very gallant pilot and ally.'

This time, Joseph Szlagowski waited in vain. Although he had grown to accept the deaths of other colleagues, Zig's was different: 'I grieved very much.'

In the winter of 1940, Margot Myers, still stranded in France just inside the occupied zone, was concerned with the gathering of food; where she stayed there was no petrol, bicycles were precious and new tyres were not available. When it snowed, Margot had to walk three miles into the village for bread.

For six months now, Margot had received no news of her husband. The Battle of Britain had come and gone. If Geoff had been killed she would probably have heard, but she could not be certain. As for Geoff in Britain, that private notebook was the only place where he could show his true feelings:

> The thought of you, my darling, keeps me going.
> I adore you. I long to see you and my little ones. But there is no horizon.
>
> God bless you, my family.

For the sake of the young men in the squadron, Geoff Myers could not betray his concern about his family's safety. He had to remain solid and reliable, but inwardly he held onto the hope that he could somehow get a coded message through to them.

In France the pressure on Jews was tightening. Some newspapers had grown openly hostile both to the Jews and to Britain. Stories filtered through from Paris of the rounding-up of Jewish children. To Margot's horror, some of her relatives were pro-Pétain.

The new developments convinced Margot that she had to leave. Initially, her mother tried to deter her because of the danger: 'It needed every ounce of my courage to carry the plan through, and so I begged my mother not to hinder me,' remembered Margot, 'and she said no more.' At about this time, a coded message finally arrived from Geoff, suggesting that the family should attempt to escape via Lisbon.

Soon after Christmas, Margot noticed that the grocer's son from the nearby village of La Chapelle-aux-Chasses had disappeared and so she discreetly approached the grocer for help. It was tricky, he replied, but he would try.

On the appointed date, the grocer told Margot and the children to dress as if going for a walk, to carry no luggage; he drove them to nearby Dompierre, where he introduced them to a gamekeeper responsible for a forest half inside the occupied zone and half outside.

The family gave the gamekeeper their passports and, in return, Margot received the identity cards of a French woman living in the unoccupied zone. The gamekeeper's wife took charge of two-year-old Anne in her pushchair, while Margot pushed Robert on his bicycle. The rain thundered down, soaking the small band of escapers but allowing them to slip past guards, who were more concerned with staying dry than arresting refugees. After a cut through some fields, they arrived in the unoccupied zone and decided to shelter in a local café, but the proprietor was hostile so Margot found a room in a local hotel and dried off the soddenclothes. Next day, she got a lift to Moulins, where she had friends – although they were Pétainists, they welcomed the arrivals warmly. For the time being, Margot, Anne and Robert Myers were safe.

Ulrich Steinhilper was on the move again. Eventually realising that the car he was travelling in was passing through the outskirts of London, he watched with interest for signs of blitz damage and was surprised that the centre appeared to have got off so lightly. His destination was a tall, good-looking building near a park, also fenced in with barbed wire. Steinhilper was disappointed to find that Schieverhofer was not among the twenty prisoners there.

At the farm the atmosphere had been one of terror. At the park camp the regime was more relaxed and more sophisticated. Steinhilper sensed that his interrogators here were cleverer and more subtle than those he had hitherto encountered, but he still refused to divulge information. The prisoners discovered that some of the rooms were bugged with hidden microphones, and they suspected that one of their number, an Italian who tried to talk at length to Steinhilper, had been employed by the British to dig out information. Every night, heavy shooting from anti-aircraft guns shook the whole building, and when the air-raid alarms sounded, the prisoners were not taken into a shelter, but left to the fear that they would be bombed by their own side.

After what seemed like a week or so, Steinhilper was moved from the centre of London, away from the Luftwaffe bombing raids, to a railway station. As the citizens of London poured out of the shelters in the early morning, he was struck by how tired and grey they looked. On the platform people began waving their fists and shouting at him. Frightened, he was for once relieved to be under armed guard.

As the train pulled out, the German prisoner, accompanied by three friendly escorts, was pleased to see green fields and countryside. The train truck passed an airfield, and he noted the rows of aircraft the RAF appeared to have available: intelligence information on British losses must have been exaggerated, he thought – the German newspapers had described Britain as 'a dying lion'. The further the train sped from London the more the hatred in people's eyes diminished. Eventually, they arrived at another camp, in a town called Sheffield.

* * *

Bob Doe was still in hospital when he heard the news that he had been awarded a bar to his DFC. 'He has shot down sixteen skyrats confirmed,' said the squadron records.

When his Achilles tendon had mended enough to enable him to fly, Doe rejoined his squadron. Little appeared to have happened in his absence. The record for November made scant mention of fighting. 'There are no bathing facilities,' it noted, 'everyone getting very dirty.' There was an outbreak of crabs.

On 21 December, the day Doe returned to 238, it was reported that Aircraftsman O'Connell, a deserter, had been picked up in Bath and remanded for further inquiry. O'Connell had been given fourteen days detention for falsely wearing an air gunner's badge before running away. This was just one of a number of incidents recorded that month in abnormally frank squadron records. A.C.I. Wainwright, who had received twenty-eight days detention for using threatening language to a sergeant pilot, had fled and was still in hiding. In addition, a 'disquieting' number of thefts in the camp had been uncovered. All indications were that, in the post-Battle of Britain months, morale and discipline in 238 Squadron was not all it might have been.

During Christmas with 152 Squadron, 'Slug' Szlagowski felt particularly desolate: 'Everyone spoke in English and I sat in the corner listening to them, thinking that if only Zig was here what fun we would have.' Slug filled two whisky glasses, one for himself and one for Zig: 'I lifted one up and said, "Cheerio Zig, Merry Christmas."' Then he started to weep.

The station warrant officer had noticed Szlagowski sitting alone; to cheer him up, he brought in a huge dish, on which was a whole turkey. 'If you don't eat that,' he said to the maudlin pilot, 'I don't know what to do with you. Now come and have a drink.'

On Boxing Day Bob Doe was to fly again for the first time since his accident; he felt as sick inside as he had before his first action with 234 back in August. With the help of a bump or two from his colleagues – he could still not walk properly – he limped across the runway and into his aircraft. When it spluttered into life, thundered down the runway and lifted into the cold night air, he was highly relieved.

The few weeks in hospital had brought home to Doe the fact that he was not infallible. He knew it was his own fault that he'd been shot down, and now, every time he prepared for take-off, his former doubts about his own ability returned. 238 Squadron, however, was pleased to see its most successful pilot back in the air, and soon after his return Bob Doe was made acting commanding officer.

With the deaths of so many of the original 257 Squadron, only two men remained whom Geoff Myers was very close to. One was Cowboy Blatchford; the other was the fresh-faced nineteen-year-old Carl Capon, whose simple courage and honesty Myers admired:

> He had become our favourite. I teased him by calling
> him our mascot. He thrived on it, and when he did
> anything awkward or silly he told everybody and
> giggled heartily at himself. He did not think that
> he was much good and I tried to encourage him by
> telling him what I really thought of his keenness and
> bravery. Tuck has recommended him for a mention in
> dispatches.

For 257, the New Year began with the usual round of patrols. On New Year's Day the cloud was low and there were snow flurries. Stanford Tuck had disappeared to France in his aircraft to 'beat up the other side', so the more mundane task of organizing convoy patrols was left to Flight Lieutenant Yates. Carl Capon volunteered to assist him.

With snow blowing hard into his face, Geoff Myers watched the returning aircraft come in to land. One landed beautifully, then Myers noticed another:

> It shouldn't be there. Oh! Stop – No! I bit my lips in agony. The aircraft suddenly appeared to be drunk, reeled to port, banked to starboard. Red, green, white lights whirled round. A gust of snow slapped in my face. God, the aircraft was going down. There was a great cracking up as it dived nose first into the ground.
>
> . . . [The aircraftsmen stood in silence], awed by the suddenness, the stillness, and the death. Steaming glycol was poured out of the wreckage. 'You'll have to get an axe to hack him out,' said one aircraftsman. 'It's John Yates,' said one pilot. 'They told me that Carl Capon's gone through to dispersal. Poor old John.'

A few minutes later, Geoff thought: have I gone mad? There, in the beam of spotlight, was John Yates. 'It's all right, Geoff,' he said. 'Don't worry about me. He's dead. It's poor old Carl. He must have got caught in the snow squall as he was circling in to land.'

That night Geoff Myers wrote a letter to his small son, Robert:

Perhaps you will read this one day and ponder over Carl Capon. Perhaps you will say, 'Oh, why should he of all the boys have been killed in this futile way? He had so much to live for. He was the best of the lot. It seems so unfair.'

Don't say that, my little boy. Capon was pure and upright. His code of conduct was based on his conscience . . . perhaps you will gain through me inspiration from his death to help you in your pattern of life.

I will not forget Carl Capon. He has helped me, and perhaps he will help you.

Your loving Dad

As the German night raids grew more serious over the New Year, the RAF decided to send two pilots from each squadron up in the hope of offering the airfields some kind of night-time protection. In his new role, Bob Doe insisted on going himself.

3 January was very cold, with frost lying on the ground. Doe was vectored off over the Channel in his Spitfire, but at about eighteen thousand feet odd things started happening to his instruments. The oil pressure was dropping but its temperature remained constant. At the same time, the radiator temperature was going up. Puzzled, Doe opened up the radiator. It was the worst thing he could have done. In fact, the oil in the cooler had frozen – the first time such a thing had happened; the correct action would have been to shut the radiator and boil it out.

Doe turned round and headed back towards Warmwell, Middle Wallop's satellite airfield, which was on the coast and therefore nearer. When his ailing plane was down to about six thousand feet, its engine stopped completely. Doe contacted the ground to explain the crisis and was told that the duty pilot would send up rockets through the cloud to enable him to locate Warmwell.

As Doe glided towards Warmwell, no rockets could be seen: the duty pilot was in the pub having a beer. Doe realised that he would have to land on his own. As he came through the cloud, he could just make out the long thin grass airfield, which was covered in snow. He swung round, missing the hangars beautifully. Thinking he was safe, Doe decided to put the Spitfire down. Unfortunately, since he had last been at Warmwell, before his accident, a dug-out had been built. His plane went straight down the dug-out entrance, smashing its front in.

Inside the plane, Bob Doe's sutton harness broke and he was thrown forward. His face hit the gunsight, and a sharp pain told him that his arm was broken. Still conscious, he looked up at the sky, which slowly blacked out as his face began to swell. Then he put his hand up to make an unspeakable discovery: the crash had smashed in half his face, forcing his nose right up onto the top of his head.

21

THE INTELLIGENCE OFFICER II

In the *Daily Mail* of 17 January 1941, Geoff Myers read that the Germans in occupied France were rounding up Englishwomen and placing them in concentration camps close to RAF bombing targets. For Myers it was a new source of worry about his family:

> For weeks I have been trying to train myself to be cheerful and calm. Now this. Men can keep up their spirits with their limbs shot away. This sort of torture is different.

Two days later, the *Sunday Dispatch* carried a story about three thousand British subjects, many of them women, being interned in France. *The Times* later confirmed the figure:

> I have been through nights of torture, searching my mind what to do. I wrote to the Red Cross and the Foreign Office asking for any information about the women interned in France.

Myers took the train to London. At the British Red Cross Society, they added his name to the long list of people making inquiries about internment in occupied France.

Anxious, Myers returned to base, where a telegram was waiting. It confirmed that Margot was still at Beaurepaire and conditions remained 'good'. The telegram, which had been sent via a friend in Clermont-Ferrand, asked whether it was wise to return to Britain.

It was the first news of his family that Geoff Myers had received since 10 September, but he could not tell how long the message had taken to be smuggled out of unoccupied France. Margot could since have been interned or perhaps she had tried to escape. He talked about his dilemma with John, a friend:

> John screwed his eyes up in delight and laughed. 'You needn't worry what Margot will do at her end,' he said, 'I know how sensible she is.'

Myers knew that sooner or later the Germans would find out Margot's identity, and that she was 'the wife of a Jew and journalist, the combination of all that is hated by the Nazis'. He wired France: 'Advise immediate return.'

In early February, he received a message from his mother's home in Oxfordshire: Margot and the children had crossed safely into unoccupied France and were intending to travel to England via Lisbon.

> The grey fog that had been hovering around my head had lifted. The early spring day seemed so lovely.
> I forgot the war for a few minutes.

Next day he went to London, booked air passages from Lisbon to London, and sent telegrams to the *Daily Telegraph* correspondents in Lisbon and Madrid, asking them to help his wife and children.

Margot Myers and her children had stayed in the country-side near Moulins for three months. Margot ha cautious and uncertain, knowing that she had to keep one step ahead of the Germans, but had no idea how next to proceed. Her mother managed to smuggle a cardboard box of clothes out to them via the grocer.

The house at Moulins was isolated, which meant that Margot had to cycle everywhere. Discreetly, she asked for help and advice. Francs were worth nothing and she realised that she would need dollars. After several fruitless efforts to discover the best way out, she went to the American consulate in Lyon, who helped her obtain train tickets and visas.

The train which was to take them via Toulouse to Barcelona was exceptionally crowded, with people literally piled one on top of another. Yet in adversity the fellow travellers were kind and pleasant to Margot's children. It was a dreadful journey, but Robert and Anne coped well.

In Spain, Margot contacted the *Daily Telegraph* correspondent, and was able to send a cable to Geoff assuring him that she was safe before she travelled on to Lisbon. Although she had plane tickets to London, the waiting list was so long she knew that a plane home was impossible.

The consular authorities informed her that, if the family wanted to be repatriated, they would have to go home by boat; it was her last chance, otherwise the authorities could no longer accept responsibility. It was a difficult decision. About half the convoys were being sunk at the time, but being stranded without consular protection was also risky. By cable, Geoff Myers advised his wife to take a boat.

While the Myers family waited in Lisbon for a passage home, both the children fell very ill, particularly Robert, whom Margot was seriously worried about. The *Daily Telegraph* correspondent and his Spanish wife came to their aid but, when news of a refugee boat being available to evacuate British subjects came through, it looked as if Robert would be too ill to travel and the family would be marooned.

Fortunately, the boat was cancelled and British subjects were told to wait two more months, until June 1941. In those months the children's health improved and the family had a pleasant time staying in a little pension and going to the beach.

Eventually, the British group took a small boat to Gibraltar, where they waited for a convoy to be formed. For two weeks they had drills on deck wearing lifebelts. They were shouted at and bullied by a sergeant major, but everyone, including the children, learned what to do if the boat sank. Margot was very scared – the risk of mines, or submarines, was all too apparent.

They left Gibraltar one evening in late June, during the blackout. In many ways it was a nightmare expedition: the boat was jam-packed with refugees and wounded servicemen; there was little space and a chronic water shortage. Yet, everyone was escaping, and they all helped each other. Among the passengers were some elderly, British spinsters who had been living on the Riviera; dismayed by the water rationing, all they wanted was a bath. Margot heard one sailor say, 'They should be on their hands and knees saying their prayers, and here they are clamouring for baths.'

The two refugee ships were escorted by an aircraft carrier and two or three destroyers, and they were later joined by a cruiser. Planes from the aircraft carrier provided aerial cover.

Throughout the journey, Margot would not get undressed at night in case there was an emergency alarm.

On 28 June, Geoff Myers wrote in his private notebook:

My Darling,

It is just three months since you arrived in Lisbon. Now I am sure you are on your way home. I have had to pump down my feelings for so many weeks now, that I am determined not to let them bubble over until you are home. The period of deferred hope is over.

I have been praying for your safety.

After a long and frightening journey, the atmosphere of excitement on deck began to intensify. Ahead, Margot Myers could just make out the dim outline of England. That night, she threw caution to the wind and undressed for the first time. The next morning the ship sailed up the Clyde. It was Sunday, 14 July 1941.

Geoff Myers agonised over his family's journey:

A colleague at Group whose wife is still in Unoccupied France asked me whether I had agreed to your going by sea. I told him that I had. Then he started saying, 'I wouldn't want to do that. It is so dangerous by sea . . . torpedoes and things.' I interrupted him, saying, 'Good night, I'm off.' What else did he think I had in my thoughts? Of course I have followed the statistics of enemy sinkings and I can't get the danger of it all out of my head.

This evening while I was at the farm next door, the telephone rang and everything in me hurt. I thought it

might be news of you, but it was a local farmer. Perhaps
I shall have to wait a fortnight.

At first, Myers had received incorrect information and followed
the progress of the wrong convoy. When he went to meet the
convoy, Margot wasn't there; he imagined his wife and children at the bottom of the sea. He tried hard to find out what
might have happened. Then, on 14 July, a telegram arrived
from Glasgow: they were alive.

To Margot, wartime Glasgow looked dismal and grey, but
she was so thrilled to have arrived safely that she gave the
porter a ten-shilling note for a tip. He was so shocked that he
said, 'Oh, madam, haven't you got anything smaller?'

She and the children spent the night in a small city-centre
hotel. The next morning there was a knock on the door.
Margot, Robert and Anne jumped up and clung round Geoff's
neck. The children had grown up so much, he thought; while
war had raged on, the family had been separated for fifteen
months. 'Glasgow,' said Geoff Myers, 'has always seemed a
blessed place to me.'

'. . . Mummy is at my side, my little ones, and you are
sleeping a few yards away. Mummy has asked me to go on
writing so that you will know how things were,' he wrote. 'I
want you to realise how Mummy and I are utterly soaked in
thankfulness for this deliverance.'

Three months after Margot Myers arrived with her children in
England, the family moved into a house near Bletchley Park,
about fifty miles north-west of London.

It is only in recent years, since the records of Bletchley were made available, that the true significance of its work has become known. It was here that the codes and cyphers of the German Enigma machine were broken, and the intelligence gathered from the decoding – known as Ultra – was assessed. The impact of the Ultra secret on the war was enormous, enabling Britain and the allies to have access to high-level secret intelligence.

The Myers family were together again, but still under pressure. Geoff seemed to be working all the time. As always, he was deeply conscientious and Margot saw all too little of him. Although she had visited London often when Geoff worked in Fleet Street, she still felt that she was living in an alien environment. News from her family in France was non-existent and she was forced to avoid attempting contact for fear that her Jewish connection would endanger them.

Geoff Myers worked in the famous Hut 3 at the heart of the operation. At first, he was assigned to the Watch, as it was called, which performed the complex task of translating the sometimes incomplete German messages. Many of the dozen or so other intelligence officers there were schoolteachers; all possessed a high skill in German language. As Peter Calvocoressi, who also worked in Hut 3, stresses, the Watch were not just translators but 'they needed to be familiar with the whole intelligence picture in order not to miss a significant clue hidden in the seemingly prosaic message on the scrap of paper before them'.[*]

---

[*]Peter Calvocoressi, *Top Secret Ultra,* Cassell, 1980.

Later, Myers worked in 3A, the air intelligence part of Hut 3, as an air advisor. All of the men there were RAF or USAF officers with experience in the Watch. They operated in pairs, sifting the material that passed through the Watch before transmitting the most important information onwards.

Even within Bletchley itself, Hut 3 was largely isolated. The nature of the work, both in its secrecy and complexity, meant that no air advisor or member of the Watch could talk about their job freely. As Calvocoressi put it, 'One of the consequences of war is to allow the workplace to usurp many of the hours which a more tranquil dispensation allots to domesticity.' Geoff and Margot Myers felt exactly that, but they both understood that the work at Bletchley Park was crucial to the war effort and sacrifices had to be made so that the job could be done with the necessary commitment.

22

The Sergeant Pilot II

Only late in the day did the British fully wake up to the potential strategic significance of Malta. Despite its importance as a
base, in June 1940 the island did not have a single RAF fighter.
For some time the enemy were held at bay by four Gladiator
aircraft and a few anti-aircraft guns. Outnumbered by the
Italian air forces, they clung on until the end of the month
when a few Hurricanes started to trickle in. If Malta had been
lost in that brief, almost undefended period, the consequences
for Britain would have been dire.

By the time Bam arrived on the island, the Hurricanes had
taken over as its main defence, but dockyards and aerodromes
had been under heavy attack from bombers, and Malta was still
extremely vulnerable. Initially, Bam was based at Takali near
Medina in the centre of the island. He found it odd fighting over
a foreign land – at least the Battle of Britain had been fought
over British fields, British houses – but more demoralising was
the lack of leadership from some of those in charge.

On one occasion, Bam and another pilot, Chubby Elliott,
were scrambled at night on the south-west coast of the island
at about twenty thousand feet. It was a pleasant, quiet,

moonlit night. Then Bam noticed that his fuel was low and asked the Takali control tower if he could come down. They said no: there had been an air-raid warning. A little later, Bam repeated the request – and received the same answer. He became desperate but the tower refused to switch on either the big chance lights or the runway lights. Rather than run out of fuel, Bam was forced to land. There was a heavy price to pay if he failed, but he had no choice, so, using the hill as a guide, he slid slowly down in the moonlight and landed safely. Bam wanted to shout his relief at someone, but everyone was in bed.

By early 1941, the enemy had called Me 109s into battle. They had a tremendous numerical advantage and Bam and his colleagues were always struggling, always on the defensive. It became obvious that the RAF were slowly losing the battle; destroyed planes were not replaced while the Luftwaffe continued to throw more 109s into the fray. One victim was Flight Lieutenant MacLachlan, who had led the tragic flight of Hurricanes off HMS *Argus*. He was hit by two 109s and his arm was shot off from the elbow. MacLachlan recalled in his diary: 'My left arm was dripping with blood, and when I tried to raise it, only the top part moved; the rest hung limply by my side.' MacLachlan had become very friendly with Bam, despite their difference in rank. 'Then,' said Bam, 'this stupid officer thing raised its ugly head again. I went to see Mac in hospital. They wouldn't let me in because I was only a sergeant.' By then MacLachlan's arm had been amputated: 'My whole arm [had begun] to smell positively revolting and the pain was almost unbearable . . . By the third morning I was so weak and the pain so unbearable they had little difficulty in taking me up to operating theatre and performing the necessary operation.'

By now Bam had suffered several near misses. He had been shot at on the ground ten times alone. The dwindling supply of serviceable aircraft became intolerable: 'Most of the time we kept the planes airborne just to prevent them being shot at.'

As the situation worsened, twelve Hurricane Mark IIs were flown to Malta from the *Ark Royal*. In early May a scratch Squadron 185 was formed with the Hurricanes and based at Hal Far, an ex-naval base in the south of the island. Cyril Bamberger joined them. By this time, Rommel was active in North Africa and the strategic importance of the island had become undeniable.

185 was carefully divided into pairs of pilots. Bam was one of the most experienced there; nonetheless, even if he had been paired with an officer of only a week or two's experience, that officer would have been the leader in the sky. 'That was crazy, but fortunately they managed to find another sergeant for me to team up with.'

Most of the time, 185 could get only a handful of planes into the air, and the supplies situation was critical. 'We often had only four or five aircraft serviceable,' said Bam. 'We just couldn't seem to get the supplies through. Yet the sky sometimes seemed full of Messerschmitts. It was worse than the Battle of Britain.'

By the first few days of June, 185 Squadron had only two serviceable planes left, then a sergeant was killed in one of them. Bam was pleased when, on 12 June, he was sent home.

Back in Britain, Cyril Bamberger eventually joined the Central Gunnery School at Sutton Bridge, a small village on the north of the Wash. Then he was posted to Northern Ireland, where he worked as a gunnery officer with American pilots who were converting to Spitfires. This marked the beginning of a long love affair with Northern Ireland and its people, which stretched way beyond the war. Nevertheless, Bam was anxious to return to active service. In March 1943, he volunteered to fly in North Africa, and within weeks he had begun sixteen months of intensive and dangerous flying, mainly with 93 Squadron, that was to take him from Algeria through Tunisia, Malta, Sicily, Italy, Egypt, Palestine, Syria, Cyprus and Corsica. By now promoted to flight lieutenant, he had matured into a brave and very skilful pilot.

After a highly intensive period in Sicily providing cover for the Salerno landings, in September 1943 Bam, now stationed at Tusciano in Italy, heard the news that 'Flight Lieutenant C. S. Bamberger has been awarded the Distinguished Flying Cross.' Bam was twenty-five and had shot down five enemy planes and damaged several more. He was cited for his 'courage, determination and devotion to duty'. Letters of congratulation arrived from the Mayor of Port Sunlight, the Chairman of Lever Brothers and Lord Leverhulme himself.

Not long afterwards, however, Bam began to feel a sense of disillusionment; it was sparked off by something very simple. In February 1944, at the Endor Cinema in Haifa, he heard the Palestine Orchestra play Beethoven's 9th Symphony. The beauty of the music and the skill of the musicians disconcerted the newly decorated flight lieutenant and left him with a profound sense of unease. For an evening, Beethoven had transported him into a world so sharply contrasting with the war all around, that 'it shook me up, almost undermined my morale. What was man doing out there, when he could create and play this, I thought.'

Bam's uneasiness lay dormant for a few months while the squadron was re-equipped. Then, in March 1944, he led the squadron – the squadron leader had engine trouble – to Corsica, where they teamed up with the American 12th air force. On the island the squadron lived mostly under canvas at Calenzana, and the rural tranquillity was frequently disturbed by German raids using fragmentation bombs. On the ground Bam's tension was obvious – one day a wild-looking dog came into the tent while he was asleep, reducing him to a state of panic – but, despite intense activity, it never showed in the air. Although he had had a slow start in the Battle of Britain, Bam had recently been almost constantly at the centre of some of the most dangerous activities of the war in the air.

On 25 May 1944, while based at Poretta in Corsica, Bam shot down his sixth enemy plane, a Me 109, during a fighter sweep over Viterbo in Italy. His combat report notes, 'Closing on two hundred yards I fired a long burst as the enemy aircraft was in a climbing turn. The enemy aircraft burst into flames and disintegrated at approx. twelve thousand feet.'

Two particular incidents from this time exemplify Bam's skill and courage as a pilot – though they must have added to his stress. One day in June, as he headed in his Spitfire towards the Italian coast, his fuel tank was hit by a shell. Immediately he opened the hood. The stench of petrol was everywhere. The undercarriage had been badly damaged, but Bam was unable to bail out because his parachute was soaked with petrol from the fountain started by the hit on the tank – as were his clothes. Although he was a hundred and twenty miles from base, Bam crept home, but on arrival he realised that he could not lower the undercarriage. With petrol everywhere, one spark would be enough to ignite the plane, but Bam managed to perform an emergency landing in a Corsican field and throw himself out of the Spitfire to safety. A month later, he was hit on a flight over Pisa. He stayed in the air as the others landed, then lowered his undercarriage, only to discover that one of his wheels had been shot off. As he landed, for a frightening moment the Spitfire seemed almost to stand on its nose, but it toppled back to safety.

Bam was worried about how the strain he was under was affecting his physical well-being, particularly his heart. He went to the American Field Hospital, where he was told there was no physical problem, but that he had been on so many operational sorties that he was 'stretched like a piece of elastic'. About two hundred operational flying hours were average: Cyril Bamberger had flown over four hundred and sixty.

Bam was sent to Naples, and then on leave to Rome, where he tried to convalesce in a monastery. Perhaps the peace of the monastery unsettled him further: 'I could have taken holy orders in no time at all, it was such an escape. I wanted to go back to Corsica, but in the end my nervous system would not stand it.'

He returned to Britain still very tense and was given leave by the Central Medical Board. The doctor suggested he went to a nursing home, but Bam refused because he thought he would go mad. Instead, he asked for limited flying duties and was sent on a course for flying instructors.

In November 1944, Cyril Bamberger was awarded a bar to his DFC. He spent the last months of the war at the gunnery school at Catfoss near Driffield teaching gunnery instructors, pleased that he could continue his distinguished flying career, but relieved finally to be out of the front line. On 3 July 1945 he was presented with his medal at Buckingham Palace. The citation in *Flight* magazine read:

> This officer has flown on numerous sorties against the enemy and has invariably shown himself to be a most efficient and determined pilot. He has destroyed six enemy aircraft and damaged others. On one occasion his aircraft was severely damaged by anti-aircraft fire when 120 miles from base. Flt Lt Bamberger, though his clothing was soaked in petrol, nevertheless flew his aircraft across many miles of sea and made a successful crash landing.

23

THE GUINEA PIG II

Mindful of the problems that they all would face when they left McIndoe's care, a group of patients in Ward 3 decided to form the Guinea Pig Club. The club was not designed to cut McIndoe's army off from the world outside but to offer mutual help and support if that world became too hostile. Geoffrey Page, still in a wheelchair, was one of its founder members, as was Tom Gleave, the Chief Guinea Pig and mainstay of the club. Archibald McIndoe was elected life president. Club membership was restricted to aircrew hurt in action who had been through the hospital at East Grinstead, requiring the skill of the maxillo-facial and plastic surgeons. It now has six hundred members all over the world. In the Guinea Pig spirit, the first treasurer was elected because his legs were in plaster – so he could not run away with the funds.

In the cold winter months, during which Carl Capon and Zig Klein were killed and Bob Doe smashed his face, the prospect of ever flying again seemed an increasingly remote possibility for Geoffrey Page. But, between the agony and tension of the operations which took place at East Grinstead once every six weeks, he was happy. This was partly because he developed a warm friendship with Archibald McIndoe and often spent time at his cottage. Page was McIndoe's favourite; some air-crew thought they resembled father and son, others that the two were more like younger and older brothers. The friendship was cemented by the fact that both men liked McIndoe's surgery sister, Jill Mullins. A tall, blonde woman with a delightful sense of humour, her skill was one of the cornerstones of McIndoe's success. Geoffrey Page fell in love with her and despite his injuries, his affection was reciprocated, until the relationship broke up two years later.

Page was lucky enough to surmount such a hurdle, but for many Guinea Pigs their confidence with women was shattered with their faces. Edward Blacksell, who has dealt with many of the injured pilots' problems, summed it up thus: 'How were they going to cope? How were they going to work? To eat? How were they going to attract a pretty girl? How were they going to manage courtship, making love? One firm offered a number of jobs for liftmen. How can you ask a squadron leader to become a liftman? One famous London store expressed an interest in placing Guinea Pigs in proper employment but, once they'd met one of the Guinea Pigs, they contacted us and said: "We'd love to help. But could you arrange for the men to wear some kind of mask?" '*

The difficulties were in some ways worse for those of McIndoe's men who were married. One married man, who was a little older than many of the others in Ward 3, occupied the next bed to Geoffrey Page. His face was badly burned in a crash in 1940. His eyelids had gone. His legs and feet were burned and his hands were charred stumps. An agonizing ten

*Peter Williams and Ted Harrison, *McIndoe's Army*, Pelham, 1979.

months of being shifted from one French hospital to another had preceded his arrival at East Grinstead. Intelligent and interesting, he brooded deeply, and found it less easy to behave like an undergraduate than the rest of Ward 3. One day, his attractive wife came to see him. Perhaps she had a romantic view of her husband as a wounded hero, for Page noticed in a flash her expression of real horror as she saw the pulped mess of her husband. She literally could not look at him. Next to the bed was a photograph of the handsome young man he had been before the crash. 'That was it,' said Geoffrey Page. 'She just couldn't take it. They were divorced. You can't blame her really. He was a different man from the one she'd married. But it took him a long time to get over it.'

Oddly, McIndoe was more worried about ruined hands than scarred faces. 'Faces – women, bless 'em, don't seem to notice it after a time. Mutilated hands – those are what you never stop noticing: when he lights a cigarette, when he tries to do up his flies, when he holds out his hand to be shaken.' One wife of a Guinea Pig told resettlement officer Edward Blacksell, 'I do love him, I'm sure I do, but there comes a moment when he touches me with those hands and I can't help it – I cringe.'

One evening, after his eleventh operation, Geoffrey Page plucked up the courage to ask Archibald McIndoe the crucial question:

'How long do you think it will be before I can return to flying?'

'You can forget about flying,' replied the surgeon. 'You've done your stuff, now the other silly sods can get on with it.'

Page discussed McIndoe's attitude with Richard Hillary, who was equally determined to fly again. Hillary, for all his superciliousness, was a courageous man who had just finished writing a book about his ordeal called *The Last Enemy*. Together the two injured pilots continued to pester McIndoe until he gave in.

Page was sent to the central medical establishment on the second floor of a rather nondescript building at the Middlesex Hospital, tucked away behind Oxford Street. Here he faced a much more difficult hurdle than his friend McIndoe's reluctance.

The adjutant was mean-faced and cold:

'. . . Third-degree burns, hands, face and legs; gun-shot wound left leg. You should get your bowler hat without any trouble.'

'I've come here to fly, not to be invalided out,' said Page firmly.

'You haven't got a chance,' replied the adjutant.

After a careful medical examination, Page was ushered into the president of the Medical Board's office. 'Apart from your injuries you seem fit enough, Page. What would you like us to do: invalid you out or give you a limited category – fit for ground duties in the UK only?' he asked pleasantly.

The young pilot's heart sank. Steeling himself, he told the air commodore that he wanted to fly, even lying about having had some experience in a friend's plane recently. The air commodore asked Page to grip his hands. Fortunately, the hard work kneading a rubber ball in every spare second had paid off. Page leaped across the desk and gripped the air commodore's hands with every ounce of strength he could summon.

The older man was surprised. 'More strength in those hands than I could imagine possible.'

There was a silence, interrupted only by the scratching of his fountain pen as he wrote. 'I am passing you fit for non-operational single-engine aircraft only. At the end of three months you will be boarded again, and, if you've coped all right, we'll give you an operational category.'

As the words 'Good luck, don't let me down' echoed in his ears, Geoffrey Page danced down the street, tears of joy rolling slowly down his scarred cheeks.

Page was initially posted to No. 3 Anti-aircraft Co-operation Unit housed at a grass airfield on the outskirts of Cardiff. It was a dull place, where pilots spent their time flying along pre-arranged routes so that anti-aircraft personnel could be trained.

On the second day came the crucial test: Page's first flight since that horrific crash two years earlier. As he started to prime the engine, working the pump nine times, he was in considerable pain, feeling faint and sweating profusely. Yet, once he was in the cockpit, his knowledge of flying returned automatically. He belted up the runway and, without thinking of what had happened last time, he lifted the little plane gently into the air.

For a moment, he relaxed, but then as he looked down his mind drifted back: he saw himself bailing out, the flames burning his flesh, and then lying on the ground dead, a charred corpse . . . But the instructor's sharp voice cut through his grisly memories and from that moment he never dwelled on them again. Three months later he was granted an operational flying category and was posted to Martlesham Heath to fly Spitfires.

Life at Martlesham was then a mundane but essential routine of convoy patrols. Compared to the drama of the summer of 1940, it seemed dull, deadly dull – especially if, like Geoffrey Page, you were trying to make up for two lost years in a hospital bed.

Consumed by hatred for the Germans that had grown during his stay in hospital, Page was thirsting for action. He maintained his resolve to shoot down one German for every operation – and he had been under the surgeon's knife eleven times so far. He applied for a posting to North Africa, but after a few weeks the heat of the African sun began to have a deleterious effect on his newly grafted sin, and eventually became too uncomfortable to bear. After just three months he returned to Britain, where he met up with Squadron Leader James MacLachlan, the remarkable pilot who had been friendly with Bam in Malta, but had subsequently lost an arm. Page might still be suffering pain in his hands, but when he saw Mac he was quick to appreciate the fact that he still had both of them.

MacLachlan and Page were in the Air-Fighting Development Unit, a non-operational organisation set up to assess all types of fighter aircraft, a task which the two men found tedious. Among the aircraft they tested were Mustangs, believed to be the fastest low-level fighters in existence. MacLachlan, supported by Page, persuaded the authorities to let them try a two-man low-level daylight raid on enemy territory. Their targets would be the Luftwaffe night-fighter bases south of Paris. The month was June 1943, almost three years since Geoffrey Page had been in an air battle with enemy aircraft.

The two pilots – one with burned hands, the other with only one arm – must have been a bizarre sight as they clambered into their freshly camouflaged green Mustangs. When they were airborne, Page's old fears returned. But alongside him was a one-armed man skilfully threading his way across the fields and rooftops of France. Mac flew with his artificial metal arm clamped onto the throttle. That was all it could be used for, so radio intercommunication was impossible. A map lay on Mac's lap. Flying fast above the treetops while reading a map at the same time is extremely difficult at the best of times but even in his disabled state Mac was a superb pilot.

Suddenly, ten miles ahead and just above them, they spotted three enemy fighters. Page steeled himself, automatically going through the routine he knew so well from 1940. Mac hit a Junkers 88, and Page watched it wheel gently to earth. After shooting down two more fighters, the men turned for home. Almost immediately, they caught sight of another plane. Mac hit it and Page dived with pleasure to finish it off before it splattered on the ground. Mac hit the other Junkers again as it was trying to land, transforming the plane into a ball of flame.

Page was elated. He later wrote:[*]

> I felt my blood boiling with the exultation of our
> recent killings. I gloated in my mind over the hideous
> scenes of violent death we had meted out. Vengeance
> was mine, and I was enjoying every moment of it.
> I felt my years in the hospital had not been in vain .
> . . Youthful innocence had died alongside Luftwaffe
> aircrews that eventful morning over northern France.

The success of the raid was marred, however, by what happened during the two men's second operation. Crossing the French

[*]Geoffrey Page, *Tale of a Guinea Pig,* Pelham, 1981.

coast once again, Mac was hit by machine-gun fire. He must have thought about bailing out and then changed his mind, because his landing speed was too fast and the Mustang smashed into an orchard, its wheels still retracted.

Page hovered above like a bird, circling hopelessly around the wrecked plane for signs of life, then he turned for home. In fact, MacLachlan had survived the crash, but he died in a French hospital three weeks later.

MacLachlan's death hardened Geoffrey Page even more: he meant to make the Germans pay a high price – not only for his own ghastly injuries but also for the death of Mac, the extraordinary pilot with one arm.

After yet another operation at East Grinstead on his crippled hands, Page, still only twenty-four years old, took over his own squadron, 132, which then moved to Ford in Sussex, where preparations for D-Day were in hand. As the momentous day dawned, Page felt weary with war, and alone. Although he was only a couple of years older than his flight commander, the men under his command seemed to him innocent and boyish: in the few years since his crash, in 1940, Page had grown middle-aged.

As he flew over the Channel, Page was deeply moved by the sight of hundreds of ships of every shape and size that bobbed below him. Remembering Dunkirk, he was thrilled to be reminded how much the tide of war had turned in Britain's favour.

Soon after D-Day, 132 was dispatched to a single-strip runway, torn out of a field of wheat by bulldozer, near Bayeux in northern France. The squadron flew daily from dawn until dusk destroying any legitimate targets on the roads behind enemy lines; their guns raked into lorries and armoured cars, causing a bloodbath. For Page, any time spent on the ground was frustrating when there was killing to be done.

One day, thirty miles behind enemy lines, Page ran into a large group of 109s. Suddenly, he found his role reversed: no longer the hunter but the hunted. As he headed for the cover of the treetops, one 109 doggedly pursued the Spitfire. What followed was quite simply, a duel – kill or be killed. Page decided to exploit the superior turning circle of the Spitfire to ease it round into the tail of the German. But he was still ahead of the 109 as the enemy pulled his nose back and fired. Fortunately for Page, the pilot had fired while on the edge of a stall; the plane slowed further with the recoil and slewed into the trees twenty feet below. Another operation on his burned body paid for with a German plane. Geoffrey Page circled slowly, almost smugly, as the smoke curled upwards from the woods below.

The destruction of two more planes, both Focke-Wulf 190s, evened the score: fifteen operations, fifteen enemy aircraft accounted for.

The fifteenth victim was a turning point, the climax of a long individual battle powered by a hatred that was sometimes so cold and all-consuming that it threatened to destroy him:[*]

> Although only twenty-four years old, I felt like an old, old man. It all seemed so purposeless now. I had left hospital with a seething desire to destroy; this ambition seemed shallow and puerile. Nevertheless the deed was now done and where did I go from here? I was

[*] *Tale of a Guinea Pig.*

tired, dead tired, both physically and mentally. The
girlfriends I'd had since leaving East Grinstead hospital
I'd treated as doormats. Hate had filled my heart. Now
hate was spent, leaving a void.

The people Page had killed in ground-strafing, dive-bombing
and air-to-air fights had never appeared human to him. Then,
on one 'cannon test' sortie, he spotted a lone German dispatch rider on the road below: a legitimate military target,
quietly studying a map. Lining up the rider in the sights,
Page caught a final glance of the man as he looked up and
realised what was happening. As the bullets ripped into him,
he threw his left arm up as if to shield his face. This simple,
almost hopeless gesture, haunted Page long afterwards. The
life of a frail human being had been brutally extinguished
in a hail of bullets. Somehow it wasn't the same as killing a
German pilot, whose death mask would have been hidden
by the metal of his aircraft. Suddenly Page's hatred was no
longer directed towards the Germans but towards himself. For several days after the incident, he found it hard
to talk to anyone. As a result of this experience, he became
a better leader, more humane and more concerned for the
private problems of his men, but his efficiency as a pilot was
undiminished.

The Luftwaffe had made a good recovery from their defeat
in northern France and had re-equipped rapidly as their factories turned out a record number of single-engined fighters.
So, as British troops attempted to establish a bridgehead by
securing river crossings over the Neder Rijn, the Waal and
the Maas, their enemy was a long way from being beaten. As
preparations for the Battle of Arnhem began, the First Airborne

Division, dropped too far from their objective, were badly hit. Liaison with the ground was poor, little attention seems to have been paid to the requirements for close support from the RAF, and bad weather meant delays. Page was conscious that paratroopers were being massacred.

In the air, too, the danger was ever-present. The autumn leaves had not yet dropped and the thickly wooded areas near Arnhem provided excellent cover for anti-aircraft personnel.

When the bad weather lifted, Page attacked enemy ground positions close to the bridgehead, and headed for home unaware that his aileron controls had been damaged in the fight. As he came in to land, his aircraft went out of control; it dived into the ground, cartwheeled across the airfield and broke in half.

At least there were no flames – but the aircraft smashed into bits as if it was made of Lego. Page was pulled from the wreckage with his back broken and blood pouring from his cheek. Geoffrey Page's war was finally over.

Three years had passed since Page had first arrived at the Queen Victoria Hospital. Now he was back there again, to become that rare creature: a Guinea Pig twice over.

'My goodness, not you again,' said Sister Hall, almost in despair.

'The trouble with you is that you're just plain clumsy,' laughed McIndoe.

In many ways it was like returning to his old school. And yet the place had changed. It was not just that the impressive new Canadian wing had been built or that the slightly lavatorial decor had been replaced with something more soft and homely; the atmosphere had altered. In the new intake at East

Grinstead, Page could see that the prewar character of the RAF had disappeared for ever. The public schoolboys such as him, the men from the University Air Squadrons, and those who had seen the early Guinea Pigs as an elite club had almost all gone. Their replacements were from a different world. As the public schoolboys had been killed, grammar schoolboys and sergeant pilots had been promoted in their place. Although McIndoe's wards had never been divided along lines of ranks, the dominant mood had been that of an officers' club. That, too, had gone.

Geoffrey Page prepared for yet another operation. Only this time, when he recovered, there wouldn't be much of the war left for him to exact revenge – but by now he didn't want to any more.

24

The Pole II

By early 1941 Joseph Szlagowski's English had improved enormously, and he was on the verge of rising from the rank of sergeant pilot to take a commission: a big leap forward for the apprentice electrician from Poland. In January, he received a visit from the Polish air force liaison officer, who was in the process of tracking down the first group of eighteen Polish pilots to reach England – of which Szlagowski had been one. The officer turned out to be Szlagowski's old flight commander from his days as an instructor at the Officer Cadet Training School in Poland. His former boss was surprised and delighted to see him.

Two weeks later, Szlagowski heard that he was to be posted to 303 Polish Squadron at Northolt. Despite the recent death of his friend Zig, he was privately appalled by the prospect of joining a completely Polish squadron. He had grown to enjoy being part of an English squadron. Even worse, the prospect of that hard-earned commission would recede: 303 Squadron already had their own officers from Poland, and the number of new commissions was small. 'I was also concerned,' said Szlagowski, 'about the class distinction between the officers and the ranks. I knew what the divisions in Polish society meant. It was much more snobbish than I'd found life in the RAF. The officers in Poland believed they were a different class.'

Although he was distressed by the turn of events, Szlagowski had no choice. His former flight commander had clearly been keen to recruit him, particularly as 303 were soon to be converted from Hurricanes to Spitfires: a pilot with Szlagowski's Spitfire experience would be invaluable.

So, on 5 March 1941, Szlagowski flew his own Spitfire from St Eval up to Northolt. Determined to show off his skill to his fellow Poles, he flew ostentatiously between the Northolt hangars, performing loops and rolls, before landing. As he descended from his Spitfire, 303's ordinary pilots were cheering and laughing – some of them were his old friends and acquaintances from before the war. Before a smiling Szlagowski could reach his billet, he was approached by a Polish officer who told him off in no uncertain terms: 'I thought I was being court-martialled for endangering others.' He was taken immediately to see the English commanding officer: 'He wasn't too strong about it. Told me to be careful. It would have been worse punishment if the Poles had dealt it out.' However, the reluctant arrival soon settled in, pleased to be reunited with old friends such as Eugene Szapeonikow, whom he knew from Thorin.

On 13 March, 303 were sent to escort Blenheim bombers heading for a railway junction in Holland and encountered intense fighting. There were several squadrons of Hurricanes and Spitfires on the escort duty, and they soon attracted large numbers of Me 109s. The action split into individual fights and Szlagowski was about to shoot at one 109, when a pilot flying above him, displaying characteristic Polish urgency, suddenly flew down to attack a 109 below his compatriot. On his way down, the pilot's right wing tip hit Szlagowski's left tailplane, cutting it off, smashing the rudder, and causing the plane to go into a spin: 'My rudder looked like a collapsed accordion.' Unable to get out of the spin as his Spitfire inexorably lost height, Szlagowski began to prepare for bailing out. He was up and about to bail, when he looked down and thought of Germans and the prospect of becoming a prisoner, and changed his mind. He crawled back and forced the rudder forward, managing to level the plane out a little. The left tailplane was only just hanging on.

As the plane continued its downward path, albeit more slowly, Szlagowski grimly concentrated on trying to save himself. He slid the Spitfire underneath three Blenheims, only to find himself in the midst of anti-aircraft fire. He then turned his crippled plane sharply left to move away from the Blenheims but, as he did so, he saw an Me 109 which had obviously spotted that the damaged Spitfire would make an easy target. On the RT a voice shouted, 'Look out, look out, he's behind you,' but Szlagowski could do little. Suddenly there was a bang, and the Me 109 splintered into pieces that seemed to drop out of the sky in slow motion, like feathers turned out of a pillow. Szlagowski had been saved by his friend Eugene Szapocznikow. Relieved, he limped slowly home, escorted across the Channel by a Hurricane and a Spitfire. The Hurricane pilot flew alongside and gestured that Szlagowski's tailplane had been hit. Near the coast, the escort checked that he was all right and turned for home.

Szlagowski flew on to Manston, the nearest RAF station. In order to land his plane safely, he could not afford to drop his speed much below 140 mph, lest the nose dropped, causing him to go down like a stone. He virtually hedge-jumped at rapid speed releasing the undercarriage just before hitting the start of the runway. The huge hangars seemed to loom up frighteningly quickly. His tail dropped down, then he swerved left just in front of the hangars and came to a halt. As he stepped out of the Spitfire, Szlagowski was literally shaking. Men were all around him taking photographs of the damage.

He had seen the smashed rudder in his mirror, but when he walked unsteadily around the back of the aircraft he was astonished to see that the tailplane, which was normally attached by more than thirty bolts, was hanging limply on the plane by just three.

Joseph Szlagowski's stay at 303 was relatively short. When the rest of 303 Squadron had been converted on to Spitfires, he was posted again, this time to the No. 1 Gunnery School at Manby, as a prelude to attending an instructor's course at the Central Flying School at Upavon in Wiltshire. Once again, his old flight commander from Poland, knowing Szlagowski's abilities as a teacher of young pilots, was behind the moves.

Just before he left Northolt, another significant event occurred in Szlagowski's life. The Polish pilots would often go dancing at a pub near Ruislip called The Orchard. Handsome and daring, the squadron of young Poles were magnets for the local girls. One night, Szlagowski danced with a pretty seventeen-year-old called Doreen Villiers. Half English and half French, Doreen had come to the dance with an officer, but she left with Szlagowski. It was old-fashioned and romantic love at first sight. From then on Joseph and Doreen were never parted.

In February 1942, Szlagowski was posted to the No. 16 Polish Flying Training School at Newton near Newark in Nottinghamshire: he realised that this was what he had been prepared for ever since the Polish liaison officer had discovered him at Middle Wallop. His logbook records that, as an instructor, he was 'above average'. He enjoyed teaching. There was always tension when the instructor had to decide how much to trust his pupils, but Szlagowski possessed a sure nose for ability and was increasingly given responsibility for the more difficult pupils; he was always proud when they passed or did particularly well.

Later that year, he and Doreen married. At first they lived in East Bridgford, then moved into married quarters at RAF Newton, when his son, Joseph Jnr, was born. As a married man, Szlagowski's perspective on the war altered. Where once he had been desperate to get at the Germans and willing to take risks, now he was aware that, with his new family responsibilities, training younger men to fly into battle was a much safer job, though still important. He spent the rest of the war at Newton, continuing to enjoy his role as an instructor. Doreen gave birth to a daughter, and family life seemed as happy and settled as it could be in the context of wartime.

25

The Flying Ace II

In January 1941, Bob Doe was just about to embark on the slow repair process that Geoffrey Page had begun several months before. Fortunately, his aircraft had not caught alight, so he had avoided the horrors of burning, but his nose had been ripped off, his jaw was impacted and his eye was closed and pushed back into his face.

At the local hospital near Warmwell in Hampshire an army surgeon did what he could to save bits of Doe's skin. Then he stitched the missing nose back on his face, and moved his eye back as near as possible to the correct level.

Next morning, the surgeon told Doe that he was definitely blind in one eye and possibly would be in the other. Remembering that he had briefly seen the sky after the crash, Doe clung to the belief that he would see again.

Eventually, Bob Doe was taken to Park Prewitt Hospital near Basingstoke, where one wing of a mental hospital had been designated for burns cases, and put under the care of Sir Harold Gillies, a distinguished plastic surgeon who had been Archibald McIndoe's early inspiration.

Then began a long round of operations, twenty-seven in all. Doe's face had to be rebuilt almost completely. His upper jaw had been smashed so badly that it rotated; it had to be wired to the bottom jaw. To feed him, the hospital staff removed one of Doe's teeth, allowing him to suck a mixture of brandy, egg and milk through the tube. Occasionally, he would bribe a friend to bring in some very finely minced beef as an alternative.

Gillies decided that the only way to stop Doe's nose flopping about on his face was to add to it a piece of bone taken from inside his hip. Understanding the psychological as well as the physical problems of repairing smashed faces, Gillies visited the ward with a bottle of whisky and a book illustrating various noses. After some of the whisky had been consumed, he went through the book explaining the operation and asking Doe which nose he would prefer.

The surgeon succeeded in holding in Doe's eye with thin strips of what seemed like very fine wire. To the patient's relief, he discovered that he was not blind, but he found that coming to terms with his injuries a terrible ordeal. 'When something happens to your face,' he said, 'you lose yourself. You see your face in the mirror and it's a stranger's. I dreaded every operation. I felt a different person.'

In December 1940, Doe had married a girl he had met in a hotel in Newquay, where she and her mother had moved from Sussex to get away from the Luftwaffe's assault on that corner of England. At the time Bob was twenty-one, and his wife, Sheila, just nineteen. They had been married for less than three weeks when Bob had his horrific accident. Eighteen months later, the marriage was virtually over: 'It was mainly due to my losing my face. My wife could not take the way it now looked. The marriage might have worked without the accident.'

The couple had a baby daughter, but that pushed them further apart, and eventually Sheila left to live with her mother: 'I don't blame her. It was my fault. She had married a handsome, confident young pilot. Now my face looked badly bashed about and, even worse, I was terribly self-conscious. I was unsettled and irritable. I must have been hell to live with.'

After twenty-two operations at Park Prewitt, late in 1941 Doe eventually managed to return to flying Spitfires, this time on convoy protection patrols based at Perranporth in Cornwall. Having made one earlier comeback, he was again able to overcome the pressures and fears that inevitably afflicted him. But he discovered that aerial warfare had changed in his absence. The opportunities to indulge in the individual style of aerial combat that he had pursued so successfully during the Battle of Britain were much less frequent now. His main job after the accident was to fly fighter sweeps over France; the techniques for this were so well-established that there was little room for personal flair.

After a couple of interesting but unexciting spells in 1941 and 1942 commanding squadrons at gunnery schools, first in Cheshire, then in Northumberland, Doe was delighted when, in September 1943, he was posted to Burma. This was his chance to make a fresh start somewhere where his style of flying would be fully utilized. The posting also enabled him to escape from the aftermath of his broken marriage.

Arriving in Bombay in December 1943, Doe was immediately asked to form an Indian Air Force Squadron. His pilots were a mixed bunch – eighteen were Indians straight from training school; the other seven were from England, Australia and Canada – but he thrived on the challenge of welding them into a coherent unit. He concentrated on a highly disciplined form of training, putting particular emphasis on formation flying.

After training in the North West Frontier and at the gunnery school at Armada Road, No. 10 Squadron of the Royal Indian Air Force were dispatched to Chittagong in Burma. Their Hurricanes were equipped with 2 × 250 lb bombs and they spent their time in support work, strafing bridges and ships. This was part of the intensive push to re-take Akyab; an essential strategic prerequisite for an attack on Rangoon over three hundred miles away, because Akyab's airfields were the only place which could provide adequate air cover.

In Burma, Doe was asked to try and relieve the 51st West African Division, who were almost surrounded by the Japanese in the Burmese hinterland. The plan was to land the bomb-carrying Hurricanes into a specially created airstrip in the jungle, so that the 51st could be offered instantaneous cover and support.

Unfortunately, the planners had failed to realise that the makeshift runway concealed an underground river. As the Hurricanes landed, the runway collapsed and seven aircraft crashed into the river. No one was badly hurt, but the West African troops had to retrieve the damaged Hurricanes. Despite a frightening night under shellfire, the remaining seven Hurricanes were next day able to take off and bomb a gap in the jungle big enough to allow the West Africans to move out.

Doe enjoyed the Burma campaign. Shouldering the responsibility for his Indian squadron gave him a sense of purpose, and the style of flying required, which often relied on initiative and quick thinking, kept him contented.

By April 1945, he was back in India, waiting for Spitfires to be re-equipped for the invasion of Rangoon. In the event, he was never needed, and moved on instead to the Army Staff College at Quetta, where he heard that he had been one of only two men awarded an Indian DSO, for his leadership and individual success with his Indian squadron in Burma.

In August of that year, Doe moved to Delhi as chief air force planner. The war in Europe was over, and a few days earlier victory in Japan had been celebrated, but there was still a good deal of useful and interesting work to do. Among other achievements, he organized the aerial contribution to the huge victory celebrations in Delhi – which at that time was the biggest air display ever seen in India.

Doe was then faced with the decision of whether or not to stay in the RAF. Although he sensed that the excitement he had enjoyed in the Battle of Britain and Burma was no longer available, there was no feasible alternative. His last job had been as an office boy at the *News of the World*. Squadron Leader Doe would hardly have been happy to return to that.

26

THE GERMAN II

At the Redmires POW camp in Sheffield, Ulrich Steinhilper finally acknowledged that the German invasion was far from imminent and that he must reconcile himself to captivity for some time to come.

Built as a training camp in the 1914–18 War, Redmires had been used as an isolation hospital for smallpox between the wars. On the outside of the city in a wild, barren spot, the camp had been largely rebuilt to house thousands of prisoners in rows of Nissen huts, surrounded by barbed-wire fences and searchlight towers. From here, the German POWs watched with fascinated horror the bomb attacks on Sheffield, Nottingham and Derby.

Among Steinhilper's fellow prisoners was Albert Waller, his old friend from training school and 3/JG 52, whom he was delighted to see alive. Waller and Steinhilper discussed escaping, but Steinhilper still limped badly and all he could do was offer to provide assistance. During their time at the camp, however, Franz von Werra, the daredevil pilot later to be immortalized as 'the one who got away', led five men to escape through a tunnel believed to be the first one built in England. The tunnel digging had been covered up by the noisy singing of the camp choir. All five men were recaptured, but von Werra had bluffed his way on to an RAF station and the POWs heard that he was arrested while sitting in a Hurricane which he could not start. When his leg was properly mended, Steinhilper resolved, he too would attempt escape.

As the war progressed, Steinhilper, like thousands of other POWs, was evacuated to Canada, where the burden of containing and feeding the enemy could be more easily undertaken. As his train chugged on its slow journey from Sheffield to the Port of Glasgow, the prisoner noticed that all the stations displayed signs saying Guinness. Had the British called all their stations by the same name deliberately to confuse any potential invaders, he wondered.

In mid-Atlantic the eight hundred Germans imprisoned on board the *Duchess of York* tried to work out how to take over the ship – their guards were very seasick – but they could never get their hands on sufficient weapons to overpower the hundreds of airforce-men also aboard, and eventually the *Duchess of York* pulled into Halifax, Nova Scotia, intact. After months in wartime Britain, it was a remarkable sight. There was no blackout and the city was ablaze with light.

Even the train that took the prisoners south was modern and luxurious, with sleepers and couchettes. The food was of a quality and variety they hadn't tasted in a long time. At mealtimes the prisoners were served by civilian waitresses dressed in elegant white uniforms.

But, as always, the talk was of escape. Franz von Werra had told everyone on the way over that he would not be a prisoner in Canada for more than six weeks. Before the train had even reached its destination, von Werra had jumped out of a window while it was passing near the St Lawrence and stolen a boat. He eventually succeeded in reaching the USA, who were not yet at war. Von Werra made it back to Germany, but was killed later in the war while flying over the Channel.

Deeply impressed by his compatriot's bold escape, Steinhilper was determined to emulate him, but his heart sank when they reached Camp Schreiber: it was on the edge of Lake Superior, out in the wilderness. He knew instinctively that he would be a POW for at least a year: 'I couldn't imagine how I would survive the boredom for so long, but slowly and sadly I adjusted myself to the long term. The real problem for me was the uncertainty – when would I ever be able to take my destiny into my own hands again?' The one man who did escape from Schreiber was found dead with a bullet hole in his head; the prisoners were dubious about the explanation that he had been shot by Indians.

In November 1941, the prisoners were moved from Camp Schreiber to Bowmanville, about fifty miles outside Toronto, and much closer to civilisation. Surprisingly comfortable, Bowmanville was housed in a former school for difficult children, inside which was a theatre and a small swimming pool.

After two days there, Steinhilper received his first parcel from his parents. He was delighted to learn that they were alive and well, but the parcel made him so desperate with homesickness that he could not restrain himself, although his leg was still not completely healed: 'I informed my friend Paul that I was fed up and that I was leaving tonight.'

Luckily, the safety fence around the camp had not yet been properly established, and the guards had not yet taken up watch in their towers. With the help of six fellow prisoners, who would create a diversion to attract the guards' attention, Steinhilper planned to prop up the two barbed-wire fences with sticks and slide under them. He had to be quick, because there was only a few seconds when the two guards would both be turned away. The camp was illuminated by searchlights, and there was no doubt that the guards would shoot before asking questions.

As he received a signal that the sentry was looking the other way, Steinhilper propped up the wire. The stick collapsed. He tried again with a spare stick. This time it worked. Under the barbed wire he slipped, and sweat dripped down his forehead as a sentry turned, moved back towards him, completed his circuit, then moved away again. As the German pulled through the first fence, his overcoat caught on the barbs. There was a ripping sound, which, to the escaping prisoner, sounded as if it was echoing around the whole camp, but the sentry did not react.

On his stomach, Steinhilper slid across to the second lot of barbed wire. Once again the stick broke. If his last replacement did not take the strain, he would be caught in no-man's land between the two fences, like a mouse in a trap. Initially, the stick held the weight, then collapsed when he was halfway there. The overcoat was lost for ever, but Steinhilper was through the fence.

The German made a break for it, his shoes causing a terrible racket as he ran. Behind him he heard a voice shout 'Halt!' But it was too late. He was off down the hill, seeking cover in the dark moonless night, away from the constant probings of the Canadian searchlights. The alarm cried out insistently, and the searchlights made sinister patterns on the hillside, but he kept going. Over fences, through a stream, up a hill, he headed for the lights of Bowmanville.

With his overcoat discarded, Steinhilper moved swiftly and easily. When he reached the first houses on the edge of town, he slowed to a walk. He was conspicuous in his tatty air force trousers and grey air force pullover and did not want to arouse suspicion.

The station at Bowmanville was deathly still. Apart from one light, there was no sign of life. The German was aware of the level of public alarm created at this time by POW escapes: he had to move fast before the roads and railways were thick with police. When it became apparent that there was no immediate prospect of a train arriving, he decided that he had to risk escape by road. Visible in the distance was traffic on a highway, presumably heading for Toronto. Very cold now and missing his overcoat, Steinhilper set off in its direction. Doing his best to smarten up his ragged appearance, he positioned himself at a point by the side of the highway where the traffic had to slow down a little.

He attempted to jump onto the back of passing trucks. Eventually he made it onto the running board of one that was moving very slowly. He opened the door and asked for a lift. 'No. There's a war on,' the driver replied. But in his desperation Steinhilper was already in the seat. 'But I am a Norwegian,' he said and closed the door.

For a moment everything was silent. What would the driver do? He looked like a good man. To the German's relief, he continued driving.

Steinhilper knew that he must talk even though he only spoke English with a thick accent. He had recently read in a magazine the story of an escape from Norway. Now he repeated it for the inquisitive driver. On the ride to Toronto, the driver grew to like the man beside him and gave Steinhilper some money for a warm supper and shook his hand. For a moment, the German nearly told him the truth to save his newfound friend trouble and embarrassment when he read the real story in the papers next day, but his common sense overcame his guilt.

The United States had not yet entered the war and Steinhilper's plan was to find a train to take him over the border. It was midnight when he arrived at Union station: 'It was a beauty to me: inviting shops with flowers, chocolate and newspapers laughed at me in a warm glow.' From the noticeboard he worked out that there was probably a night train to Buffalo, just the other side of the border. He could not get through the ticket barrier, so he went around the back of the station and found a way through a fence into the railway yard.

For nearly two hours Steinhilper hovered in the shadows of the yard waiting in vain for the Buffalo train. He eventually settled for the night in the warmth of a passenger carriage in a siding, where he even found an iced-water machine.

By morning, the escaping prisoner was desperate. Very few trains had stopped – most had simply scuttled through the station. In the grip of a kind of madness, he decided to move away from the yard and return to the heart of the station itself. Suddenly he saw a freight train rolling towards him. With a leap born of despair, he almost fell into an open car as the train rattled past, clinging on with his cold fingers. To his relief, as he pulled himself up into the car, which was carpeted with coal dust, the train gathered speed; he hid in the corner, his face occasionally lit up by splashes of light from trains passing on the next track. All too soon, however, the freight train stopped in a factory yard and the engine pulled away, leaving Steinhilper and the freight carriages behind.

It had been a wasted ride. It was late afternoon as he slipped back into the station at Toronto and searched once again for a hiding place, this time inside a stationary America-bound passenger train. He tried the kitchen, the maintenance cupboard, even underneath a bench in the elegant ladies' powder room, but all were too risky. He finally elected to hide in the sandbox underneath the carriage, but waited until the train was slowly pulling out before jumping on board.

As he lay in the darkness beneath the car, his body about four inches from the ground, Steinhilper enjoyed a rather pleasant view and an exciting sensation as the train picked up speed. After so many false starts, he felt happy; he was overwhelmed with an exhilarating sense of freedom, as he watched the rail tracks ahead run away like a glittering snake.

Though underneath the carriage, the German was still visible from certain angles. At one station another train pulled up alongside his and a young couple inside it noticed Steinhilper, who at the time was eating a sausage he had brought with him. To his relief, the couple simply waved at this strange figure clinging to the belly of the train. He waved back with his half-eaten sausage.

The stations were dangerous. At the next one, a pair of shiny shoes stopped by the sandbox. They belonged to a railway official, who told him to get out, but did nothing more.

Steinhilper walked away from the train, not looking back, and headed for the nearby road, where he asked a passerby for directions. Hamilton was forty miles away, he learned: the train had not taken him far from the centre of Toronto.

It was a long walk, but Steinhilper resisted the temptation to spend the truck driver's dinner money and set out for Hamilton. He stumbled on all day and into the night, sometimes nervous, sometimes excited, always cold, hungry and tired. Fourteen hours later he was embraced by the warm air of Hamilton railway station. Yet, as he again waited for the Buffalo train, the German's mind was in turmoil. His nerves felt strained and he began to remember his family. What would they think if he was killed on some hare-brained escape? Perhaps he should give himself up? At least he had got this far. On the other hand, he was only two hours from the border.

His thoughts were interrupted by the arrival of the long-awaited train cloaked in steam and covered in ice. As the engine moved back towards the carriages, having filled up with water, Steinhilper was alongside. On the engine was an iron ladder. A few steps later, he had found a place to hide, between the boiler and the windshield. He had to lie down, but fortunately the pipes in the space were not too hot – just warm enough for some comfort in the freezing air.

As Steinhilper heard the sound of the engine whistle cutting through the thumping of his heart, he once again felt the exhilaration of the journey. Beneath him the engine throbbed as it swiftly left the bright lights of Hamilton behind.

When the train gathered speed, however, the wind cut through the fugitive's clothes and, as he tried to close the openings of his trouser-legs with his socks, he almost fell off. Then bells and sirens blasted in his ears, and black dust from the funnel rained relentlessly on his face. I'm in hell, he thought at that moment.

From his high vantage-point, Steinhilper could see Lake Ontario ahead and knew he was heading in the right direction. Then he saw the station sign NIAGARA FALLS (ONT.). This was the border: anything could happen. The train stopped and men with floodlights inspected beneath the carriages very carefully. Then, just below him, the German was shocked to see the top of the train engineer's blond head as he oiled the wheels. To his relief, the train re-started and rolled slowly across the border. Here is a neutral country, he thought to himself. No war, but freedom. Prison life has ended.

But caution was still essential, he reminded himself, as the train crossed the bridge and he caught a glimpse of the cascading water of Niagara Falls. This was all too much for the German, who released a wild cry of joy, which was carried on the wind and drowned by the noise of the waterfall.

Steinhilper decided to stay in his lair until Buffalo because he felt uncertain about the attitude of the American police. But at the first station over the bridge the engine uncoupled and moved slowly out. After a brief stop, however, it began to roll back into the station, and Steinhilper's worry evaporated: in a minute the engine would be re-coupled and away they would speed to Buffalo. NIAGARA FALLS (N.Y.), read the sign, and the platform was full of Americans. Perhaps, thought Steinhilper, one of them will help me. To his horror, instead of slowing down at the station to pick up its carriages, the engine gathered speed. Even though it was now travelling at almost 40 mph, he had to jump off before the border. He climbed down the iron ladder, but on the front of the engine were five railwaymen: they would be bound to catch him.

A few minutes later the engine sped back across the bridge where not so long before he had let out his whoop of joy: they were back in Canada.

Steinhilper felt defeated, but perhaps, he reasoned, he could hide and try to slip across the border again on another train. He waited until it was quiet before descending from his perch. As he shuffled away, a man suddenly appeared and challenged him. The man gripped him by the arm and within seconds, it seemed, more men were running out of the station, one of them armed with a gun. The German no longer had the energy or the will to run; instead, he tried to pretend that he was an illegal immigrant from the USA.

The story did not wash. After a while, Steinhilper told them that he was an escaped officer. Everyone laughed and he was told to look in the mirror. He laughed too when he saw his face: it was completely black with soot, except for the eyes and teeth.

Next day, an officer and some guards arrived to take the escaper back to Bowmanville. Sitting in the station wagon driving north, Steinhilper was heartbroken to see how far he had come, only to be caught at the last. It all felt like a dream.

* * *

Despite the disappointment of his first escape attempt, it was only a few weeks before Steinhilper tried again. This time, in preparation, he made himself a suit and head-covering mask from the white bed linen. In the deep snow of the Canadian winter, it was the perfect camouflage.

Having cut through the wire at night with stolen wire-cutters, the German once again headed for the railway. Hiding in an empty ice car, he travelled as far as Montreal, where, at Windsor station, he found a suitable train for the onward journey. Underneath the passenger cars were two T-bars. Using scarves and four belts, he strapped himself to the T-bars, so he was neatly secured, with his back just above the track.

As departure time approached, Steinhilper tested his fastenings for a last time. One of his feet slipped out of the scarves and onto the track. A few minutes later, he saw feet standing alongside where he was strapped. Then a torchlight was shone in his face.

The German was handcuffed and taken to the local police station, where he was locked in an iron cage in the centre of the room. He was desperately disappointed. For a second time, he thought, he had been extremely unlucky.

The Canadian police, however, took the opposite view. They told him that he would certainly have been killed travelling through the Appalachian mountains strapped beneath the train. He would either have been hit by thrown-up lumps of ice or he would have simply frozen to death.

Back at Bowmanville, Steinhilper was welcomed by his fellow prisoners as a hero. To the authorities, he was now regarded as the most dangerous man in the camp, and a guard was assigned to watch over him personally virtually all the time. His only free moment was the guard's hour-long lunchbreak.

The next escape plan involved the prisoners' dressing-up in costumes from the theatre to resemble Canadian workmen who were going to paint the perimeter fence. The written official permission to paint the fence was forged. Some of the prisoners thought the plan too bold and the risk of being shot too high. So Steinhilper recruited his old friend Albert Waller, who was frightened at first but finally agreed to join the escape attempt.

On the appointed day, 24 November 1941, the two friends
waited until Steinhilper's personal guard was taking his lunchbreak. Although Waller was so nervous that he dropped his
paint pot, the plan worked beautifully. Using heavy painter's
ladders, the two men made good their escape, and soon reached
the railway station. This time, the escapers climbed onto the
top of a train, but after a very near miss, when they almost hit
a bridge, the two men jumped off.

The snow underfoot was so thick that progress was exceptionally difficult. Uncertain of their bearings, both men were
soon frozen and exhausted. They sheltered from the bitter weather by hiding in a broken hut, where they made some cocoa by
heating up snow in a tin can. Shuddering with cold, they clung
to each other for warmth. Although Waller vomited most of the
first night, they had to go on. For two days they moved slowly
across country, sleeping in barnyards. Waller was able to use his
experience as a farmer's son by milking cows on the way.

The escapers wore woollen skiing masks and hats but this
was scarcely adequate protection against the heavy blizzards
and biting cold. Steinhilper noticed icicles hanging from his
friend's body and wondered how long they would survive.

But by the third night the two men had reached Watertown,
just inside New York State. By travelling across country, they
had negotiated the border without being noticed. As America
was now in the war, it was no longer necessarily safe, so,
after they had worked out the location of the railway station,
the men hid up in another barn. The plan was to head for
New York, where they had addresses of some sympathetic
Americans. Once again, Waller made for the cowshed, where
he saw a bowl of milk. A job saved, he thought, and started to

drink. It was disinfectant. Waller vomited severely again, and Steinhilper thought he was going to die. But, next morning, he was still alive, and the two Luftwaffe pilots decided to walk to New York.

At Watertown itself the men realised that they were lost, so they stopped and asked a man getting out of a black Ford the way to Carthage. Half an hour later they heard a police siren. 'Isn't that interesting,' said Steinhilper. 'Now we can see an American police chase.' Instead, the car screeched to a halt and Patrolman William J. McIntyre levelled his gun at the two escapers. After a brief discussion, the two men were arrested and driven to the police station at gunpoint, where they discovered, to their horror and amazement, that the man in the black car had been a police teletype operator. Only that day he had taken a message regarding the escape. The *Watertown Daily Times* proudly boasted 'Two escaped Nazi airmen captured by City Police'. The story stated that Steinhilper was 'a veteran escaper' and 'the calmer of the two prisoners'. Patrolmen Berrow and McIntyre were pictured filing their report over a caption reading 'Officers who captured Nazis'.

The local police were very pleasant to the Germans, but Steinhilper could not believe his misfortune. Out of the hundred thousand people in Watertown, it seemed incredible to have asked the police teletype operator for directions. Destiny, he thought, is against me.

When he was subsequently moved to Gravenhurst, north of Toronto, a camp for prisoners who had misbehaved, Steinhilper thought his chances of freedom might be at an end. But he soon took part in his fourth escape, this time a group breakout, for which the Germans built a snow tunnel propped up with bread boxes. Steinhilper was far down the list for the escape but he just managed to make it.

At Gravenhurst the nearby railhead was of little use, so Steinhilper had to hitchhike in the freezing cold. He managed to knock on a farmer's house to ask for shelter and was given a bed and a good pancake and maple syrup breakfast. Even when news of his escape came on the radio, the farmer believed the German's story that he was a sailor. But his luck was too good to last. The only way of making progress was to hitchhike, and soon a police car stopped. The policeman took one look at the German's prison-camp boots and said, 'You'll get a ride, but not the way you want.'

Still, Steinhilper was not deterred: he felt it was his duty to liberate himself; even if he was caught, he reasoned, guarding an escaper occupied Allied manpower. For his next attempt, the wire was cut in advance and a diversion created as he slipped through. This time, he heard 'Halt! Halt! Halt!' as he had just negotiated the third fence. He thought he would be shot, but kept on running for the nearby woods. He ran straight into the arms of a Canadian guard.

In the long, golden summer of 1943, Ulrich Steinhilper reflected on his five escape attempts. Apart from his friend von Werra, no German escaper had made it back to his homeland, or even to a neutral country, despite the developing sophistication of escape methods.

That summer had seen the first exchange of prisoners between Britain and Germany. Ten Germans from Gravenhurst who were ill were to be sent home via Switzerland. The exchange gave Steinhilper, who had grown increasingly desperate after so many failures, an idea. As autumn gave way to the icy blast of winter, his chance came.

In the hope of persuading the exchange commission to put him on their list, he decided to feign serious mental illness. One night, he shoved his right arm through the hall window. Although his arm was already bleeding, he took a shard of glass and slashed himself from temple to chin. Then he jumped out of the window and, with the warm blood running down his face, neck and chest, ran off into the snow.

Most of the camp were astonished when they heard the story. Steinhilper was so tough, so single-minded; how could he, of all people, possibly have cracked? Only a few close friends understood what was going on. For the six weeks that followed, the prisoner almost starved himself, losing fifteen pounds in an effort to take on the physical appearance of a man who was going mad. Then, in the first-floor lecture room one day, he screamed out, 'I've had enough . . .' and threw himself through the window, smashing against the mesh wire of the fence. He lay on the ground, crying out loudly.

In the sick bay, the German doctor, who was in on the plan, was stunned by Steinhilper's convincing act, and told him that he was lucky to have survived the jump. The doctor was informed that his patient was to be moved into a psychiatric hospital and would probably be exchanged in four weeks' time. Steinhilper was delighted, but the doctor warned him that, however tough he was, it would be dangerous to keep up his crazed behaviour for longer than a month.

On arrival at the asylum his confidence faltered, for he saw there faces of such wretched humanity – some curious, some hostile – that he found his act of deception among these people who were genuinely ill hard to maintain. But after a night in a locked room, his resolve had strengthened again.

At breakfast the next day he feigned an attack, smashing the breakfast tray into the nurse's face. As a result, he was set upon and hit by several men in white coats, and tied to a bed so he could cause no more trouble.

For four weeks Steinhilper kept up the pattern of two fits each week. Survival in the asylum required greater tenacity and courage than escaping by train or road. In his previous escape attempts there had been danger and excitement; this time he was pushing himself to the edge of his mental limit. It would be all too easy to go over that edge.

Then the prisoner was given a date for his exchange but the day before it was due to take place the list was changed and his name swapped. In a black depression, he took some sleeping tablets and was very ill.

The haunted faces of the insane, the sounds of screeching in the night, the shuffling shapes of the other inmates, all made Steinhilper feel that he had landed in hell. As he sensed himself in danger of slipping into insanity, he set himself difficult sums, or recited multiplication tables, or wrote poems. But after five months of playing a madman he had had enough. Either, he reasoned, he would die in the hell-hole or, if he was returned home, he would be such a mental and physical wreck that he would be incapable of re-establishing ordinary life. So he began deliberately to exhibit signs of sanity and told the Canadian hospital doctor that he wanted to return to the camp. The doctor decided that there was hope after all for Steinhilper and that it would be a real medical achievement if he could restore his sanity completely; he was too interesting a psychiatric case to let go. A week later, three merchant sailors with minor ailments were repatriated. Steinhilper, top of the exchange list until a few days earlier, was left in the lunatic asylum.

The German built up strength again, still hoping for repatriation, but eventually the news broke that no more prisoners would be exchanged because the Allied troops had blocked all routes into neutral Switzerland. By now it was Spring 1945 and the war in Europe was almost over. When the prisoner realised that if he was repatriated he would probably be just in time to be captured by the Russians, he gave up hope. He had finally lost the struggle to control his own destiny, a struggle that had preoccupied him since 27 October 1940, when he had landed in the marshes at Chislet.

It wasn't until May 1945, when it was announced that the Germans had capitulated, that Steinhilper started to live again, acting like a complete human being for the first time since his arrival in the psychiatric hospital. The hospital were delighted with the progress he had made over his fifteen months as a patient, and never suspected that his serious illness had been faked. They thought that their care and attention had brought about a remarkable cure.

On 21 July 1945, Steinhilper was returned to a POW camp in Grande Ligne, Quebec. His life in the hospital had left him physically weak and mentally uncertain, but at Grande Ligne he regained strength. Here, for the first time, the prisoners learned from films the full horror of what had happened in the Nazi concentration camps. The rumours they had heard while incarcerated, but had not wanted to believe, were sickeningly confirmed.

It was nearly a year later before the POWs were put on a boat in Nova Scotia and returned to England, where Steinhilper was sent to another prison camp in Sheffield and worked on the potato harvest for two months. The weather was bitter but the pleasure of doing some productive work again more than compensated for cold fingers.

Then the prisoners were taken by ferry to Hamburg. Back on German soil after so long, Steinhilper felt alternately deep sadness and great pleasure: the city had been devastated by bombs and arriving in Germany as a prisoner was ignominious; but it was his homeland.

On a train south the prisoners were informed that they were being taken to a camp called Dachau. During the journey the American guards allowed Steinhilper to ask a stationmaster to telephone his parents and tell them what was happening. Just outside Dachau, the train came to a halt beside several others. Suddenly the voice of a man running along outside could be heard crying, 'Where is Steinhilper? Where is he?' It was his father. The two fell into each other's arms.

But Steinhilper was forced to stay with the other POWs in Dachau for three weeks. The men knew what evils had been perpetrated in the camp; it was a disturbing place to be and some wondered if they would ever get out.

On 6 December 1946 Ulrich Steinhilper was allowed home to Ludwigsburg. Unable to contact his parents in advance, he arrived at the station at 11.00 p.m. and had to walk the final four miles. At midnight he knocked on the door of his house for the first time in six years. He had left in 1940 at the age of twenty-two; now he was twenty-eight. But he was home.

27

End of an Era

As the excitement of the war in Europe subsided, the fighter pilots of the RAF began to return to the relatively mundane peacetime world. Terry Hunt, reunited with her injured husband David from 257 Squadron, summed up the mood of the time:

> It was four o'clock in the morning in Cardiganshire,
> VE Day. The victory beacons were going out.
> I thought of those who weren't there to share that
> moment, and then I realised that the golden years had
> gone, they had dried out with that fire.[*]

Those who had survived the war were irrevocably changed; they had seen great horror and at the same time felt great elation. Many had interrupted their university education, and now, six years later, it seemed impossible to go back; for others, embryonic careers had been rudely interrupted. Men who had been propelled by war up through the rigid British class system – in 1939 sergeant pilots, six years later squadron leaders or even wing commanders – were now confused about their exact position within the social hierarchy.

[*]Esther Terry Wright, *Pilot's Wife's Tale,* Bodley Head, 1942.

Many fighter pilots were able to readapt successfully – the qualities of character that saw them through the war stood them in good stead in civilian life – but a few found it impossible. One distinguished Battle of Britain pilot, widely recognized as a man of enormous moral courage, became an alcoholic – a lonely, rather incoherent old man living in a tiny flat.

Before 1939, the dreams of Cyril Bamberger had not stretched much beyond a lifetime at Lever Brothers. Now he had travelled widely, won a DFC and bar, and made decisions that affected the life of others, he saw that the rigid class structure which had characterised the early war years of the RAF was a nonsense. Men like Bam had been forced into responsible positions because so many leaders had been killed in the Battle of Britain, and they had shown that eligibility for leadership was not simply determined by birth. Yet, when the war finished, even heroes with DFCs and bars discovered that many of the old prewar standards and attitudes came back into operation. Life outside the RAF began to seem attractive, but Bam felt ill-equipped for anything except flying and wanted to stay in. The best he could hope for was a short-service commission, for which other former sergeant pilots had already been turned down. With Bam's lack of education, his chances of acceptance seemed slim, so he decided to opt out of the RAF rather than risk the ignominy of rejection.

When he returned to work at Lever Brothers, Bam was given a marvellous welcome, but the management failed to understand how the war had changed him. They wanted him to resume his apprenticeship where he had left off six years previously. When he did not agree, the firm gave the returned hero a job as a clerk in the sales department. One minute Bam had been tearing through the skies in a modern war-machine, the next he was sitting at a desk in a huge room with about two hundred other people, charged with responsibility for four representatives and the awesome task of ticking off sales on a series of white cards. Despite the valiant efforts of the personnel department, Bam came to the conclusion that he had had enough.

Bam's next job was as a management trainee for a brewery firm in Liverpool, but he resigned on principle when the manager sacked two employees unjustly. He then took a job he did not enjoy much, as a bottling store manager in Wrexham. His one escape was flying. In 1947 he returned to Hooton Park and rejoined 610 Auxiliary Squadron where his career had begun eleven years before. He flew every weekend and was eventually made commanding officer of the squadron of which he had once been the humblest member.

When the Korean Crisis blew up, Bam – to his delight – was called up again, and managed, in February 1951 to earn himself a permanent commission, initially with 610 Squadron. In May 1952, he moved to an intelligence unit, where he assessed the battle order and strike capabilities of the Chinese and the Koreans. It was a fascinating job, working with some of the best minds in the RAF.

In September 1954, when Bam was thirty-nine, he was given an all-weather course on Meteors by the Ministry of Defence, which included several hours in a decompression chamber. Inside the chamber Bam's wrists hurt and he had severe pains in his head; he was rushed out of the chamber and for a short time was on the critical list. Although he returned to fly helicopters, that was the end of a disappointed Cyril Bamberger's career as a pilot of jet planes.

After a spell at photo-reconnaissance and then testing helicopters, Bam retired from the RAF. He went on to become managing director of a small company he started in 1954 making packaging materials, before retiring from business to run an antique shop in Hampshire, becoming an expert in English porcelain.

Each year, on the nearest Sunday to 15 September – officially designated Battle of Britain day – a service of commemoration is held at Westminster Abbey. Twice Cyril Bamberger was chosen for the escort party – he was very proud to take part in this poignant occasion.

Bam had a restless, driving energy and took tranquillizers to quell his nerves and hyperactivity. The stretched elastic referred to by the doctor at the end of his service career became a little more slack, but the tension he still struggled against was a direct consequence of his wartime experience.

As a result of the love he had developed for Northern Ireland – where, during his six months there in 1942, he was almost adopted by a Protestant family, even though he was a Catholic – Bam spent much of the seventies on a one-man peace mission to the province, trying to promote greater understanding. He hoped that, as a Catholic who had very close contacts with the Protestant community, he might be able to see the problem through the eyes of both sides. He visited Belfast regularly, talking to church and community leaders. He even showed Mother Theresa around Ballymurphy and the other Catholic areas of Belfast during her visit to the province. He wrote and talked to political groups of both religions, regularly suggesting creative ways forward for Northern Ireland.

Merlyn Rees, then the Minister for Northern Ireland, invited Bam to lunch to discuss his proposals.

In spare moments between running his business, visiting his family and travelling to Belfast, Bam spent a great deal of time raising money for charity, particularly for Mother Theresa. He did voluntary social work for the Society of St Vincent and St Paul, and he was chairman of the League of Friends of Lord Mayor Trelaor School for the physically handicapped. After the war, Cyril Bamberger devoted himself to caring for others and to the cause of peace.

Bob Doe returned to England in 1946. As the ship on which he was sailing slid past the Isle of Wight he was astonished to be reminded how green his homeland was. Only then did he realise how much he had missed it during his four-year absence.

Doe joined the staff at the School of Combined Operations in Barnstaple, where he decided that the anti-climax of postwar service life was more than compensated for by the pleasures of peacetime. He enjoyed the Devon countryside and took up cricket again. In 1948, before moving to the HQ of Reserve Command, he married for the second time.

By 1950, Doe was back in action. He was moved to Egypt where he flew jets for the first time and was involved in a spectacular assault on Khartoum. Three years later he returned to Britain to command a squadron at the Central Gunnery School on Humberside. He saw out his distinguished service career by alternating between spells of teaching gunnery and sitting on planning units at the Ministry of Defence.

In 1966 Bob Doe retired from the RAF with the rank of Wing Commander. He could have remained within the service but he had become very unhappy in one particular job and many serious rows with his boss had convinced him that retirement would be wise. After twenty-nine years in the air force, it could have been a difficult wrench, but, as usual, Doe took things in his stride and became a director of an old family car firm in Tunbridge Wells. At 8.00 a.m. every morning, the third highest-ranked RAF scorer in the Battle of Britain was out on the forecourt serving petrol.

After his remarkable wartime career, such an occupation might seem incongruous, but Bob Doe was happy with it. Occasionally, he would attend service reunions but did not enjoy the evenings: he did not wish to indulge in living in the past. A German pilot whom he shot down in the Battle of Britain asked to meet him; but Doe refused. 'What's done is done. I'd have nothing to say to him. I don't want to look back, but if I had to shoot him down again to protect my country or my family, I would.'

Bob Doe could not escape from the effects of the Battle of Britain. On cold mornings at the garage he had trouble seeing for the first half an hour, because his tear ducts were destroyed in the accident. He could not wear boots because his Achilles tendon still hurt from the damage it suffered forty-five years prior. His arm often caused great pain where the muscles had insufficient room to grow. When his damaged eye was giving severe trouble one Saturday morning, he rang up East Grinstead to see if they could help. By 8.30 that evening, a consultant surgeon was operating on him. The anaesthetist remembered him: 'Good God. I gave you the anaesthetic when Gillies gave you your nose.' They expertly inserted modern thread to hold the eye socket in place more firmly, and less than twenty-four hours later Doe was home.

The Battle of Britain changed Bob Doe's life for ever in other ways. He had gone into it as a timid Fleet Street office boy who saw himself as a nobody. The Battle of Britain gave him a chance to achieve something, to prove to himself and to everyone else that he could be mature and responsible – in short, it gave him the chance to become a somebody.

The end of the war found the Polish pilots with no jobs to go back to, no housing of their own, no British educational qualifications. But Joseph Szlagowski was determined to continue flying, and he successfully applied to join Air Canada. His family prepared to pack up and depart, but at the last minute Doreen, who was still only twenty-one, changed her mind: she did not want to leave her home country. Szlagowski told Air Canada that he could not take the job. Even if he had wanted to, it now seemed too late for him to remain in the RAF, so he decided to move to Doreen's home town of London. By the time he was demobbed in November 1946, Szlagowski had flown for six years in Poland and eight in England.

He started work on the shop floor at the Wilkinson's Sword razorblade factory in Acton, eventually rising to the position of foreman, but at first he found it difficult to settle after the excitement of flying fighter aircraft.

Such problems were common among Polish fighter pilots. The war was over and the hated Germans defeated, but the Poles were caught between two nations. Some went back to Poland, only to be harshly treated by the Russians. A number were executed. Others, such as Szlagowski, liked England, had married English girls and put down roots. Yet, during the war, they had had an identity, a uniform; they had been part of a group, and a successful group at that. Outside that circle, and with so many other young men returning from war, they became in some ways aliens again. Several were quite shocked by the treatment they received. Jean Zumbach, a tough and successful pilot who had shot down thirteen German planes, wanted to stay in England, but when it was discovered that he was in fact a Swiss citizen, he was refused permission. Zumbach protested that he had been in England since 1940 and had many friends he wanted to say goodbye to, but he was told that he had to leave within a few days. Zumbach handed back all his air force issue belongings, such as his gun and parachute, and headed for France, where he was made welcome. In Zumbach's words, the British authorities seemed to be saying, 'The negro did his job, the negro can go – and I was upset.'

He was not alone. George Palusinski, also from 303 Squadron, felt that 'the British wanted to keep all the glory for themselves. We were made to feel very unwelcome.' He claimed that signs were posted on factories saying: POLES, NO NEED TO APPLY. In Poland he had been his own boss, but in Britain his identity card stated that he could not be self-employed. For two years he was unemployed, until the self-employment rule was relaxed and he took up pig farming.

Another Pole to suffer in this way was Gandy Drobinski, a squadron leader with a distinguished war record, including a string of medals. After the war, he stayed in the services for a couple of years at Uxbridge, and then at Tangmere, but, like so many Battle of Britain pilots, he was bored by the routine training of peacetime. He had been commanding officer of 303 Squadron so, when the RAF offered him a role as a flight lieutenant in 1948, he asked for his discharge papers. Drobinski went to the Aliens Office in Piccadilly and stated that he wanted to become a British subject. The residency requirement was five years and, as he had been in Britain for eight years, he felt confident. He explained how he had arrived on 27 January 1940 – only to be told that he had landed without permission and that the eight years he had spent in the RAF did not count towards any residential qualification: 'I was speechless. I was very, very disappointed after all this to be treated like a foe rather than friend.'

Squadron Leader Drobinski was sent to a Nissen-hutted Polish resettlement camp near Ipswich to be successfully integrated into the British way of life. There he found over two hundred Poles cooped up together feeling downhearted and bitter. They saw what was happening in Poland and felt that the Polish people had been let down.

But men such as Gandy Drobinski and Joseph Szlagowski refused to be permanently affected by bitterness. The official indifference shown them in the immediate postwar period might have been shameful, but the young men exiled from their own land had to concentrate on building a new life in England.

In 1956, Wilkinson's Sword opened a razorblade factory in Poland. Joseph Szlagowski was the obvious person to send to instruct the Polish workers how to operate the machinery. He was thrilled to be back in Koscierzyna, and to see his brothers and sisters again. Yet he was filled with sadness too: food and clothing were difficult to find and the country seemed overwhelmed by tragedy. He left his family with cases full of Marks and Spencer's clothing and returned to England deeply concerned about his suffering homeland.

At seventy-one, Szlagowski had been a widower for several years and lived with his daughter in a council flat on the ninth floor of a tower block in Fulham. As a pensioner, money was tight so he could not always afford to go to the Polish Air Force Association reunion. In 1984, an old friend from Poland was coming up from Cardiff so he scraped the money together. Before the reunion, he laid his wreath with veterans of 303 at the Polish War Memorial, with its never-ending list of the deceased on the back, which stands gaunt on the edge of the busy A40. Guest of honour on this occasion was the frail Count Krystni, then in his nineties, who was the President of the Polish government-in-exile. Afterwards, the Polish Cultural centre in Hammersmith provided a lunch which was well attended by Battle of Britain veterans – Drobinski, Palusinski, even, sometimes, Jean Zumbach from France. Plenty of wine and red cabbage was consumed. In an emotional moment, the room stood as one to sing the Polish anthem.

Szlagowski, who still regarded himself as a Pole, but chose not to spend his time socializing with other Poles, enjoyed the event, particularly as he met there a man who had recently visited his home town of Koscierzyna. Yet the day always had an air of sadness. It is not just that thoughts were dominated by the memories of dead colleagues. So many of the guests were men caught between two worlds. Their careers over, their families grown up, their need for England had diminished. They loved England but their roots were in Poland and they sometimes ached for their homeland.

The reunion was the high spot of Joseph Szlagowski's year. For the rest of the time, he led a quiet life, walking everywhere to keep fit and to escape from his flat. In the summer he walked down to the river, and sat on the bank. In winter he stuck to shopping centres to keep warm and save on his heating bill. When at home, he sat on the corner of the settee by the window and watched the planes flying in and out of Heathrow: 'I can't stop watching them day and night. When Concorde comes over it tickles my heart. Sometimes I sit here and imagine that it's the Battle of Britain all over again. That I'm up there dog-fighting. It's lovely.'

Geoffrey Page was sorry to see the war come to an end: 'I know I was badly burned up, but I was sad when it was all over. I was lucky, I didn't suffer any personal loss, like so many families, but it gave us young men a sense of purpose and brought the best out in so many people.'

Page applied for a service commission. As a Cranwell graduate, he had much more reason to feel optimistic about success than Cyril Bamberger had – and his optimism proved justified. After a pleasant interlude as a test pilot, the RAF put him behind a desk: he was appointed personal assistant to the senior RAF officer on the Military Staff Commission to the newly formed United Nations in New York. Despite Air Chief Marshal Sir Guy Garrod's patience, Page hated the new job: 'I wasn't cut out for paperwork. It was extremely boring. I spent most of my time putting out place names at dinner parties.'

The closest Page came to flying in this job was to make paper aeroplanes and throw them out of his office window on the sixty-fourth floor. There was, however, one consolation. On an earlier lecture tour he had become friendly with several members of the acting fraternity in Los Angeles, particularly English actor Nigel Bruce and his wife. His time in New York gave Wing Commander Page a chance to look up his old friends. On his previous stay with them, their daughter Pauline had been in Canada; now she was back, and her tall, dark-haired good looks stunned the British pilot. Nigel Bruce had joked about Geoffrey coming back to marry their daughter. Little had he known that his wish would come true.

After a year in New York, Page approached Sir Guy Garrod and told him that he wanted to fly again. The Air Chief Marshal was understanding and eventually it was arranged that Wing Commander Page could return to England to take over a fighter squadron.

With his new wife from California, Geoffrey Page was posted to RAF Linton-on-Ouse in the flat Yorkshire countryside. Although he had returned to his first love, flying, RAF Fighter Command in peacetime seemed an anti-climax. Page stayed at Linton for over two years, but gradually disillusionment set in. Morale at the base was low, largely because of serious teething problems with Hornet fighters: during training, four of the young pilots of the already half-strength squadron were killed. By now, Geoffrey and Pauline had been happily married for two years, and were expecting their first child. As Pauline saw the pilots being killed one by one, she increasingly wondered whether her husband would be next. Sensitive to his wife's feelings, and realising that, after his stint at Linton, he would certainly be sent back to an administrative job, Page decided to leave the force he had loved so much.

In 1950, Page emigrated to California, where he had a personal contact in the chairman of the giant American aviation company Lockheed – so there was at least a chance of returning to test flying.

The Californian sunshine and the new baby seemed to mark the beginning of a fresh, more optimistic, era for Geoffrey Page. Lockheed's chairman was charming and helpful. He was keen to offer this extraordinary Englishman a job, but, he said, there were hundreds of American pilots from the last war looking for work, and he just could not justify giving the job to a foreigner.

As Page walked out into the California sun after the interview, he was overcome with disappointment. He had given up his flying career in England and now the first door he had tried in California had, however politely, been shut in his face. 'From the moment I walked out of Lockheed's,' he says, 'I suppose I've been out of place. I've been happy. I have a wonderful family and many friends, but I've never quite found my niche, never quite found anything I enjoyed as much as flying Hurricanes, or working as a test pilot.'

In desperation, he took a manual job at Technicolor Laboratories, pushing around trolleys of film cans in the bowels of the building. After three and a half years, he had risen to the dizzy heights of a printer. 'I loathed every minute of it,' he says without a trace of bitterness. 'With a family to keep, I just couldn't afford to be without a job – but I hadn't cheated death twice and recovered from those horrible injuries just to end up as a manual labourer.'

After years of trying to find a better job, Page eventually passed a correspondence course in stockbroking, and joined a big firm in Los Angeles. He preferred stockbroking to life as a factory hand, but it was not the ex-fighter pilot's natural territory. Once again, it was Sir Archibald McIndoe who came to the rescue.

McIndoe came to California and immediately looked up the patient who he had been almost a father to. McIndoe recognised Page's misery and, a month after his departure, Page received a letter saying, 'Come back to England and make up your mind.' Enclosed was an air ticket. 'It was not only generous, but sensitive,' says Page. 'It was absolutely typical of the man.'

In London, courtesy of McIndoe, Geoffrey Page found a job selling commercial jets for Vickers Armstrong, which later became the British Aircraft Corporation. He was delighted to be back in the aviation world again – even if he wasn't flying. He was eventually promoted to sales manager for Europe and Africa. But the pay was low and, with two small sons at prep school, money was tight. In addition, the English winters were no good for his war wounds: the cold and damp made his hands ache severely. So Page persuaded the BAC to give him the agency for selling in Switzerland, and the family moved to Geneva, where the winters were cold but dry. The agency ran successfully for three years – until the development of the Anglo-French Concorde, when either an English or a French agent were required in Switzerland – in a French-speaking country, Page was obviously going to be second choice.

Forty-five years after the Battle of Britain, Geoffrey Page has various business ventures, including an aviation consultancy for a firm of Lloyds underwriters. He led a comfortable life in Geneva for sixteen years, but always felt out of place there. He and Pauline eventually moved back to England: 'We've been so long away we've rather missed out on housing, and the cold and damp will be bad on my hands, but it's home.'

Coming home enabled Page to become more involved in the club he helped found: the Guinea Pigs. Every autumn they would hold their annual reunion weekend in a modern, impersonal hotel near Gatwick airport. The reunion traditionally became known as the Lost Weekend, because of the amount of alcohol consumed.

Geoffrey Page, with his hands that never straightened and the bright scar down his face, was one of the least damaged among them. Some faces, completely rebuilt, were a mass of colour and tissue. One man held his drink with fingerless stumps. Another smoked with his pipe wedged in his iron-hooked hand. A couple who were blinded in the war were led through to the dining room on the arms of others.

Everyone seemed delighted to meet again; the common bond was still strong. The after-dinner jokes were received with roaring approval, and the assembled company enjoyed themselves.

The main guest was a senior member of the RAF hierarchy. To an outsider, his gung-ho speech sounded resoundingly inappropriate in a room littered with the human wreckage of war, but the Guinea Pigs scarcely seemed to notice – or didn't make it obvious if they did.

At the end of Tom Gleave's update on the Guinea Pig year, he drew particular attention to three guests in the body of the hall, men badly injured in the Falklands War. One was blind, another was crippled; both were helped to their feet. The third had both his legs blown off and sat still. All three young men were visibly touched by the warm applause.

The presence of Falklands victims drew attention to the dilemma facing the Guinea Pigs: the club was quite literally dying. Some members wanted to keep it as an exclusive group. Others, such as Geoffrey Page, one of the founders, wanted the Club to welcome in new people who may have had no connection with East Grinstead.

The poignant climax of the evening was the singing of the Guinea Pig anthem to the tune of 'The Church's One Foundation'. This is a moment when shared memories and self-deprecating humour welded together Guinea Pigs from far and wide:

'We are McIndoe's Army,
We are his Guinea Pigs,
With dermatomes and pediciles
Glass eyes, false teeth and wigs
And when we get our discharge
We'll start with all our might
"Per ardua ad astra",
We'd rather drink than fight.
'John Hunter runs the gas works,
Ross Tilley wields the knife
And if they are not careful
They'll have your ruddy life.
So Guinea Pigs, stand ready
For all your surgeon's calls;
And if their hands aren't steady,
They whip off both your [mock pause] ears.'
etc.

Yet, between the dinner and cocktail parties, the problems of the Guinea Pigs were not forgotten. Geoffrey Page had been having bad pains in his damaged hands. There appeared to be something wrong with the nerves. In a consulting room he talked to a consultant surgeon, who examined the hand: 'I'm afraid you'll need an operation. I'll do it here at East Grinstead. How many operations is that since the crash?' Page paused for a moment: 'Thirty-seven, I think, and I'm not looking for a half-century.'

The thirty-seventh operation was not Page's last. He still needed daily painkillers, particularly for the back he broke at Arnhem – 'but that's the price you pay for bashing about your body when you're young. Some of my friends never got that chance.'

Although he was once infected with hatred and a thirst for killing the Germans, Page finally had friends who were Luftwaffe pilots. 'My enemy isn't the Germans any more,' he said, 'It's small boys on trains and buses who say, "Look at that man's face, Mum."'

As an intelligence officer, Geoff Myers had lived in a world of secrets and confidential information for seven years. Back in civilian life he found it hard to re-adjust to the constant journalistic pressure to publish. As an air advisor, his job was to select, assess and weigh up accurately the importance of intelligence material. In newspapers, the impetus was the opposite: to make stories bigger than they really were. This was not the only reason that Myers found his new life on the *Daily Telegraph* in Paris unsatisfactory, for – like Cyril Bamberger at Lever Brothers – he had been taken back on at the same level as he had left the paper in 1939.

Though Paris had changed greatly, Margot was delighted to be in reach of her mother at Beaurepaire, but Geoff was depressed. He found it almost impossible to shake off the chains of obsessive secrecy. He had also lost many of his journalistic contacts, and some of his prewar colleagues had overtaken him as a result of successful careers as war correspondents.

Yet Geoff Myers was as determined and punctilious as ever, and he worked hard and diligently for the *Daily Telegraph*. When the *Sunday Telegraph* started, he was promoted to their number one correspondent; although he was never as happy with features as he had been with the more precise requirements of daily news, he spent virtually all his working life with the *Telegraph* group.

Six years before retirement, Myers was offered the job of correspondent at the United Nations in New York. It was an exciting and dramatic change, and he worked happily there until the age of sixty-five.

I knew Geoff Myers only in retirement. It was sometimes hard to reconcile the picture of the rather severe and serious intelligence officer that emerged from his own notebooks with the lively and amusing retired journalist. Small and darting, with wavy grey hair and twinkling eyes, Myers seemed gentle and warm-hearted. He was a man who cared deeply about other people and the world. In retirement he was always on the move, visiting his children, or looking after his grandchildren, while Margot gave music lessons in their flat in Paris.

The last time I saw him was for lunch in a small French restaurant in 1984, just around the corner from his son's flat in Notting Hill Gate. He had a huge suitcase with him, and was on his way to visit his daughter in the USA before returning to France, where he was to look after his elderly mother-in-law at Beaurepaire during the winter. It was typical of the careful and conscientious nature of the man that he had spent that morning at the Public Records Office in Kew reading afresh the 257 Squadron records to ensure that all the information he gave me was accurate. During a warm, friendly lunch he confided one or two remarkable pieces of information about the war that he had told no one else. They chiefly concerned the exploits of a couple of famous pilots. 'Someone needs to know about these things,' he kept insisting. He also gave me permission to publish his letters.

I should have realised what was happening. Just before our lunch, Geoff Myers had been told he had cancer and had only a year to live. It was typical of Geoff's dignity and courage that he never told me he was ill, and that throughout our lunch he was laughing and cheerful.

Geoff Myers never had the final year he was promised. Six weeks after our lunch, he died in France.

Back in Germany, after his six years as a POW, Ulrich Steinhilper, desiring to make up for lost time, rushed into a marriage which turned out unhappily. His working life was more successful, however, and he finally retired as a senior executive with IBM.

Forty-five years after the Battle of Britain, Steinhilper still looked as fit as he must have been when he was a famous escaper. He lived contentedly in a flat in Stuttgart with his second wife. Despite his Battle of Britain limp, he was still physically active in his later life, walking, cycling and even water-skiing.

In the early 1980's Steinhilper was contacted by British aviation enthusiasts. He was astonished to hear that, forty years after his crash, the Kent Battle of Britain Museum recovery team had successfully reclaimed the remains of his Me 109. By borrowing deep-location equipment from a bomb-disposal squad, they had been able to pinpoint exactly where in the marshes the plane had crashed. Apparently, the aircraft was surprisingly well preserved: the cockpit, undercarriage, guns, ammunition, propeller blades and engine were all successfully recovered.

Steinhilper became fascinated by a chapter of his life that had long since closed. When Yorkshire Television asked him to appear in a television documentary about the Battle of Britain, he decided to take up Chislet's invitation to return. He wondered how he would be received after all those years.

In fact, he was welcomed back by the villagers as a hero. The return of the German pilot seemed to have been the most exciting event in Chislet since his crash in 1940. But it was a strange moment for him to stand again on the exact spot where he had crashed. 'That one moment changed your life,' he said. 'You were all alone. You had no control over your own destiny. Then we were shooting each other. Today we behave normally towards each other.'

The Me 109 remains are now housed in the Kent Battle of Britain Museum at Hawkinge airfield near Folkestone. To see the remains again, to see the bullet holes and to realise how lucky he was to have survived shook Steinhilper: 'It got much closer than I wanted. I was more touched than I expected to be. It's important to remind people today that war isn't glorious. There is also death and blood. It's a situation we should not repeat.'

Along the coast at Brighton lived Bill Skinner, the man who, it seems from the records, was the most likely to have shot Steinhilper down: small and thin with a tiny grey moustache and half-moon spectacles, he was a former bank manager and looked the part. Ulrich and Bill were keen to meet, to come face to face after so many years. Once, they had tried to kill each other; now they sat in a Brighton flat drinking whisky and comparing notes. Neither of them could really believe it.

EPILOGUE

After the Wealden Aviation Archaeological Group had reported the discovery of 'human remains' to the police, the response was swift, if perplexed. The police arrived in mid-afternoon in force – two inspectors, a sergeant and a constable.

Perhaps they thought that in their quiet corner of England they had run across a major crime. They were appalled by the smell and confused by what had happened and about what to do next. Finding bits of body forty years on was not a regular event in the lives of the Sheppey police. Scratching their heads, they took away Hugh Beresford's remains in black plastic sacks and handed the case over to the coroner.

The Ministry of Defence set out to inform Hugh Beresford's relatives. His wife had remarried and died in 1966. His only surviving relative was his sixty-two-year-old sister Pamela. Quiet, unmarried, almost a recluse, she lived in the pleasant Leicestershire village of Hoby near Melton Mowbray. One quiet September day the doorbell rang: it was a man from the RAF to tell her that Hugh's body had been dug up at Sheppey. She was numbed. 'I know it sounds strange, but I don't think I ever fully accepted that Hugh was dead. All through the war we kept hoping that somehow he was still alive, that one day he'd walk through the door again . . . The last time I saw my brother was when he came home on leave about three weeks before he died. He mentioned that he had been working hard – but did not go into detail. I suppose you always hope, no matter what people say. I thought he might have been a prisoner of war – and that was why we never heard from him.'

Flight Lieutenant Beresford's inquest was held in Sittingbourne on 19 October 1979. Lionel Skingley, the coroner for north-west Kent, was told by the RAF that, on 7 September 1940, '257 Squadron attacked a formation of bombers and then were attacked by 109s coming out of the sun.'

The pathologist, Dr John Dales, revealed that Hugh Beresford had died instantly, and that he had been shot in the back: 'A hole on the right hand side of his back had been the entry point.' Whether the bullet in the back or the plane crash had been the cause of death was now impossible to tell. The bones of his legs and pelvis had been fractured and his feet had been found still in his boots where the crash impact had sheared his legs off at the shin.

The coroner described Flight Lieutenant Beresford as 'one of our national heroes . . . There were those who with undoubted courage and determination were prepared to sacrifice them-selves for their country.'

News of the discovery of Beresford's death was noted in several newspapers and spread to his former colleagues and friends. Sergeant Pilot Ronnie Forward remembers: 'It hit me right out of the blue. I can't believe it. Forty years later, buried in all that muck.'

A few weeks after Hugh Beresford was dug out of the mud, by an extraordinary coincidence there was a funeral of a German war hero who had died peacefully at his Austrian home. His name: Oberleutnant (later Major) Josef Fozo, leader of an Me 109 Jagdgeschwader. Fozo was the man who, on 7 September 1940, had shot and killed Hugh Beresford.

Then it was Hugh Beresford's turn finally to be laid to rest. He was buried at Brookwood Military Cemetery in Surrey with full military honours on 16 November 1979.

To the men of the Wealden Aviation Archaeological Group it was a correct and satisfying conclusion to the mystery of Beresford's disappearance. To his sister Pamela it opened the wounds anew, but she was pleased to see her brother receive a proper military burial.

On the long march to Grave No. 14 in Row D of Plot 24, Squadron Leader the Reverend Roger Huddleston walked in front of the funeral car carrying the coffin, which was flanked by six serving RAF officers and six airmen from the Queen's Colour Squadron.

At the graveside, the Reverend Huddleston said that Hugh Beresford 'was one of the few to whom so many owe so much'.

The fifteen-man escort party from the Queen's Colour Squadron fired a three-volley salute and the band of RAF Cranwell played the Last Post. As they turned and departed, each member of the bearer party saluted the grave.

Four months later the neat headstone made of Botticino limestone was fixed in place. Thirty-nine years after his death, the story of Flight Lieutenant Hugh Beresford, one of Churchill's Few, was finally over.

POSTSCRIPT

As the British Airways plane headed towards London the pilot said, 'Air traffic control has asked us to hold here at a little airfield called Biggin Hill for five minutes.' I looked round the plane full of families heading home from the sunshine and wondered how many, if any, understood the historical significance of Biggin Hill. The pilot might have thought it was 'little' but Biggin's role in the Battle of Britain was immense.

It was one of the principal frontline airfields in the fight against the Luftwaffe. During the Second World War, 435 aircrew based at Biggin Hill died. Biggin Hill, or Biggin On the Bump as pilots liked to call it, was of huge strategic importance because it was situated on the edge of London. It was no wonder that the Germans saw destroying Biggin as vital so they could attack the capital itself with impunity. On 30 August during the Battle of Britain, the Luftwaffe brutally smashed Biggin Hill in a raid that cost thirty-nine lives and destroyed much of the base. The next day survivors reported for duty as usual.

Today, full-sized replicas, one of a Spitfire and the other of a Hurricane, stand like immense guardians at the gate of what was RAF Biggin Hill.

As we head towards the 80th anniversary of the Battle of Britain, that is almost all that is left – replicas and ruined runways, memorials and museums. Famous airbases have become light industrial units or housing estates. Biggin Hill is one of the few to remain as an airfield. That is why the memories contained in this book are precious. When I wrote this Postscript in June 2019, only six of the pilots who flew in the Battle of Britain were still alive. That tiny handful were in their late nineties or over a hundred. In February 2019, one of those six survivors, Pilot Officer Archie McInnes, was given a flight in a Spitfire over Kent to mark his ninety-ninth birthday.

Finalising this Postscript in September 2019, the number of surviving pilots is now down to four. Archie McInnes himself died in July 2019, just a few hours after celebrating his 100th birthday. Given that he was shot down by the Germans in October 1941 and lost is arm in a serious crash, it was something of a miracle that Archie made it anywhere near one hundred years of age.

In June 2019, Squadron Leader John Hart died, although news of his passing did not emerge until more recently. John was one hundred and two, and the last Canadian survivor of the Battle of Britain. Both men were described in their obituaries as courageous and modest.

The pilots featured in *Churchill's Few* have all died. In the time I spent with them I never heard any of the men complain. During the Battle of Britain, over five hundred RAF personnel were killed and the men in this book felt lucky to have survived when so many of their friends and colleagues were shot down in their twenties or even their teens. As Geoffey Page put it, as he faced up to his thirty seventh operation since the Battle of Britain, 'People complain about growing old but so many were denied the privilege.'

Geoffrey died in 2000 at the age of eighty. He had been one of the founders of the legendary Guinea Pig Club. His obituary in the *Daily Telegraph* noted that he had recorded the minutes of the very first meeting.

He was also the moving force behind the creation of the Battle of Britain Memorial which was erected in 1993 on the cliffs near Folkestone and Dover. He was awarded the OBE in 1995 which sat alongside his wartime DFC and bar and his DSO.

Joseph Slagowski had a much lower profile but the contribution of the Polish pilots to the success of the Battle of Britain was immense and out of all proportion to their numbers. Joe died in London in 1993 at the age of seventy-nine.

Cyril Bamberger, the humble Sergeant Pilot from Cheshire, went on after the Battle of Britain to have a brilliant flying career in Malta and then in the Korean War. He served the RAF for nearly thirty years. He too was awarded a DFC and bar and died in Hampshire in 2008 at the age of eighty-eight. He lived to see the proud moment when his granddaughter presented the Duchess of Cornwall with a posy at the unveiling of the Battle of Britain monument in 2005.

Bob Doe, the pilot who never considered himself to be a hero but was exactly that, died at the age of eighty-nine in 2010. After the crash described in this book, Bob had twenty-two operations at East Grinstead but continued his remarkable flying career in India and Burma, adding a DSO to his DFC and bar. In 2015 his historian daughter, Helen Doe, wrote his biography which was simply called *Fighter Pilot*.

As recorded earlier in *Churchill's Few*, the Intelligence Officer, Geoffrey Myers, a man of great sensitivity and thoughtfulness, died a few weeks after we had cheerful lunch to discuss his diaries. He knew he did not have long to live but never told me. His letters to his family had been kept private for more than forty years but their unflinching portrait of his squadron had been gnawing away at him all that time. Now, he said, it was time for them to be published.

Ulrich Steinhilper, the great Luftwaffe escaper, died in his native Stuttgart in 2009 at the age of ninety-one after a successful career at IBM.

All these men, having survived the Battle of Britain, led long and active lives and several continued to fly. Time has deepened my respect for them all both as servicemen and as human beings.

It is easy to see why Churchill said that 'never in the field of human conflict was so much owed by so many to so few.' Less often quoted are Churchill's sentences before this famous quote, words that sum up the achievements of the men in this book, 'The gratitude of every home in our Island, in our Empire and indeed throughout the world, except in the abodes of the guilty, goes out to the British airmen who, undaunted by odds, unwearied in their constant challenge and mortal danger, are turning the tide of the world war by their prowess and by their devotion.'

John Willis, 2019

ACKNOWLEDGEMENTS

There are several excellent books of various types about the Battle to which any chronicler of the period must be indebted. The standard reference books, Francis K. Mason's *Battle Over Britain* (McWhirter Twins) and the encyclopaedic *The Battle of Britain – Then and Now* by Winston G. Ramsey (After The Battle) were particularly useful.

Since the original publication, many more excellent books have been published including helpful overviews like the *The Battle of Britain* by James Holland (Bantam) and *Fighter Boys* by Patrick Bishop (Harper Collins). Geoffrey Wellum's autobiography *First Light* (Penguin) was inspiring. Ulrich Steinhilper (with Peter Osborne) published his own memoirs *Spitfire On My Tail* and *Ten Minutes to Buffalo* (Independent). Bob Doe's historian daughter, Helen, wrote a first-class biography of her father called *Fighter Pilot* (Amberley). All these compliment *Churchill's Few*.

Thanks again to my colleagues at Yorkshire Television, particularly those who worked on the film that the book accompanied. Their support was invaluable. I owe a particular debt to Jane Nairac and Janet Willis for their superb research efforts, and to Peter Gordon, Peter Moore, Andy Saunders and Edwina Tarply for initial assistance. Carole Sedler supplied not only typing skills, but encouragement and initiative.

For this new, updated edition thanks again to Janet Willis for her research efforts and general help and to Mairi Hutchinson for her computer skills. Thanks, too, to my agent, David Grossman and to Richard Charkin at Mensch for their support. I am indebted to Phillip Beresford for his excellent work on the cover and to Miranda Vaughan Jones for her first-class editing skills.

But the real inspiration was supplied by Ted Willis, my father. In the 1930s he spoke out against Nazism and Fascism so vigorously that he was among 2300 men and women put on Hitler's Black (or Special Search) list, the Gestapo's notorious Sonderfahndungsliste GB. If the invasion had been successful, the men and women on the list would have been the first citizens to be arrested and presumably killed. So, without Churchill's Few, I might not have been born, let alone written this book.

A NOTE ON THE AUTHOR

John Willis is one of Britain's best known television executives. He is former director of programmes at Channel 4 and director of factual and learning at the BBC. He was vice president for national programs at WGBH Boston. In 2012 he was elected chair of the British Academy of Film and Television Arts (BAFTA).

He was educated at Eltham College and FitzwilliamCollege, Cambridge where he read History. He started his career as a documentary maker and won a string of awards for his films including Johnny Go Home, Alice: A Fight for Life, Rampton: The Secret Hospital, and First Tuesday: Return to Nagasaki.

He was Chief Executive of Mentorn Media –producers of Question Time for the BBC – and he now chairs the board of governors at the Royal Central School of Speech and Drama.

He divides his time between London and Norfolk.